Arthur Schopenhauer
PHILOSOPHICAL WRITINGS

Edited by Wolfgang Schirmacher

CONTINUUM · NEW YORK

1998

The Continuum Publishing Company
370 Lexington Avenue, New York, NY 10017

The German Library
is published in cooperation with Deutsches Haus,
New York University.
This volume has been supported by Inter Nationes, and a grant from
the funds of Stifterverband für die Deutsche Wissenschaft.

Printed in the United States of America

Library of Congress Cataloging-in-Publication Data

Schopenhauer, Arthur, 1788–1860.
  [Selections. English. 1994]
  Philosophical writings / Arthur Schopenhauer ; edited by Wolfgang
Schirmacher.
     p.   cm. — (German library ; v. 27)
  Includes bibliographical references.
  ISBN 0-8264-0728-5 (hard : alk. paper) — ISBN
0-8264-0729-3 (pbk. : alk. paper)
     1. Philosophy.   I. Schirmacher, Wolfgang.   II. Title.
III. Series.
B3108.S3   1994
193—dc20   93-40616
                                                         CIP

Acknowledgments will be found on page xxiv,
which constitutes an extension of the copyright page.

Contents

PART 2

PART 3

All translated by E. F. J. Payne

Introduction

Arthur Schopenhauer (born 1788, Danzig, died 1860, Frankfurt am Main) is to this day the most widely read philosopher in Germany. While the audience of his contemporaries Kant, Fichte, Schelling, and Hegel is largely restricted to academic philosophers, new editions of Schopenhauer's works continue to be published, and he still finds tens of thousands of readers with his *Manuscript Remains*. The realistic as well as intuitive thinker Schopenhauer seems to see with undiminished clarity what we too discover when we have courage enough to endure the truth of human existence. As composer Richard Wagner noted in relief, with Schopenhauer one may finally give voice to the secretly held belief that the world is bad. This blunt honesty was Schopenhauer's trademark. Quite in contrast to the "gentlemen of the philosophical trade," the second oldest profession in the world. Philosophy professors were in Schopenhauer's judgment, "too poor to be honorable and straightforward"[1] and had to deny their convictions to keep their employers and patrons in state and society satisfied. The "mask of obscurity and unintelligibility"[2] served the "sham philosophers" and their "scribbling nonsense" exceptionally well, as Schopenhauer phrased his famed reproach of his colleagues. Introduced by Fichte and perfected by Schelling, this nonunderstanding reached its peak with Hegel. Nothing is "easier than to

---

1. Arthur Schopenhauer, *Parerga and Paralipomena*, vol. 2, trans. E. F. J. Payne (Oxford, 1974), 483.
2. Ibid., 2:560–61.

write so that no one understands."[3] Schopenhauer did not want to
be a "conjuror of ideas" *(Volker Spierling),* but instead to return
to "the only living source of perception,"[4] without falling into a
naive empiricism. Schopenhauer belonged to post-Kantian philosophy and thought within the horizon of its problems. Despite all his
claims to the contrary, Schopenhauer's philosophy had its place
in German Idealism, and the "pitiful charlatan" Hegel is merely
Schopenhauer's antagonistic brother, closely bound to him in negation. While Hegel designed the influential concept of a dialectical
progress of society, Schopenhauer founded the tradition of a radical
critique of progress that reaches from Friedrich Nietzsche and Sig-
mund Freud into the postmodern era. Hegel's conviction—shared
by the industrial age—that there is a "progress in the awareness
of freedom"[5] elicited the sobering comment from Schopenhauer:

> The continuous and perpetual existence of the human race is
> merely proof of its exuberance and wantonness.[6]

To speak of "reason in history" seemed to Schopenhauer like
shameless derision of the suffering of all beings.

Schopenhauer's Originality
in the Post-Kantian Age

Schopenhauer's main concept of a *World as Will and Representation* had in common with post-Kantian philosophy the idea that
reality, as we experience it in its seeming originality through perception, is in truth the result of a process of cognition. It cannot
be disputed that "I think" must accompany all my thoughts. The
world is a "brain-activity,"[7] and Schopenhauer does not want to
fall back behind Kant's *Critique of Pure Reason.* For the human

---

3. Schopenhauer, op cit., 2:561.
4. Arthur Schopenhauer, *The World as Will and Representation,* vol. 2, trans.
E. F. J. Payne (New York, 1966), 81.
5. Georg Wilhelm Friedrich Hegel, *Vorlesungen uber die Philosophie der
Geschichte, Suhrkamp Theorie-Ausgabe Bd. 12* (Frankfurt, 1974), 32.
6. Arthur Schopenhauer, *Manuscript Remains,* vol. 4, trans. E. F. J. Payne
(Oxford, 1990), 349.
7. Schopenhauer, *World as Will,* 2:81.

being does not know "a sun and an earth; but only an eye that sees a sun, a hand that feels an earth." Kant's critique convincingly demonstrated to the individual

> that the world around him is there only as representation, in other words, only in reference to another thing, namely that which represents, and that is himself.[8]

But like other post-Kantian thinkers of German Idealism, Schopenhauer is satisfied neither with Kant's ethics nor his metaphysics and anthropology. The "inner essence of nature" that as thing-in-itself remains forever unattainable to knowledge may well be accessible to the human individual in other ways. The "metaphysical need" does not vanish, but is kept alive through the consciousness of death. The weakness of reason, which limits our experience, is no excuse for philistines who dare not transcend everyday experiences for fear of risking their comfortable lives. Ethics is central for Schopenhauer, but he rejects—as does Hegel—an "ought-to-be" ethics, which must preach good and is therefore better suited to "beautiful souls" than to harsh reality.

But here ends the common ground between Schopenhauer and the post-Kantian philosophers, for his teachings are in no way a variation of German Idealism evoking the delight of philosophy professors through its subtlety. The opposite is the case. Schopenhauer's philosophy, which pursues one main thought through ever-new approaches, was for a long time dismissed as too simply constructed and as too easily understood. Yet writers and artists were magnetically drawn to Schopenhauer's style, and philosophical outsiders from Wittgenstein to Horkheimer took encouragement from it. What is new in Schopenhauer's thought, and where does his originality lie? Three aspects stand out. Firstly, Schopenhauer introduced Indian thought into German philosophy and combined it with Western mysticism. Schopenhauer's pessimism is then not cynicism, but a metaphysics arising from inner experience of the emptiness of existence, as expressed in the *Upanishads*.[9] This opens the door to a transformed understanding of ethics as intuitive

8. Ibid., 1:3.
9. See Schopenhauer, *Parerga*, vol. 2, chapter 16.

practice. Secondly, Schopenhauer revealed the will as the true essence of the world and outlined a descriptive anthropology that for the first time recognizes human nature as one of "concrete sexual impulses"[10] and reverses the relationship of primacy between body and soul. This corporeal anthropology became the realistic basis of an ethics of compassion and anticipated the psychoanalytic doctrines of the subconscious. And thirdly, Schopenhauer's thinking changed in the end; it took the form of an unwritten philosophy, one that led to his becoming Nietzsche's "Educator," and that is to be understood not as an abstract construct but as an intrinsically practical philosophy to be lived aesthetically as everyday mysticism.

Pessimism and Indian Thought

Schopenhauer's immense and still-undiminished influence cannot be explained by simply stating that he was right. To be sure, just as Schopenhauer predicted the price of progress would be, the present world bears a closer resemblance to hell each passing day. And even the ecological crisis—which is often discussed but never tackled from its roots—is irrefutable proof of the stupidity and shortsightedness of the human race, driven by short-term needs and desires. And it is true, the life of the people of the third world, like that lived by the homeless of the first world, is day after day "an enterprise that does not cover its expenses," as Schopenhauer, the businessman's son, pragmatically observed. But this is still not a convincing explanation for the lasting fascination with Schopenhauer's philosophy. Only academic philosophers, whose books no one reads anyway, would try to dismiss Schopenhauer as a philosopher of adolescent weltschmerz. The dogmatism of doomsayers was never very attractive, and as Cassandra's brother Schopenhauer would scarcely make an impression on us today. That life means suffering, that our fellow humans are capable of every abomination, and that progress is a fraud: we have accepted and tolerated with brutalizing indifference all this and more for too long. Serial murderers excite our morbid curiosity. And who but a

10. Schopenhauer, *World as Will*, 2:568.

vegetarian can be moved by Schopenhauer's grim observation that every "beast of prey," first and foremost carnivorous man, "is the living grave of thousands of others, and its self-maintenance is a chain of torturing deaths."[11] We "active nihilists" (Nietzsche) have seen literally everything in horror films and celebrate—thoroughly postmodern—the ugly together with the cruel. Pessimism has for us a purely aesthetic quality, not an ethical one, and urges us toward pleasure, not to change our ways.

But is this opposition of ethics and aesthetics at all tenable? Truth does not follow from the concept of pessimism, but from the under-the-skin perception of unceasing suffering. At the same time victims and perpetrators of this suffering, the irony of truth catches up with us. Schopenhauer is not a pessimist in the dogmatic sense, for he does not believe our world is the worst of all worlds. The "black" Schopenhauer describes what he sees and persistently re-fuses to close his eyes to the daily murders, only all too avoidable. But his phenomenology of suffering also lays bare the breach, the point at which "the will turns" and an "entirely different world" becomes visible. At the end of Schopenhauer's principal work, *The World as Will and Representation*, the mask of pessimism falls away, in book 1, written at thirty, as well as in book 2, completed when he was fifty-five. There is a cheerfulness in the serenity with which Schopenhauer bids farewell to "the world as we see it" and an expressiveness in the silence he keeps about our true home, the "world in itself." We may prepare ourselves for this world through ascetic reason and in living an ethics of "holiness," but, as Witt-genstein, an admirer of Schopenhauer, concisely put it, we cannot speak about it. Every "intellectual concept" that seeks to fathom the Absolute, as Schelling had hoped, is, to Schopenhauer's mind, charlatanry. But living "from within" is something that cannot be sustained "from without" and is where "all knowledge necessar-ily ceases."[12]

Schopenhauer's teachings take on a "negative character" just as their "highest point" is reached, but this "nothingness" is "only relative."[13] In Indian thought as in occidental mysticism, in the

11. Ibid., 2:581.
12. Ibid., 2:610.
13. Ibid., 2:612.

Islamic gnosis of the Sufis as well as in the negative theology of Plotinus, Schopenhauer finds ways of life that revel in the consciousness of being one with the "kernel of the world" and the "source of all existence."[14] All "European systems" with the exception of his own philosophy, explained Schopenhauer, held the "representatives" of this "mode of thought" to be "impostors or madmen," and in so doing they set themselves against the "oldest and most numerous" peoples of the earth. But for Schopenhauer the correspondence of his thought with the doctrines of "Brahmanism and Buddhism" (Schopenhauer was the first to acknowledge them on an intellectual level befitting their significance) was evidence of the truth of his own philosophy.[15]

Quietism and asceticism, the "giving up of all willing," and the "intentional mortification of one's own will" lead to "consciousness of the identity of one's own inner being with that of all things."[16] Schopenhauer's pessimism expresses existential nothingness in philosophical concepts and shows cause for the nature of the world and the ethical importance of turning from it. In this discursive perspective, life presents itself "as a process of purification, the purifying lye of which is pain." Then, "if the process is carried out," the insignificance of our works and endeavors becomes evident, nothingness "appears"[17] and opens to us the path toward an intuitive way of living. "Black" Schopenhauer's so very "white" closing passage of volume 1 of *The World as Will and Representation* deals with this intuitive living that has no need of a written doctrine:

> Before us there is certainly left only nothing; . . . But now we turn our glance from our own needy and perplexed nature to those who have overcome the world, . . . instead of the restless pressure and effort, . . . instead of the never-satisfied and never-dying hope, . . . we see that peace that is higher than all reason, that ocean-like calmness of the spirit, that deep tranquility, that unshakable confidence and serenity, whose mere reflection in the countenance, as depicted by Raphael and Correggio, is a

14. Ibid., 613.
15. Ibid., 615.
16. Ibid., 613.
17. Ibid., 639.

complete and certain gospel. Only knowledge remains; the will has vanished.[18]

Life as suffering does not exclude the "fullness of the void"; "life is bad" does not follow from this as the last word. Death can take on the color black or white, can herald rupture or "the closure of Being" (Martin Heidegger). One holds a key to understanding Schopenhauer if one combines the most superficial interpretation, his pessimism, with the hiddenmost sense of his philosophy. Behind the mask of the arrant pessimist Schopenhauer was the most important mystic of the nineteenth century, and it is upon us to begin where he left off, in order to do full justice to his thinking, to bring it to fruition.

The Will to Live and the Primacy of the Body

The will to live is the "keynote" of all living creatures. Schopenhauer did not describe man in terms of the world, but the "world from man."[19] The head experiences the world as representation, the body experiences the world as a will at variance with itself, as eternal struggle for survival. Sexuality is the "invisible central point of all action and conduct,"[20] and through the genitals the individual is connected with the species. Our intellect is merely a tool of this blind will to survive, and we experience this anew each time we recognize what is right and still do wrong. Submission to our carnal instincts and the control of the subconscious over us: an all too familiar fact of human existence that many feel the need to repress. The ego was never master in its own house, but was always the slave of the will. The anthropological defect lies in our wanting. It makes no difference *what* we want, the fact *that* we want is decisive and our misfortune. For our wanting can never be fulfilled.

In his *Critique of Pure Reason* Kant determined not only the idea of reason but its limitations as well—and Schopenhauer followed him this far—but did not dispute the primacy of the spirit.

18. Ibid., 1:411.
19. Ibid., 2:350, 642.
20. Ibid., 510.

It was Schopenhauer's metaphysics of the will that first broke through the anthropological self-lie of "homo sapiens," the thinking being, who autonomously determines his own laws of reason. Although for Kant, too, the human individual was "hewn from crooked timber," his ethical maxim was "you should, so then you can." But the ontological primacy of the mind remained intact, and Hegel, for all his realism, never questioned it. In the radical interpretation of the self, realized as descriptive anthropology, Schopenhauer found a way to heed and at the same time get around Kant's categorical insistence that the thing-in-itself is unknowable.

Schopenhauer wondered at human vanity and folly, and in the age of cancer and AIDS his reflections ring true for us as well:

> Look at the rigid terror with which a sentence of death is heard, the profound dread with which we view the preparations for carrying it out, and the heartrending pity that seizes us at the execution itself. We might then imagine that it was a question of something quite different from merely a few years less of an empty, sad existence embittered by worries and troubles of every kind, and always uncertain.[21]

It is our body that acts, that is enslaved to the will and that gives evidence of the existence of the will. This is also and especially true if the body is not the object of our representation. Where do we find the most intimate knowledge of that inner nature of the world, of that thing-in-itself that Schopenhauer called the will to live?

> The act of procreation is further related to the world as the solution to the riddle. . . . Yet all this is only the phenomenon of the will-to-live; and the concentration, the focus of this will is the act of generation. Hence in this act the inner nature of the world most distinctly expresses itself.[22]

Where are we most conscious of it? Schopenhauer posed this question and answered: In the sensual pleasure we experience in the act of copulation.

21. Ibid., 2:351.
22. Ibid., 570.

I have called the genitals the focus of the will. Indeed, it may be said that man is concrete sexual impulse, for his origin is an act of copulation, and the desire of his desires is an act of copulation.[23]

This observation can no longer unnerve us today, for we live within the horizon of this new and realistic image of the human being that Schopenhauer had begun to sketch. His philosophy of the body remains in two respects a thorn in the side of this century's philosophical anthropology.

For one, Schopenhauer refused to derive from the ontological inferiority of the intellect an ethical indifference toward the dictates of reason. A key insight of Schopenhauer's is that, "with the appearance of reason" the will does

finally attain to reflection for the first time, that is, in man . . . it stands consciously face to face with *death*, and besides the finiteness of all existence, the vanity and fruitlessness of all effort force themselves on it . . .[24]

And the will feels disgust for itself in every individual for whom universal suffering is unbearable, inhuman, and irreconcilable with reason. In the denial of the will to live, in the ethical phenomena of compassion and the love for humans as well as for animals, the will does deny itself through us and wants its turning. Arnold Gehlen, one of the founders of modern philosophical anthropology, wanted nothing to do with such a "metaphysics from inner experience." Thus the turning of the will is possible not in the scientist, but in the philosopher, the artist, and the saint.

The other reason Schopenhauer remains a nuisance is that he deals "with the actual conduct of man, and not with the a priori building of houses of cards,"[25] and he therefore identifies egoism without embellishment as "this nearest, ever ready, original, and living standard of all acts of will."[26] As if this were not enough, Schopenhauer declares compassion to be the only force that can overcome this egoism and claims compassion to be

23. Ibid., 2:514.
24. Ibid., 160.
25. Arthur Schopenhauer, *On the Basis of Morality,* trans. E. F. J. Payne (Indianapolis, 1965), 75.
26. Ibid., 89.

something our faculty of reason can give no direct account of, and its grounds cannot be discovered on the path of experience.[27]

On what then should an ethics of discourse be founded? How can we pursue a rational anthropology? Yet Schopenhauer saw the decisive advantage of his ethics of compassion in its having its basis in the body and in its ability to overcome every rationalization easily. The phenomena of compassion and of human love appear suddenly and without having been evoked—they leave us no choice. Even the most hard-hearted individual can never be certain that compassion will not take possession of him unexpectedly. Schopenhauer's compassion tears away the veil of the *Maya*, as the Indian pundits say, tears through the illusion of the multiplicity of the world of appearances. The delusion that we are protected by our individuality from the suffering of all creatures is shattered, and victim and victimizer recognize themselves as being one in the same: *Tat tvam asi*—"This thou art." The act of compassion is ethically significant precisely because it is not oriented to each situation individually, but to the "world's entire existence and man's destiny,"[28] which, for Schopenhauer, includes "boundless compassion for all living beings."[29] Schopenhauer's metaphysics of the will, which sustains his ethics, is not an absolute truth that one can contentedly acknowledge and believe to possess, but a "ray of light" that falls upon "the darkness of our existence." Through compassion our body, to which we owe the immediate familiarity with our desires, holds the assurance of the way out of the world of representation and of will, always this world of suffering. In intuitive acts, in negative thinking, in the "will-less perception"[30] of the work of art, above all in music, we speak of an "entirely different world"—be the theory as abstruse as it may. *Pre-emptive non-sequitor. He's on to something useful and makes sure people superior to the upper class won't use it.*

Aesthetic Experience and Everyday Mysticism

Schopenhauer is not a fatalist, for "the act of will, from which the world springs, is our own. It is free . . .," so read the closing lines

27. Ibid., 166.
28. Schopenhauer, *Basis of Morality,* 200.
29. Ibid., 172.
30. Schopenhauer, *World as Will,* 1:198.

of the second book of *The World as Will and Representation*. Schopenhauer's last word is the beginning of an ethics to be lived: we can "will otherwise."[31] Only to our consciousness does the thing-in-itself present itself as the will to live. In "mystical intuition" (Nietzsche), in will-less aesthetic experience, in compassion as immediate bodily experience we can "glimpse the 'other,' sense its existence even in the false, the untrue."[32] It is futile to speak about this completely different other; it must be fostered in silence and comes to presence alone in our acts. Schopenhauer perceived in art a realm in which this entirely different world is lived by us for moments all too rare, lived by creative artists as well as by neo-creative viewers, by writers and empathetic readers. Through its transition to ethics Schopenhauer's "gnostically tinted aesthetics of worldlessness," as found in his philosophy of art, becomes an "aesthetics of aliveness" that in the "experience of otherness" overcomes the stagnation of the given world.[33] But in "pure knowing" as well, in the work of philosophical genius, we can become "the clear eye of the world."[34] Compassion is a way of life enabling us to put into practice the "turning" of the will, and thus achieve its suspension. *Escape from the duty to destroy the enemies*

Philosophical knowledge, aesthetic experience, and ethics of *of* compassion culminate in mystical practice whose theory can only *talent.* be negative. This negativity heightens, does not diminish its effectiveness. In the pre-technological world, mystics were more often than not incapable of surviving and had to be sheltered in cloisters from a world certain to mean their death. Those who lacked the will to survive inevitably became victims. Schopenhauer's great achievement lies in having foreseen at the beginning of the industrial revolution the consequences of the approaching technological world for human life. Schopenhauer perceived that an ideology of progress, in trying to improve things, only makes our situation worse and intensifies our suffering. At the same time, Schopenhauer intuitively understood that with the dawn of technology the

31. Ibid., 2:646.

32. Martin Hielscher, "Der Rang der Kunst in der Philosophie Schopenhauers," *Schopenhauer in der Postmoderne,* in Wolfgang Schirmacher, ed. (Vienna, 1989), 192.

33. Andreas Steffens, "Lebensversicherungen," in *Schopenhauer in der Postmoderne,* 186.

34. Schopenhauer, *World as Will,* 1:186.

struggle for survival and the war against nature had become obsolete. And with this, technology gives humankind for the first time the potential to contribute to harmony in the cosmos. What once only a few were capable of, and for which they often paid with their lives, can now become for all humankind the one humane form of life: "everyday mysticism." In the present ecological crisis we are learning the hard way that Schopenhauer strikes the core of our difficulties when his philosophical intuition tells him nothing is as dangerous for the human race as the will to survive. It is up to us to pursue Schopenhauer's way out and transform the negation of the will into a living ethics. On the threshold of the twenty-first century let us live as "everyday mystics."

W. S.

Translated by Virginia Cutrufelli

Chronology

1788 22 February: Arthur Schopenhauer is born in Danzig, the son of the patrician merchant Heinrich Floris Schopenhauer and his wife Johanna.

1793 Because of the independent city's occupation by the Prussians the family moves to Hamburg.

1797 Arthur travels to Paris and Le Havre, and stays in Le Havre for two wonderful years with a French family.

1799 Arthur returns to Hamburg where he attends a *prep* private school.

1803 Promised a four-month tour of Europe with his parents, Arthur decides against a career as scholar in favor of training as a merchant.

1804–7 Apprenticed to the merchants Kabrun in Danzig and Jenisch in Hamburg.

1805 Suicide of his father.

1807 Arthur leaves Hamburg to acquire university entrance qualification at the Gotha Gymnasium.

1809–11   Studies at Göttingen University: natural sciences, Plato, Kant.

1811–13   Studies at Berlin University. Attends lectures by Johann Fichte, and Friedrich Schleiermacher.

1813   Writes his dissertation *On the Fourfold Root of the Principle of Sufficient Reason* and has conversations with Goethe on color theory.

1814   Final break with his mother, a well-known novelist.

1814–18   Lives in Dresden.

1815   *On Seeing and Colors.*

1818   Completes the first version of his principal work, *The World as Will and Representation* (published 1819) and starts his Italian journey (Florence, Rome, Naples, Venice).

1819   Family financial crisis owing to the collapse of a Danzig banking house. Schopenhauer applies for a lectureship at Berlin University and, with the help of Hegel, is accepted.

1820   Start of lecture with very low student attendance (attempts to give lectures without success in the following years).

1821   Falls in love with the singer Caroline Medon.

1822   Second Italian journey (Milan, Florence, Venice).

1831   Flees from Berlin because of a cholera epidemic that causes Hegel's death.

1833   Settles in Frankfurt-am-Main for the next twenty-eight years, until the end of his life.

1835   *On the Will in Nature.*

1841   *The Two Fundamental Problems of Ethics, Treated in Two Academic Prize Essays.*

1844   *The World as Will and Representation:* second edition, amplified by a volume.

1852   *Parerga and Paralipomena.*

1853   Beginning of Schopenhauer's fame.

1860   21 September: death of Arthur Schopenhauer in Frankfurt.

Works on Schopenhauer

Atwell, John E. *Schopenhauer: The Human Character*. Philadelphia, 1990.

Hamlyn, David Walter. *Schopenhauer*. London, 1985.

Hübscher, Arthur. *The Philosophy of Schopenhauer in Its Intellectual Context: Thinker against the Tide*. Transl. J. T. Baer and D. E. Cartwright. Lewistone, New York, 1989.

Janaway, Charles *Self and World in Schopenhauer's Philosophy*. Oxford, 1989.

Magee, Brian. *The Philosophy of Schopenhauer*. Oxford, 1983.

Safranski, Rüdiger. *Schopenhauer and the Wild Years of Philosophy*. Transl. E. Oser. Cambridge, Massachusetts, 1990.

Schopenhauer: New Essays in Honor of His Two Hundredth Birthday. Ed. Eric von der Luft. Lewiston, New York, 1986.

Schopenhauer: His Philosophical Achievement. Ed. Michael Fox. Brighton, 1980.

Simmel, Georg. *Schopenhauer and Nietzsche*. Transl. H. Lioskandl. Amherst, 1986.

Young, Julian. *Willing and Unwilling: A Study in the Philosophy of Arthur Schopenhauer*. Dordrecht, 1987.

ACKNOWLEDGMENTS

Every reasonable effort has been made to locate the owners of rights to previously published translations printed here. We gratefully acknowledge permission to reprint the following material:

From *The World as Will and Representation*, volume 2, by Arthur Schopenhauer, translated by E. F. J. Payne. New York: Dover Publications, 1969.

Reprinted with the permission of Macmillan Publishing Company from *On the Basis of Morality* by Arthur Schopenhauer and edited by E. F. J. Payne. Copyright © 1965 by Macmillan Publishing Company.

© Oxford University Press 1974. Reprinted from *Parerga and Paralimpomena* by Arthur Schopenhauer translated by E. F. J. Payne (1974), vols. 1 and 2 by permission of Oxford University Press.

From *Arthur Schopenhauer: Manuscript Remains in Four Volumes:* volume 1: *Early Manuscripts,* edited by Arthur Hübscher, translated by E. F. J. Payne. Reprinted with permission of Berg Publishers, Ltd., Oxford/New York, 1988.

PART 1

1

On Thinking for Oneself

257

J ust as the largest library, badly arranged, is not so useful as a very moderate one that is well arranged, so the greatest amount of knowledge, if not elaborated by our own thoughts, is worth much less than a far smaller volume that has been abundantly and repeatedly thought over. For only by universally combining what we know, by comparing every truth with every other, do we fully assimilate our own knowledge and get it into our power. We can think over only what we know, and so we should learn something; but we know only what we have thought out.

Now it is true that we can arbitrarily apply ourselves to reading and learning, but not really to thinking. Thus just as a fire is kindled and sustained by a draft of air, so too must thinking be through some interest in its theme, which may be either purely objective or merely subjective. The latter exists solely in connection with our personal affairs; the former, however, is only for minds who think by nature, to whom thinking is as natural as breathing, but who are very rare. Thus with most scholars there is so little of it. Exactly what the will is for, not a chain but a booster.

258

The difference between the effect produced on the mind by thinking for oneself and that produced by reading is incredibly great;

and thus it is forever increasing the original disparity between
minds, by virtue whereof we are driven to the one or to the other.
Thus reading forces on the mind ideas that are as foreign and
heterogeneous to the tendency and mood it has at the moment, as
is the seal to the wax whereon it impresses its stamp. Thus the
mind is totally compelled from without to think first of one thing
and then of another, for which it has absolutely no inclination or
disposition. When, on the other hand, a man thinks for himself,
his mind follows its own natural impulse, as this has been more
specifically determined for the moment either by external environment or by some recollection. Thus the environment of intuitive
perception does not impress on the mind one definite idea as does
reading, but gives it merely the material and the occasion to think
what is in accordance with its nature and present disposition.
Therefore the mind is deprived of all its elasticity by *much* reading
as is a spring when a weight is continually applied to it; and the
surest way not to have thoughts of our own is for us at once to
take up a book when we have a moment to spare. This practice is
the reason why erudition makes most men more stupid and simple
than they are by nature and also deprives their literary careers of
every success.[1] As Pope says, they remain:

> For ever reading, never to be read.
> *The Dunciad*, 3:193–94.

Not if you read with a gun pointed at the author's head

Scholars are those who have read in books, but thinkers, men
of genius, world enlighteners, and reformers of the human race are
those who have read directly in the book of the world.

259

At bottom, only our own fundamental ideas have truth and life;
for it is they alone that we really and thoroughly understand. The
ideas of someone else that we have read are the scraps and leavings
of someone else's meal, the cast-off clothes of a stranger.

The idea of another that we have read is related to our own that

---

1. Those who write are so numerous, those who think so rare—TR.

occurs to us as the impression in stone of a plant from the primeval world to the blossoming plant of spring.

260

Reading is a mere makeshift for original thinking. When we read, we allow another to guide our thoughts in leading strings. Moreover, many books merely serve to show how many false paths there are and how seriously we could go astray if we allowed ourselves to be guided by them. But whoever is guided by genius, in other words thinks for himself, thinks freely and of his own accord and thinks correctly; he has the compass for finding the right way. We should, therefore, read only when the source of our own ideas dries up, which will be the case often enough even with the best minds. On the other hand, to scare away our own original and powerful ideas in order to take up a book, is a sin against the Holy Ghost. We then resemble the man who runs away from free nature in order to look at a herbarium, or to contemplate a beautiful landscape in a copper engraving.

Even if occasionally we had been able very easily and conveniently to find in a book a truth or view that we very laboriously and slowly discovered through our own thinking and combining, it is nevertheless a hundred times more valuable if we have arrived at it through our own original thinking. Only then does it enter into the whole system of our ideas as an integral part and living member; only then is it completely and firmly connected therewith, is understood in all its grounds and consequents, bears the color, tone, and stamp of our whole mode of thought, has come at the very time when the need for it was keen, is therefore firmly established and cannot again pass away. Accordingly, Goethe's verse here finds its most perfect application and even explanation:

> What from your fathers' heritage is lent,
> Earn it anew, really to possess it![2]

Thus the man who thinks for himself only subsequently becomes acquainted with the authorities for his opinions when they serve merely to confirm him therein and to encourage him. The book-

---

2. *Faust,* part 1, Bayard Taylor's translation.

philosopher, on the other hand, starts from those authorities in that he constructs for himself an entire system from the opinions of others that he has collected in the course of his reading. Such a system is then like an automaton composed of foreign material, whereas that of the original thinker resembles a living human being. For it originated like this, since the external world fertilized the thinking mind that afterwards carried it and gave birth to it.

The truth that has been merely learned sticks to us like an artificial limb, a false tooth, a nose of wax, or at best like a rhinoplastic nose formed from someone else's flesh. On the other hand, the truth acquired through our own thinking is like the natural limb; it alone really belongs to us. On this rests the distinction between the thinker and the mere scholar. The intellectual gain of the man who thinks for himself is, therefore, like a beautiful painting that vividly stands out with correct light and shade, sustained tone, and perfect harmony of colors. The intellectual acquisition of the mere scholar, on the other hand, is like a large palette full of bright colors, systematically arranged perhaps, but without harmony, sequence, and significance.

261

Reading is equivalent to thinking with someone else's head instead of with one's own. Now for our own thinking, whence a coherent and connected whole, a system though not strictly rounded off, endeavors to evolve, nothing is more detrimental than too strong an influx of other people's ideas through constant reading. For each of them has sprung from the mind of another, belongs to another system, bears another tint; and never do they flow of themselves into a totality of thought, knowledge, insight, and conviction. On the contrary, they set up in the head a slight Babylonian confusion of tongues, and a mind so crammed is now robbed of all clear insight and thus is well-nigh disorganized. This state can be observed in many scholars and results in their being inferior to many illiterate men as regards common sense, correct judgment, and practical tact. The latter have always subordinated to, and incorporated in, their own thinking the little knowledge that has come to them from without through experience, conversation, and a little reading. Now it is just this that the scientific *thinker* also does to a greater degree. Although he needs much knowledge and must, therefore, read a great deal, his mind is nevertheless strong enough to master all this, to assimilate it, to incorporate it into his system of ideas, and thus to subordinate it to the organically consistent totality of his vast and ever-growing insight. Here his own thinking, like the ground-bass of an organ, always dominates everything and is never drowned by the notes and tones of others, as is the case with the minds of mere pundits and polyhistors, where fragments of music in all keys run into one another, so to speak, and the fundamental note can no longer be detected at all.

262

Those who have spent their lives in reading, and have drawn their wisdom from books, resemble men who have acquired precise information about a country from many descriptions of travel. They are able to give much information about things, but at bottom they have really no coherent, clear, and thorough knowledge of the nature of the country. On the other hand, those who have spent their lives in thinking are like men who have themselves been in that country. They alone really know what they are talking about; they have a consistent and coherent knowledge of things there and are truly at home in them.

263

The ordinary book-philosopher is related to the man who thinks for himself as a critical historian to an eyewitness; the latter speaks from his own immediate apprehension of things. At bottom, therefore, all who think for themselves are of one accord and their difference springs only from that of their standpoint; but where this alters nothing, they all say the same thing. For they state merely what they have objectively apprehended. To my agreeable surprise I have often subsequently found stated in the ancient works of great men propositions that, on account of their paradoxical nature, I hesitated to lay before the public. The book-philosopher, on the other hand, reports the statement of one man, the opinion of another, the objection of a third, and so on. He compares, carefully weighs, and criticizes all these and endeavors to get at the truth of things; and in this respect he is exactly like the critical historian.

Thus for example he will start investigations on whether Leibniz had for a while ever been a Spinozist, and such like. Very clear instances of what is said here are furnished for the curious admirer by Herbart's *Analytische Beleuchtung der Moral und des Naturrechts* and also by his *Briefe über die Freiheit*. We might marvel at the great trouble such a man takes, for it seems that, if only he would keep his eye on the matter itself, he would soon reach the goal through a little thinking for himself. But there is a small difficulty here since such a thing does not depend on our will; we can at any time sit down and read, but not think as well. Thus it is the same with ideas as with human beings; we cannot always send for them at will, but must wait for them to come. Thinking about a subject must occur automatically through a happy and harmonious concurrence of external occasion with inner mood and interest; and it is precisely this that will never come to those men. This finds its illustration even in those ideas that concern our personal interest. If we have to come to a decision in such a matter, we cannot sit down to it at any arbitrarily chosen moment, think over the reasons, and then decide. For at that very moment, our consideration of the matter is often not firm, but wanders to other things; and for this even our disinclination in the matter is sometimes responsible. We should, therefore, not try to force it, but wait till the mood for it comes automatically. This will often come unexpectedly and repeatedly, and every different mood at a different time casts a fresh light on the subject. It is this slow procedure that is understood by the expression *maturity of decisions*. For the task must be apportioned and in this way much that was previously overlooked will occur to us; and even the disinclination disappears since things often seem to be much more endurable when they are kept clearly in view. Likewise in what is theoretical, the proper time must be awaited and not even the man endowed with the greatest mind is capable at all times of thinking for himself. Therefore he does well to use the rest of the time for reading; but, as I have said, reading is a substitute for original thinking and supplies the mind with material, since someone else thinks for us, although always in a way that is not our own. For this reason, we should not read too much lest the mind become accustomed to the substitute and cease to know the thing itself, and thus get used to paths already well worn and become estranged from its own train of thought by following that of another. Least of all should we, for the sake of reading, withdraw entirely from the spectacle of the real world. For here the occasion and mood for original thought occur incomparably more frequently than in reading. That which is intuitively perceptual and real is, in its original nature and force, the natural object of the thinking mind and is most readily capable of deeply stimulating it.

According to these observations, it will not surprise us to learn that the man who is capable of thinking for himself and the book-philosopher can easily be recognized even by their style of delivery; the former by the stamp of earnestness, directness, and originality, by all his ideas and expressions that spring from his own perception of things; the latter, on the other hand, by the fact that everything is secondhand, consists of traditional notions, trash and rubbish, and is flat and dull, like the impression of an impression. His style, consisting of conventional, and even banal, phrases and current newfangled words, resembles a small state whose circulation consists of none but foreign coins because it does not mint any of its own.

264

Mere experience is as little able to replace thinking as is reading. Pure empiricism is related to thinking as eating to digestion and assimilation. When empiricism boasts that it alone through its discoveries has advanced human knowledge, it is as if the mouth were to boast that the existence of the body were solely its work.

265

The works of all really capable minds differ from the rest in their character of *decisiveness* and *definiteness,* together with the distinctness and clearness springing therefrom, since they at all times clearly and definitely knew what they wanted to express; it may have been in prose, verse, or tones. The rest lack that decisiveness and clearness; and in this respect they can be at once recognized.

The characteristic sign of all first-rate minds is the directness of all their judgments and opinions. All that they express and assert is the result of their own original thinking and everywhere proclaims itself as such even by the style of delivery. Accordingly, like princes, they have an imperial immediacy in the realm of the mind; the rest are all mediatized, as is already seen from their style that has no stamp of originality.

Therefore every genuine and original thinker is to this extent like a monarch; he is immediate and perceives no one who is his superior. Like the decrees of a monarch, his judgments spring from his own supreme power and come directly from himself. For he no more accepts authorities than does the monarch take orders; on the contrary, he admits nothing but what he himself has confirmed. On the other hand, minds of the common ruck who labor under all kinds of current opinions, authorities, and prejudices, are like the crowd that silently obeys laws and orders.

266

Those who are so eager and hasty to decide debatable questions by quoting authorities, are really glad when they can bring into the field the intellect and insight of someone else instead of their own, which they lack. Their number is legion; for as Seneca says: *unus quisque mavult credere, quam judicare.*[3] And so in their controversies, authorities are the weapons generally chosen with which they pitch into one another; and whoever is involved in these is ill-advised to defend himself against them with grounds and arguments. For against such weapons they are horny Siegfrieds immersed in the flood of an inability to think and judge. They will, therefore, hold up to him their authorities as an *argumentum ad verecundiam,*[4] and will cry *victoria!*

267

In the realm of reality, beautiful, happy, and agreeable as it may have been, we always move only under the influence of heaviness that must constantly be overcome; whereas in the realm of ideas we are bodiless spirits without weight and pressure. Therefore no

---

3. Everyone prefers to believe rather than to give his own opinion. (*De vita beata*, 1, 4.)

4. An argument that avails itself of human respect for great men, ancient customs and authority generally in order to strengthen one's point.

happiness on earth can compare with that which a fine and fruitful mind finds in itself at a happy hour.

268

The presence of an idea is like that of a loved one. We imagine that we shall never forget it and that the beloved can never become indifferent to us; but out of sight, out of mind! The finest thought runs the risk of being irretrievably forgotten if it is not written down, and the beloved of being taken from us unless she has been wedded.

269

There are plenty of ideas that are of value to the man who thinks them; but of them only a few have the power to act through repercussion or reflection, that is to gain the reader's interest after they have been written down.

270

But here only that is of real value that we have in the first instance thought out *for ourselves.* Thus we can divide thinkers into those who think primarily *for themselves* and those who think at once *for others.* The former are the genuine *self-thinkers* in the double meaning of the term; they are the real *philosophers.* For they alone take the matter seriously; and the pleasure and happiness of their existence consists in just thinking. The others are the *sophists;* they wish to *shine* and seek their fortune in what they hope to obtain from others in this way; this is where they are in earnest. We can soon see from his whole style and method to which of the two classes a man belongs. Lichtenberg is an example of the first; Herder belongs to the second.

271

The *problem of existence* is very great and very close to us; this existence that is dubious, questionable, tormented, fleeting, and dreamlike. It is so great and so near that, the moment we become aware of it, it overshadows and hides all other problems and purposes. Now in this connection, we see how all men, with few and rare exceptions, are not clearly conscious of the problem; in fact, they do not appear to have grasped it at all, but are much more concerned about everything else. They live for the day and think only of the scarcely longer span of their personal future, for either they expressly decline to consider the problem, or else, with regard thereto, they willingly make a compromise through some system of popular metaphysics with which they are satisfied. If we carefully consider all this, we may form the opinion that only in a much wider sense can man be called a *thinking being;* and then we shall not be very surprised at any trait of thoughtlessness or simplicity. On the contrary, we shall realize that the intellectual horizon of the normal man transcends, it is true, that of the animal that is unaware of the future and the past and whose existence is, so to speak, a single present. But we shall also realize that the human mental horizon is not so incalculably far removed from the animal's as is generally assumed.

It is in accordance with the foregoing that, even in conversation, we find the thoughts of most people to be clipped as short as chopped straw, so that out of them a longer thread cannot be spun.

If this world were populated with really thinking beings, it would be impossible for all kinds of noise to be permitted and given such unlimited scope, even the most terrible and purposeless. But if nature had intended man for thinking, she would not have given him ears, or at any rate would have furnished them with airtight flaps, as with bats whom for this reason I envy. But like the rest, man is really a poor animal whose powers are calculated merely for the maintenance of his existence. For this reason, he needs ears that are always open and, even unasked, announce the approach of a pursuer both by night and by day.

Translated by E. F. J. Payne

2

On the Affirmation of
the Will-to-Live

If the will-to-live exhibited itself merely as an impulse to self-preservation, that would be only an affirmation of the individual phenomenon for the span of time of its natural duration. The cares and troubles of such a life would not be great, and consequently existence would prove easy and cheerful. Since, on the contrary, the will wills life absolutely and for all time, it exhibits itself at the same time as sexual impulse that has an endless series of generations in view. This impulse does away with that unconcern, cheerfulness, and innocence that would accompany a merely individual existence, since it brings into consciousness unrest, uneasiness, and melancholy, and into the course of life misfortunes, cares, and misery. On the other hand, if it is voluntarily suppressed, as we see in rare exceptions, then this is the turning of the will, which changes its course. It is then absorbed in, and does not go beyond, the individual; but this can happen only through his doing a painful violence to himself. If this has taken place, that unconcern and cheerfulness of the merely individual existence are restored to consciousness, and indeed raised to a higher power. On the other hand, tied up with the satisfaction of that strongest of all impulses and desires is the origin of a new existence, and hence the carrying out of life afresh with all its burdens, cares, wants, and pains, in *another* individual, it is true; yet if the two, who are different in the phenomenon, were such absolutely and in themselves, where then would eternal justice be found? Life presents itself as a problem, a task to be worked out, and in general therefore as a constant struggle against want and affliction. Accordingly everyone tries to get through with it and come off as well as he can; he disposes of life as he does of a compulsory service that he is in duty bound to carry out. But who has contracted this debt? His begetter, in the enjoyment of sensual pleasure. Therefore, because the one has enjoyed this pleasure, the other must live, suffer, and die. However, we know and look back to the fact that the difference of the homogeneous is conditioned by space and time, which I have called in this sense the *principium individuationis;* otherwise eternal justice would be irretrievably lost. Paternal love, by virtue of which the father is ready to do, to suffer, and to take a risk more for his child than for himself, and at the same time recognizes this as his obligation, is due to the very fact that the begetter recognizes himself once more in the begotten.

The life of a man, with its endless care, want, and suffering, is to be regarded as the explanation and paraphrase of the act of procreation, of the decided affirmation of the will-to-live. Further, it is also due to this that he owes nature the debt of death, and thinks of this debt with uneasiness. Is not this evidence of the fact that our existence involves guilt? But we certainly always exist on periodical payment of the toll, birth and death, and we enjoy successively all the sorrows and joys of life, so that none can escape us. This is just the fruit of the affirmation of the will-to-live. Thus the fear of death, which holds us firmly to life in spite of all its miseries, is really illusory; but just as illusory is the impulse that has enticed us into it. This enticement itself can be objectively perceived in the reciprocal longing glances of two lovers; they are the purest expression of the will-to-live in its affirmation. How gentle and tender it is here! It wills well-being, and quiet enjoyment, and mild pleasures for itself, for others, for all. This is the theme of Anacreon. Thus by allurement and flattery it works its way into life; but when it is in life, then misery introduces crime, and crime misery; horror and desolation fill the scene. This is the theme of Aeschylus.

But the act by which the will affirms itself and man comes into existence is one of which all in their heart of hearts are ashamed, and which therefore they carefully conceal; in fact, if they are caught in the act, they are as alarmed as if they had been detected in a crime. It is an action of which, on cool reflection, we think often with repugnance, and in an exalted mood with disgust. Considerations going more closely into the matter in this sense are afforded by Montaigne in the fifth chapter of his third book under the marginal heading *Ce que c'est que l'amour.* A peculiar sadness and remorse follows close on it; yet these are felt most after the consummation of the act for the first time, and generally they are the more distinct, the nobler the character. Hence even the pagan Pliny say: *Homini tantum primi coitus poenitentia; augurium scilicet vitae, a poenitenda origine (Histoira Naturalis,* 10:83).[1] On the other hand, in Goethe's *Faust* what do devil and witches practice and sing on their Sabbath? Lewdness and obscene jokes. In the very same work (in the admirable Paralipomena to *Faust*) what does Satan incarnate preach before the assembled multitude? Lewdness and obscene talk, nothing more. But the human race continues to exist simply and solely by means of the constant practice of such an act as this. Now if optimism were right, if our existence were to be gratefully acknowledged as the gift of the highest goodness guided by wisdom, and accordingly if it were in itself praiseworthy, commendable, and delightful, then certainly the act that perpetuates it would necessarily bear quite a different complexion. If, on the other hand, this existence is a kind of false step or wrong path, if it is the work of an originally blind will, the luckiest development of which is that it comes to itself in order to abolish itself, then the act perpetuating that existence must appear precisely as in fact it does.

With regard to the first fundamental truth of my teaching, the remark merits a place here that the above-mentioned shame over the business of procreation extends even to the parts that serve it, although, like all the other parts, they are given us by nature. Once again, this is a striking proof of the fact that not merely man's actions, but even his body, are to be regarded as the phenomenon, the objectification, of his *will,* and as its work. For he could not be ashamed of a thing that existed without his will.

The act of procreation is further related to the world as the solution is to the riddle. Thus the world is wide in space and old

---

1. Only man feels remorse after the first copulation; a course characteristic of life, that we feel remorse for our origin.—TR.

in time, and has an inexhaustible multiplicity of forms. Yet all this is only the phenomenon of the will-to-live; and the concentration, the focus of this will is the act of generation. Hence in this act the inner nature of the world most distinctly expresses itself. In this respect it is even worth noting that the act itself is also positively called "the will" in the very significant German phrase: *Er verlangte von ihr, sie sollte ihm zu Willen sein.*[2] Therefore that act, as the most distinct expression of the will, is the kernel, the compendium, the quintessence of the world. Hence we obtain through it a light as to the true nature and tendency of the world; it is the solution to the riddle. Accordingly, it is understood by the "tree of knowledge"; for, after acquaintance with it, everyone begins to see life in its true light, as Byron also says:

> The tree of knowledge has been pluck'd—all's known.
> *Don Juan,* 1:128.

No less in keeping with this quality is the fact that it is the great *unspeakable,* the public secret that must never be distinctly mentioned anywhere, but is always and everywhere understood to be the main thing as a matter of course, and is therefore always present in the minds of all. For this reason, even the slightest allusion to it is instantly understood. The principal role played in the world by this act and by what is connected with it, because everywhere love-intrigues are pursued on the one hand, and assumed on the other, is quite in keeping with the importance of this *punctum saliens* of the world-egg. What is amusing is to be found only in the constant concealment of the main thing.

But see now how the young, innocent human intellect is startled at the enormity, when that great secret of the world first becomes known to it! The reason for this is that, on the long path that the will, originally without knowledge, had to traverse before it rose to intellect, especially to human, rational intellect, it became such a stranger to itself; and so it no longer knows its origin, that *poenitenda origo,* and from the standpoint of pure, hence innocent, knowledge is horrified thereat.

Now, as the focus of the will, that is to say, its concentration and highest expression, are the sexual impulse and its satisfaction,

---

2. He expected her to be willing to serve him.—Tr.

it is expressed very significantly and naively in the symbolical language of nature by the fact that individualized will, hence man and the animal, makes its entry into the world through the portal of the sexual organs.

The *affirmation of the will-to-live,* which accordingly has its center in the act of generation, is inevitable and bound to happen in the case of the animal. For the will that is the *natura naturans* first of all arrives at *reflection* in man. To arrive at reflection means not merely to know for the momentary need and necessity of the individual will, for its service in the urgent present moment—as is the case with the animal according to its completeness and its needs that go hand in hand—but to have reached a greater breadth of knowledge, by virtue of a distinct recollection of the past, of an approximate anticipation of the future, and, in this way, of a comprehensive survey of the individual life, of one's own, of another, indeed of existence generally. Actually, the life of every animal species throughout the thousands of years of its existence is to a certain extent like a single moment; for it is mere consciousness of the *present* without that of the past and of the future, and consequently without that of death. In this sense it is to be regarded as a steady and enduring moment, a *nunc stans.* Incidentally, we here see most distinctly that in general the form of life, or of the phenomenon of the will with consciousness, is primarily and immediately only the *present.* Past and future are added only in the case of man, and indeed only in the concept; they are known *in abstracto,* and are possibly illustrated by pictures of the imagination. Hence, after the will-to-live, i.e., the inner being of nature, has run through the whole series of animals in restless striving toward complete objectification and complete enjoyment—and this often happens at various intervals of successive animal series arising anew on the same planet—it ultimately arrives at *reflection* in the being endowed with the faculty of reason, namely, man. Here the matter now begins to be grave and critical for him; the question forces itself on him whence is all this and for what purpose, and principally whether the trouble and misery of his life and effort are really repaid by the profit. *Le jeu vaut-il bien la chandelle?*[3] Accordingly, here is the point where, in the light of distinct knowl-

---

3. Is the game worth the candle?—TR.

edge, he decides for the affirmation or denial of the will-to-live, although he can as a rule bring the latter to consciousness only in a mythical cloak. Consequently, we have no ground for assuming that an even more highly developed objectification of the will is reached anywhere, for it has already reached its turning point here.

Translated by E. F. J. Payne

3

Additional Remarks on the Doctrine of the Vanity of Existence

142

This vanity finds its expression in the whole form of existence; in the infinite nature of time and space as opposed to the finite nature of the individual in both; in the transitory and passing present moment as reality's sole mode of existence; in the dependence and relativity of all things; in constant becoming without being; in constant desire without satisfaction; in the constant interruption of efforts and aspirations that constitutes the course of life until such obstruction is overcome. *Time* and the *fleeting nature* of all things therein, and by means thereof, are merely the form wherein is revealed to the will-to-live, which as the thing-in-itself is imperishable, the *vanity* of that striving. *Time* is that by virtue whereof at every moment all things in our hands come to naught and thereby lose all true value.

Why clean your room when it will only get dirty again? This search for finality is infantile.

143

What has *been,* no longer *is;* it as little exists as that which has *never* been. But everything that is, is the next moment already regarded as having been. And so the most insignificant present has over the most significant past the advantage of *reality,* whereby the former is related to the latter as something to nothing.

To his astonishment, a man all of a sudden exists after countless thousands of years of nonexistence and, after a short time, must again pass into a nonexistence just as long. The heart says that this can never be right, and from considerations of this kind there must dawn even on the crude and uncultured mind a presentiment of the ideality of time. But this, together with the ideality of space, is the key to all true metaphysics because it makes way for an order of things quite different from what is found in nature. This is why Kant is so great.

Of every event in our life, only for one moment can it be said that it *is;* for ever afterwards we must say that it *was.* Every evening we are poorer by a day. Perhaps the sight of this ebbing away of our brief span of time would drive us mad, if in the very depths of our being we were not secretly conscious that the inexhaustible spring of eternity belongs to us so that from it we are forever able to renew the period of life.

On considerations such as the foregoing, we can certainly base the theory that to enjoy the present moment and to make this the object of our life is the greatest *wisdom* because the present alone is real, everything else being only the play of thought. But we could just as well call it the greatest *folly;* for that which in the next moment no longer exists, and vanishes as completely as a dream, is never worth a serious effort.

144

Our existence has no foundation to support it except the ever-fleeting and vanishing present; and so constant *motion* is essentially its form, without any possibility of that rest for which we are loafing always longing. We resemble a man running downhill who would inevitably fall if he tried to stop, and who keeps on his legs only by continuing to run; or we are like a stick balanced on a fingertip; or the planet that would fall into its sun if it ceased to hurry forward irresistibly. Thus restlessness is the original form of existence. and proud of it,

In such a world where there is no stability of any kind, no lasting state is possible but everything is involved in restless rotation and change, where everyone hurries along and keeps erect on a tight-rope by always advancing and moving, happiness is not even conceivable. It cannot dwell where Plato's "constant becoming and never being" is the only thing that occurs. In the first place, no one is happy, but everyone throughout his life strives for an alleged happiness that is rarely attained, and even then only to disappoint him. As a rule, everyone ultimately reaches port with masts and rigging gone; but then it is immaterial whether he was happy or unhappy in a life that consisted merely of a fleeting vanishing present and is now over and finished.

However, it must be a matter of surprise to us to see how, in the human and animal worlds, that exceedingly great, varied, and restless motion is produced and kept up by two simple tendencies, hunger and the sexual impulse, aided a little perhaps by boredom, and how these are able to give the *primum mobile*[1] to such a complicated machine that sets in motion the many-colored puppet-show.

Now if we consider the matter more closely, we first of all see the existence of the inorganic attacked at every moment and finally obliterated by chemical forces. On the other hand, the existence of the organic is rendered possible only through the constant change of matter that requires a continuous flow and consequently assistance from without. Thus in itself, organic life already resembles the stick that is balanced on the hand and must always be in motion; and it is, therefore, a constant need, an ever-recurring want, and an endless trouble. Yet only by means of this organic life is consciousness possible. All this is accordingly *finite existence* whose opposite would be conceivable as *infinite,* as exposed to no attack from without, or as requiring no help from without, and therefore as *ever remaining unchanged,* in eternal rest and calm, *neither coming into being or passing away,* without change, without time, without multiplicity and diversity, the negative knowledge of which is the keynote of Plato's philosophy. Such an existence must be that to which the denial of the will-to-live opens the way. to dominance by those set up from birth.

145

The scenes of our life are like pictures in rough mosaic that produce no effect if we stand close to them, but that must be viewed at a

1. "The first impulse," "the prime mover."—Tr.

distance if we are to find them beautiful. Therefore to obtain something that was eagerly desired is equivalent to finding out how empty and insubstantial it was, and if we are always living in expectation of better things, we often repent at the same time and long for the past. On the other hand, the present is accepted only for the time being, is set at naught, and looked upon merely as the path to the goal. Thus when at the end of their lives most men look back, they will find that they have lived throughout *ad interim;* they will be surprised to see that the very thing they allowed to slip by unappreciated and unenjoyed was just their life, precisely that in the expectation of which they lived. And so the course of a man's life is, as a rule, such that, having been duped by hope, he dances into the arms of death.

In addition, there is the insatiability of the individual will by virtue whereof every satisfaction creates a fresh desire and its craving, eternally insatiable, goes on forever. At bottom, however, it is due to the fact that, taken in itself, the will is lord of the worlds to whom everything belongs; and so no part could give it satisfaction, but only the whole that, however, is endless. Meanwhile, it must awaken our sympathy when we consider how very little this lord of the world obtains in its individual phenomenon; usually only just enough to maintain the individual body. Hence the profound woe and misery of the individual.

146

In the present period of intellectual impotence that is distinguished by its veneration for every species of inferiority and describes itself most appropriately by the homemade word *Jetztzeit,*[2] as cacophonous as it is pretentious, as if its Now were the Now *par excellence,* the Now for whose production alone all previous Nows have existed—in such a period even the pantheists have the effrontery to say that life is, as they call it, an "end in itself."[3] If this existence of ours were the final aim and object of the world, it would be the silliest that had ever been laid down, whether by ourselves or anyone else.

---

2. "Now-time" (a cacophonous word condemned by Schopenhauer).—Tr.
3. The German *Selbstzweck* is another cacophonous expression censured by Schopenhauer.—Tr.

Life presents itself primarily as a task, namely, that of gaining a livelihood, *de gagner sa vie*. When this problem is solved, what has been gained is a burden, and there comes the second problem of how to dispose of what we have got in order to ward off boredom. Like a bird of prey on the watch, this evil pounces on every life that has been made secure. The first problem, therefore, is to acquire something and the second is to prevent it from making itself felt after it has been acquired, otherwise it is a burden.

If we attempt to take in at a glance the whole world of humanity, we see everywhere a restless struggle, a vast contest for life and existence, with the fullest exertion of bodily and mental powers, in face of dangers and evils of every kind that threaten and strike at any moment. If we then consider the reward for all this, namely, existence and life itself, we find some intervals of painless existence that are at once attacked by boredom and rapidly brought to an end by a new affliction.

Behind *need and want* is to be found at once *boredom,* which attacks even the more intelligent animals. This is a consequence of the fact that life has no *genuine intrinsic worth,* but is kept in *motion* merely by want and illusion. But as soon as this comes to a standstill, the utter barrenness and emptiness of existence become apparent.

That human existence must be a kind of error is sufficiently clear from the simple observation that man is a concretion of needs and wants. Their satisfaction is hard to attain and yet affords him nothing but a painless state in which he is still abandoned to boredom. This, then, is a positive proof that, in itself, existence has no value; for boredom is just that feeling of its emptiness. Thus if life, in the craving for which our very essence and existence consist, had a positive value and in itself a real intrinsic worth, there could not possibly be any boredom. On the contrary, mere existence in itself would necessarily fill our hearts and satisfy us. Now we take no delight in our existence except in striving for something when the distance and obstacles make us think that the goal will be satisfactory, an illusion that vanishes when it is reached; or else in a purely intellectual occupation where we really step out of life in order to contemplate it from without, like spectators in the boxes. Even sensual pleasure itself consists in a constant striving and ceases as soon as its goal is attained. Now whenever we are not striving for something or are not intellectually occupied, but are thrown back on existence itself, its worthlessness and vanity are brought home to us; and this is what is meant by boredom. Even our inherent and ineradicable tendency to run after what is strange and extraordinary shows how glad we are to see an interruption in the natural course of things, which is so tedious. Even the pomp and splendor of the great in their luxury and entertainments are at bottom really nothing but a vain attempt to get beyond the essential wretchedness of our existence. For after all, what are precious stones, pearls, feathers, red velvet, many candles, dancers, the putting on and off of masks, and so on? No man has ever yet felt entirely happy in the present, for he would have been intoxicated.

147

The most perfect phenomenon of the will-to-live, which manifests itself in the exceedingly ingenious and complex mechanism of the human organism, must crumble to dust, and thus its whole essence and efforts are in the end obviously given over to annihilation. All this is the naive utterance of nature, always true and sincere, that the whole striving of that will is essentially empty and vain. If we were something valuable in itself, something that could be unconditioned and absolute, it would not have nonexistence as its goal. The feeling of this also underlies Goethe's fine song:

> High upon the ancient tower
> Stands the hero's noble spirit.

The *necessity of death* can be inferred primarily from the fact that man is a mere phenomenon, not a thing-in-itself and thus not *that which truly is.*[4] If he were, he could not perish. But that the thing-in-itself at the root of phenomena of this kind can manifest itself only in them, is a consequence of its nature.

What a difference there is between our beginning and our end! the former in the frenzy of desire and the ecstasy of sensual pleasure; the latter in the destruction of all the organs and the musty odor of corpses. The path from birth to death is always downhill as regards well-being and the enjoyment of life; blissfully dreaming

---

4. Expression used by Plato.—Tr.

childhood, lighthearted youth, toilsome manhood, frail and often pitiable old age, the torture of the last illness, and finally the agony of death. Does it not look exactly as if existence were a false step whose consequences gradually become more and more obvious?

We shall have the most accurate view of life if we regard it as a *desengaño*, a disillusionment; everything points to this clearly enough.

147a

Our life is of a *microscopical* nature; it is an indivisible point that we see drawn apart by the two powerful lenses of space and time, and thus very considerably magnified.

Time is a contrivance in our brain for giving the *utterly futile existence* of things and ourselves a semblance of reality by means of continuance and duration.

How foolish it is to regret and deplore the fact that in the past we let slip the opportunity for some pleasure or good fortune! For what more would we have now? Just the shriveled-up mummy of a memory. But it is the same with everything that has actually fallen to our lot. Accordingly, the *form of time* itself is precisely the means well calculated to bring home to us the *vanity* of all earthly pleasures.

Our existence and that of all animals is not something standing fast and remaining firm, at any rate temporally; on the contrary it is a *mere existentia fluxa* that continues only through constant fluctuation and change and is comparable to a whirlpool. It is true that the *form* of the body has a precarious existence for a while, but only on condition that matter constantly changes, the old being evacuated and the new assimilated. Accordingly, the principal business of all those beings is to procure at all times matter that is suitable for this influx. At the same time, they are conscious that such an existence as theirs can be maintained only for a while in the aforesaid manner and so with the approach of death, they endeavor to carry it forward to another being that will take their place. This striving appears in self-consciousness in the form of sexual impulse and manifests itself, in the consciousness of other things and thus in objective intuitive perception, in the form of genital organs. We can compare this impulse to the thread of a pearl necklace where those rapidly succeeding individuals would correspond to the pearls. If in our imagination we accelerate this succession and always see in the whole series as well as in the individuals only the form permanent, but the substance or matter constantly changing, we then become aware that we have only a quasi existence. This interpretation is also the basis of Plato's doctrine of *Ideas* that alone exist and of the shadowlike nature of the things that correspond to them.

That we are *mere phenomena* as distinct from things-in-themselves, is illustrated and exemplified by the fact that the *conditio sine qua non* of our existence is the constant excretion and accretion of matter, as nourishment the need for which is always recurring. For in this respect, we resemble phenomena that are brought about through smoke, flame, or a jet of water and that fade away or stop as soon as the supply fails.

It can also be said that the *will-to-live* manifests itself simply in phenomena that become absolutely *nothing*. But this nothing together with the phenomena remains within the will-to-live and rests on its ground. This is, of course, obscure and not easy to understand.

If from contemplating the course of the world on a large scale and especially from considering the rapid succession of generations of people and their ephemeral mock-existence we turn and look at *human life in detail,* as presented say by the comedy, then the impression this now makes is like that of a drop of water, seen through a microscope and teeming with *infusoria,* or that of an otherwise visible little heap of cheese-mites whose strenuous activity and strife make us laugh. For, as in the narrowest space, so too in the briefest span of time, great and serious activity produces a comic effect.

Translated by E. F. J. Payne

4
Additional Remarks on the Doctrine of the Suffering of the World

148

If suffering is not the first and immediate object of our life, then our existence is the most inexpedient and inappropriate thing in the world. For it is absurd to assume that the infinite pain, which everywhere abounds in the world and springs from the want and misery essential to life, could be purposeless and purely accidental. Our susceptibility to pain is well-nigh infinite; but that to pleasure has narrow limits. It is true that each separate piece of misfortune seems to be an exception, but misfortune in general is the rule.

149

Just as a brook forms no eddy so long as it meets with no obstructions, so human nature, as well as animal, is such that we do not really notice and perceive all that goes on in accordance with our will. If we were to notice it, then the reason for this would inevitably be that it did not go according to our will, but must have met with some obstacle. On the other hand, everything that obstructs, crosses, or opposes our will, and thus everything unpleasant and painful, is felt by us immediately, at once, and very plainly. Just as we *do not feel* the health of our whole body, but only the small spot where the shoe pinches, so we do not think of all our affairs that are going on perfectly well, but only of some significant trifle that annoys us. On this rests the negative nature of well-being and happiness, as opposed to the positive nature of pain, a point that I have often stressed.

Accordingly, I know of no greater absurdity than that of most metaphysical systems that declare evil to be something negative;[1] whereas it is precisely that which is positive and makes itself felt. On the other hand, that which is good, in other words, all happiness and satisfaction, is negative, that is, the mere elimination of a desire and the ending of a pain.

In agreement with this is the fact that, as a rule, we find pleasures far below, but pains far beyond, our expectation.

Whoever wants summarily to test the assertion that the pleasure in the world outweighs the pain, or at any rate that the two balance each other, should compare the feelings of an animal that is devouring another with those of that other.

150

The most effective consolation in any misfortune or suffering is to look at others who are even more unfortunate than we; and this everyone can do. But what then is the result for the whole of humanity?

We are like lambs playing in the field, while the butcher eyes them and selects first one and then another; for in our good days we do not know what calamity fate at this very moment has in store for us, sickness, persecution, impoverishment, mutilation, loss of sight, madness, death, and so on.

History shows us the life of nations and can find nothing to relate except wars and insurrections; the years of peace appear here and there only as short pauses, as intervals between the acts. And in the same way, the life of the individual is a perpetual struggle, not merely metaphorically with want and boredom but actually with others. Everywhere he finds an opponent, lives in constant conflict, and dies weapon in hand.

151

Not a little is contributed to the torment of our existence by the fact that *time* is always pressing on us, never lets us draw breath,

---

1. Leibniz is particularly strong on this point and endeavors (*Théodicée*, Section 153) to strengthen his case by a palpable and pitiable sophism.

and is behind every one of us is like a taskmaster with a whip. Only those who have been handed over to boredom are not pressed and plagued by time.

152

However, just as our body would inevitably burst if the pressure of the atmosphere were removed from it, so if the pressure of want, hardship, disappointment, and the frustration of effort were removed from the lives of men, their arrogance would rise, though not to bursting point, yet to manifestations of the most unbridled folly and even madness. At all times, everyone indeed needs a certain amount of care, anxiety, pain, or trouble, just as a ship requires ballast in order to proceed on a straight and steady course.

Work, worry, toil, and trouble are certainly the lot of almost all throughout their lives. But if all desires were fulfilled as soon as they arose, how then would people occupy their lives and spend their time? Suppose the human race were removed to Utopia where everything grew automatically and pigeons flew about ready roasted; where everyone at once found his sweetheart and had no difficulty in keeping her; then people would die of boredom or hang themselves; or else they would fight, throttle, and murder one another and so cause themselves more suffering than is now laid upon them by nature. Thus for such a race, no other scene, no other existence, is suitable.

153

On account of the negative nature of well-being and pleasure as distinct from the positive nature of pain, a fact to which I just now drew the reader's attention, the happiness of any given life is to be measured not by its joys and pleasures, but by the absence of sorrow and suffering, of what is positive. But then the lot of animals appears to be more bearable than that of man. We will consider the two somewhat more closely.

However varied the forms in which man's happiness and unhappiness appear and impel him to pursuit or escape, the material basis of all this is nevertheless physical pleasure or pain. This basis is very restricted, namely, health, nourishment, protection from wet and cold, and sexual satisfaction, or else the want of these things. Consequently, in real physical pleasure man has no more than the animal, except in so far as his more highly developed nervous system enhances the susceptibility to every pleasure but also to every pain as well. But how very much stronger are the emotions stirred in him than those aroused in the animal! How incomparably more deeply and powerfully are his feelings excited! and ultimately only to arrive at the same result, namely, health, nourishment, clothing, and so on.

This arises primarily from the fact that, with him, everything is powerfully enhanced by his thinking of the absent and the future, whereby anxiety, fear, and hope really come into existence for the first time. But then these press much more heavily on him than can the present reality of pleasures or pains, to which the animal is confined. Thus the animal lacks reflection, that condenser of pleasures and pains that, therefore, cannot be accumulated, as happens in the case of man by means of his memory and foresight. On the contrary, with the animal, the suffering of the present moment always remains, even when this again recurs innumerable times, merely the suffering of the present moment as on the first occasion, and cannot be accumulated. Hence the enviable tranquillity and placidity of animals. On the other hand, by means of reflection and everything connected therewith, there is developed in man from those same elements of pleasure and pain that he has in common with the animal, an enhancement of susceptibility to happiness and unhappiness that is capable of leading to momentary, and sometimes even fatal, ecstasy or else to the depths of despair and suicide. More closely considered, things seem to take the following course. In order to heighten his pleasure, man deliberately increases his needs that were originally only a little more difficult to satisfy than those of the animal; hence luxury, delicacies, tobacco, opium, alcoholic liquors, pomp, display, and all that goes with this. Then in addition, in consequence of reflection, there is open to man alone a source of pleasure, and of pain as well, a source that gives him an excessive amount of trouble, in fact almost more than is given by all the others. I refer to ambition and the feeling of honor and shame, in plain words, what he thinks of other people's opinion of him. Now in a thousand different and often strange forms this becomes the goal of almost all his efforts that go beyond physical pleasure or pain. It is true that he certainly has over the animal the advantage of really intellectual pleasures that admit of many degrees from the most ingenuous trifling or conversation up to the highest achievements of the mind. But as a counterweight to this on the side of suffering, boredom appears in man that is unknown to the animal, at any rate in the natural state, but that slightly attacks the most intelligent only if they are domesticated, whereas with man it becomes a real scourge. We see it in that host of miserable wretches who have always been concerned over filling their purses but never their heads, and for whom their very wealth now becomes a punishment by delivering them into the hands of tormenting boredom. To escape from this, they now rush about in all directions and travel here, there, and everywhere. No sooner do they arrive at a place, than they anxiously inquire about its *amusements and clubs,* just as does a poor man about its *sources of assistance;* for, of course, want and boredom are the two poles of human life. Finally, I have to mention that, in the case of man, there is associated with sexual satisfaction an obstinate selection, peculiar to him alone, which rises sometimes to a more or less passionate love and to which I have devoted a lengthy chapter in the second volume of my chief work. In this way, it becomes for him a source of much suffering and little pleasure.

Meanwhile, it is remarkable how, through the addition of thought that the animal lacks, so lofty and vast a structure of human happiness and unhappiness is raised on the same narrow basis of joys and sorrows that the animal also has. With reference to this, his feelings are exposed to such violent emotions, passions, and shocks, that their stamp can be read in the permanent lines on his face; and yet in the end and in reality, it is only a question of the same things that even the animal obtains, and indeed with incomparably less expenditure of emotion and distress. But through all this, the measure of pain increases in man much more than that of pleasure and is now in a special way very greatly enhanced by the fact that death is actually *known* to him. On the other hand, the animal runs away from death merely instinctively, without really knowing it and thus without ever actually coming fact-to-face with it, as does man who always has before him this prospect. And so although only a few animals die a natural death, most of them get only just enough time to propagate their species and then, if not earlier, become the prey of some other animal. On the other hand, man alone in his species has managed to make the so-called natural death the rule to which there are, however, important exceptions. Yet in spite of all this, the animals still have the advantage, for the reason I have given. Moreover, man reaches his really natural term of life just as rarely as do the animals, because his unnatural way of living, his struggles and passions, and the degeneration of the race resulting therefrom rarely enable him to succeed in this.

Animals are much more satisfied than we by mere existence; the plant is wholly satisfied, man according to the degree of his dullness. Consequently, the animal's life contains less suffering, but also less pleasure, than man's. This is due primarily to the fact that it remains free from *care and anxiety* together with their torment, on the one hand, but is also without real *hope,* on the other. And so it does not participate in that anticipation of a joyful future through ideas together with the delightful phantasmagoria, that source of most of our joys and pleasures, which accompanies those ideas and is given in addition by the imagination; consequently in this sense it is without hope. It is both these because its consciousness is restricted to what is intuitively perceived and so to the present moment. Thus only in reference to objects that already exist at this moment in intuitive perception, does the animal have an extremely short fear and hope; whereas man's consciousness has an intellectual horizon that embraces the whole of life and even goes beyond this. But in consequence of this, animals, when compared with us, seem to be really wise in one respect, namely in their calm and undisturbed enjoyment of the present moment. The animal is the embodiment of the present; the obvious peace of mind that it thus shares frequently puts us to shame with our often restless and dissatisfied state that comes from thoughts and cares. And even those pleasures of hope and anticipation we have just been discussing are not to be had for nothing. Thus what a man enjoys in advance, through hoping and expecting a satisfaction, afterwards detracts from the actual enjoyment of this, since the thing itself then satisfies him by so much the less. The animal, on the other hand, remains free from such pleasure in advance as well as from that deduction of pleasure, and therefore enjoys the real and present thing itself, whole and undiminished. In the same way, evils press on the animal merely with their own actual weight, whereas for us they are often increased tenfold by fear and foresight, what the Greeks called, *the dread of evil.*

It is just this *complete absorption in the present moment,* peculiar to animals, that contributes so much to the pleasure we derive from our domestic pets. They are the present moment personified and, to a certain extent, make us feel the value of every unburdened and unclouded hour, whereas with our thoughts we usually pass it over and leave it unheeded. But the above-mentioned capacity of animals to be more satisfied than we by mere existence is abused by egotistic and heartless man, and is often exploited to such an extent that he allows them absolutely nothing but bare existence. For example, the bird that is organized to roam through half the world, is confined to a cubic foot of space where it slowly pines to death and cries; for

> *l'uccello nella gabbia*
> *Canta non di piacre, ma di rabbia,*[2]

and the highly intelligent dog, man's truest and most faithful friend, is put on a chain by him! Never do I see such a dog without feelings of the deepest sympathy for him and of profound indignation against his master. I think with satisfaction of a case, reported some years ago in *The Times,* where Lord——kept a large dog on a chain. One day as he was walking through the yard, he took it into his head to go and pat the dog, whereupon the animal tore his arm open from top to bottom, and quite right too! What he meant by this was: "You are not my master, but my devil who makes a hell of my brief existence!" May this happen to all who chains up dogs.

154

If the result of the foregoing remarks is that the enhanced power of knowledge renders the life of man more woebegone than that of the animal, we can reduce this to a universal law and thereby obtain a much wider view.

In itself, knowledge is always painless. Pain concerns the *will* alone and consists in checking, hindering, or thwarting this; yet an additional requirement is that this checking be accompanied by knowledge. Thus just as light illuminates space only when objects exist to reflect it; just as a tone requires resonance and sound gener-

2. Ill is the humor of the bird in a cage; He signs not for pleasure, but only from rage.—TR.

ally becomes audible at a distance only through waves of the vibrating air that break on hard bodies so that its effect is strikingly feeble on isolated mountaintops and a song in the open produces little effect; so also in the same way must the checking of the *will*, in order to be felt as pain, be accompanied by knowledge that in itself, however, is a stranger to all pain.

Thus *physical* pain is already conditioned by nerves and their connection with the brain; and so an injury to a limb is not felt if its nerves leading to the brain are severed, or when the brain itself loses its powers through chloroform. For the very same reason, we consider that, as soon as consciousness is extinguished when a person is dying, all subsequent convulsions are painless. It follows as a matter of course that *mental* pain is conditioned by knowledge; and that it increases with the degree of knowledge can easily be seen, and moreover in the above remarks as also in my chief work, volume 1, section 56. We can, therefore, figuratively express the whole relationship by saying that the will is the string, its thwarting or checking the vibration thereof, knowledge the sounding board, and pain the tone.

Now according to this, only what is inorganic and also the plant are incapable of feeling pain, however often the will may be checked in both. On the other hand, every animal, even an infusorian, feels pain because knowledge, however imperfect, is the true characteristic of animal existence. As knowledge rises on the animal scale, so too does susceptibility to pain. It is, therefore, still extremely small in the case of the lowest animals; thus, for example, insects still go on eating when the back part of the body is nearly torn off and hangs by a mere thread of gut. But even in the highest animals, because of an absence of concepts and thought, pain is nothing like that which is suffered by man. Even the susceptibility to pain could reach its highest point only when, by virtue of our faculty of reason and its reflectiveness, there exists also the possibility of denying the will. For without that possibility, such susceptibility would have been purposeless cruelty.

155

In early youth we sit before the impending course of our life like children at the theater before the curtain is raised, who sit there in happy and excited expectation of the things that are to come. It is a blessing that we do not know what will actually come. For to the man who knows, the children may at times appear to be like innocent delinquents who are condemned not to death, it is true, but to life and have not yet grasped the purport of their sentence. Nevertheless everyone wants to reach old age and thus to a state of life, whereof it may be said: "It is bad today and every day it will get worse, until the worst of all happens."

156

If we picture to ourselves roughly as far as we can the sum total of misery, pain, and suffering of every kind on which the sun shines in its course, we shall admit that it would have been much better if it had been just as impossible for the sun to produce the phenomenon of life on earth as on the moon, and the surface of the earth, like that of the moon, had still been in a crystalline state.

We can also regard our life as a uselessly disturbing episode in the blissful repose of nothingness. At all events even the man who has fared tolerably well, becomes more clearly aware, the longer he lives, that life on the whole is a *disappointment, nay a cheat,*[3] in other words, bears the character of a great mystification or even a fraud. When two men who were friends in their youth meet again after the separation of a lifetime, the feeling uppermost in their minds when they see each other, in that it recalls old times, is one of complete *disappointment with the whole of life.* In former years under the rosy sunrise of their youth, life seemed to them so fair in prospect; it made so many promises and has kept so few. So definitely uppermost is this feeling when they meet that they do not even deem it necessary to express it in words, but both tacitly assume it and proceed to talk on that basis.

Whoever lives *two or three generations,* feels like the spectator who, during the fair, sees the performances of all kinds of jugglers and, if he remains seated in the booth, sees them repeated two or three times. As the tricks were meant only for one performance, they no longer make any impression after the illusion and novelty have vanished.

We should be driven crazy if we contemplated the lavish and

3. Schopenhauer's own words.—Tr.

excessive arrangements, the countless flaming fixed stars in infinite space that have nothing to do but illuminate worlds, such being the scene of misery and desolation and, in the luckiest case, yielding nothing but boredom—at any rate to judge from the specimen with which we are familiar.

No one is to be greatly *envied*, but many thousands are to be greatly *pitied*.

Life is a task to be worked off; in this sense *defunctus*[4] is a fine expression.

Let us for a moment imagine that the act of procreation were not a necessity or accompanied by intense pleasure, but a matter of pure rational deliberation; could then the human race really continue to exist? Would not everyone rather feel so much sympathy for the coming generation that he would prefer to spare it the burden of existence, or at any rate would not like to assume in cold blood the responsibility of imposing on it such a burden?

The world is just a *hell* and in it human beings are the tortured souls on the one hand, and the devils on the other.

I suppose I shall have to be told again that my philosophy is cheerless and comfortless simply because I tell the truth, whereas people want to hear that the Lord has made all things very well. Go to your churches and leave us philosophers in peace! At any rate, do not demand that they should cut their doctrines according to your pattern! This is done by knaves and philosophasters from whom you can order whatever doctrines you like.[5]

Brahma produces the world through a kind of original sin, but himself remains in it to atone for this until he has redeemed himself from it. This is quite a good idea! In *Buddhism* the world comes into being in consequence of an inexplicable disturbance (after a long period of calm) in the crystal clearness of the blessed and penitentially obtained state of *Nirvana* and hence through a kind of fatality that, however, is to be understood ultimately in a moral sense; although the matter has its exact analogue and corresponding picture in physics, in the inexplicable arising of a primordial nebula, whence a sun is formed. Accordingly, in consequence of moral lapses, it also gradually becomes physically worse and worse

4. One who has finished with the business of life.—Tr.
5. To put professors of philosophy out of countenance with their orthodox optimism is as easy as it is agreeable.

until it assumes its present sorry state. An excellent idea! To the *Greeks* the world and the gods were the work of an unfathomable necessity; this is fairly reasonable insofar as it satisfies us for the time being. *Ormuzd* lives in conflict with *Ahriman;* this seems not unreasonable. But that a God *Jehovah* creates this world of misery and affliction *animi causa*[6] and *de gaité de coeur,*[7] and then applauds himself with an "everything was very good,"[8] this is something intolerable. And so in this respect, we see the religion of the Jews occupy the lowest place among the dogmas of the civilized world, which is wholly in keeping with the fact that it is also the only religion that has absolutely no doctrine of immortality, nor has it even any trace thereof. (See vol. 1 of this work, pages 125-126.)

Even if Leibniz's demonstration were correct, that of all *possible* worlds this is nevertheless always the best, we should still not have a *Théodicée.* For the Creator has created indeed not merely the world, but also the possibility itself; accordingly, he should have arranged this with a view to its admitting of a better world.

But generally, such a view of the world as the successful work of an all-wise, all-benevolent, and moreover almighty Being is too flagrantly contradicted by the misery and wretchedness that fill the world on the one hand, and by the obvious imperfection and even burlesque distortion of the most perfect of its phenomena on the other; I refer to the human phenomenon. Here is to be found a dissonance that can never be resolved. On the other hand, these very instances will agree with, and serve as a proof of, our argument if we look upon the world as the work of our own guilt and consequently as something that it were better never to have been. Whereas on the first assumption human beings become a bitter indictment against the Creator and provide material for sarcasm, they appear on the second as a denunciation of our own true nature and will, which is calculated to humble us. For they lead us to the view that we, as the offspring of dissolute fathers, have come into the world already burdened with guilt and that, only because we have to be continually working off this debt, does our existence prove to be so wretched and have death as its finale. Nothing is

6. Because he feels inclined to.—TR.
7. Out of sheer wantonness.—TR.
8. Genesis 1:31.—TR.

more certain than that, speaking generally, it is the great *sin of the world* that produces the many and great *sufferings of the world;* and here I refer not to the physically empirical connection, but to the metaphysical. According to this view, it is only the story of the Fall of Man that reconciles me to the Old Testament. In fact, in my eyes, it is the only metaphysical truth that appears in the book, although it is clothed in allegory. For to nothing does our existence bear so close a resemblance as to the consequence of a false step and guilty lust. I cannot refrain from recommending to the thoughtful reader a popular, but exceedingly profound, dissertation on this subject by Claudius that brings to light the essentially pessimistic spirit of Christianity and appears in the fourth part of the *Wandsbecker Bote* with the title "Cursed be the ground for thy sake."

To have always in hand a sure compass for guiding us in life and enabling us always to view this in the right light without ever going astray, nothing is more suitable than to accustom ourselves to regard this world as a place of penance and hence a penal colony, so to speak, a *penetentiary,* as it was called even by the oldest philosophers (according to Clement of Alexandria, *Stromata,* lib. 3, c. 3, p. 399). Among the Christian Fathers Origen expressed it thus with commendable boldness. (See Augustine, *De civitate dei,*[9] lib. 11, c. 23.) This view of the world also finds its theoretical and objective justification not merely in my philosophy, but in the wisdom of all ages, in Brahmanism, Buddhism, Empedocles, and Pythagoras. Cicero also mentions (*Fragmenta de philosophia,* vol. 12, p. 316, *ed. Bip.*) that it was taught by ancient sages and at the initiation into the Mysteries, *nos ob aliqua scelera suscepta in vita superiore, poenarum luendarum causa natos esse.*[10] Vanini, whom it was easier to burn that to refute, gives the strongest expression to this by saying: *Tot tantisque homo repletus miseriis, ut si Christianae religioni non repugnaret, dicere auderem: si daemones dantur, ipsi, in hominum corpora transmigrantes, sceleris poenas*

---

9. Nothing can be more conducive to patience in life and to a placid endurance of men and evils than a *Buddhist* reminder of this kind: "*This is Samsara,* the world of lust and craving and thus of birth, disease, old age, and death; it is a world that ought not to be. And this is here the population of *Samsara.* Therefore what better things can you expect?" I would like to prescribe that everyone repeat this four times a day, fully conscious of what he is saying.

10. That, on account of definite mistakes made in a previous life, we are born to pay the penalty.—Tr.

luunt.[11] (*De admirandis naturae arcanis,* Dial. 50, p. 353.) But even in genuine Christianity that is properly understood, our existence is regarded as the consequence of a guilt, a false step. If we have acquired that habit, we shall adjust our expectations from life to suit the occasion and accordingly no longer regard as unexpected and abnormal its troubles, vexations, sufferings, worries, and misery, great and small. On the contrary, we shall find such things to be quite in order, well knowing that here everyone is punished for his existence and indeed each in his own way.[12] For one of the evils of a penitentiary is also the society we meet there. What this is like will be known by anyone who is worthy of a better society without my telling him. A fine nature, as well as a genius, may sometimes feel in this world like a noble state-prisoner in the galleys among common criminals; and they, like him, will therefore attempt to isolate themselves. Generally speaking, however, the above-mentioned way of looking at things will enable us to regard without surprise and certainly without indignation the so-called imperfections, that is, the wretched and contemptible nature of most men both morally and intellectually, which is accordingly stamped on their faces. For we shall always remember where we are and consequently look on everyone primarily as a being who exists only as a result of his sinfulness and whose life is the atonement for the guilt of his birth. It is just this that Christianity calls the sinful nature of man. It is, therefore, the basis of the beings whom we meet in this world as our fellows. Moreover, in consequence of the constitution of the world, they are almost all, more or less, in a state of suffering and dissatisfaction that is not calculated to make them more sympathetic and amiable. Finally, there is the fact that, in almost all cases, their intellect is barely sufficient for the service of their will. Accordingly, we have to regulate our claims on the society of this world. Whoever keeps firmly to this point of view, might call the social impulse a pernicious tendency.

11. Man is so full of many great afflictions that, if it were not repugnant to the Christian religion, I would venture to assert that, if there are demons, they are cast into human bodies and pay the penalties for their sins.—TR.

12. The correct standard for *judging any man* is to remember that he is really a being who should not exist at all, but who is atoning for his existence through many different forms of suffering and through death. What can we expect from such a being? We atone for our birth first by living and secondly by dying. This is also allegorized by *original sin.*

In fact, the conviction that the world and thus also man is something that really ought not to be, is calculated to fill us with forbearance toward one another; for what can we expect from beings in such a predicament? In fact from this point of view, it might occur to us that the really proper address between one man and another should be, instead of *Sir, Monsieur,* and so on, *Leidensgefährte, socii malorum, compagnon de misères, my fellow sufferer.* However strange this may sound, it accords with the facts, put the other man in the most correct light, and reminds us of that most necessary thing, tolerance, patience, forbearance, and love of one's neighbor, which everyone needs and each of us, therefore, owes to another.

156a

The characteristic of the things of this world and especially of the world of men is not exactly *imperfection,* as has often been said, but rather *distortion,* in everything, in what is moral, intellectual, or physical.

The excuse, sometimes made for many a vice, namely *"that it is natural to man,"* is by no means adequate, but the proper rejoinder should be: "just because it is bad, it is *natural;* and just because it is *natural* it is bad." To understand this aright, we must have grasped the meaning of the doctrine of original sin.

When judging a human individual, we should always keep to the point of view that the basis of such is something that ought not to be at all, something sinful, perverse, and absurd, that which has been understood as original sin, that on account of which he is doomed to die. This fundamentally bad nature is indeed characterized by the fact that no one can bear to be closely scrutinized. What can we expect from such a being? If, therefore, we start from this fact, we shall judge him more indulgently; we shall not be surprised when the devils lurking in him bestir themselves and peep out, and we shall be better able to appreciate any good point that has nevertheless been found in him, whether this be a consequence of his intellect or of anything else. In the second place, we should also be mindful of his position and remember that life is essentially a condition of want, distress, and often misery, where everyone has to fight and struggle for his existence and therefore cannot always put on a pleasant face. If, on the contrary, man were that which all optimistic religions and philosophies would like to make him, namely, the work or even the incarnation of a God, in fact a being that in every sense ought to be and to be as he is, what a totally different effect would inevitably be produced by the first sight, the closer acquaintance, and the continued intercourse with every human being from that which is now produced!

Pardon's the word to all (Cymbeline, act 5, sc. 5). We should treat with indulgence every human folly, failing, and vice, bearing in mind that what we have before us are simply our own follies, failings, and vices. For they are just the failings of mankind to which we also belong; accordingly, we have in ourselves all its failings, and so those at which we are just now indignant, merely because they do not appear in us at this particular moment. Thus they are not on the surface, but lie deep down within us and will come up and show themselves on the first occasion, just as we see them in others; although one failing is conspicuous in one man and another in another, and the sum total of all bad qualities is undoubtedly very much greater in one man than in another. For the difference in individualities is incalculably great.

Translated by E. F. J. Payne

5

On Suicide

A s far as I can see, it is only the monotheistic, and hence Jewish, religions whose followers regard suicide as a crime. This is the more surprising since neither in the Old Testament nor in the New is there to be found any prohibition or even merely a definite condemnation of suicide. Teachers of religion have, therefore, to base their objection to suicide on their own philosophical grounds; but their arguments are in such a bad way that they try to make up for what these lack in strength by the vigorous expressions of their abhorrence and thus by being abusive. We then of necessity hear that suicide is the greatest cowardice, that it is possible only in madness, and suchlike absurdities; or else the wholly meaningless phrase that suicide is "wrong," whereas there is obviously nothing in the world over which every man has such an indisputable *right* as his own person and life. (Cf. section 121.) As I have said, suicide is even accounted a crime and connected with this, especially in vulgar bigoted England, are an ignominious burial and the confiscation of legacies; for which reason a jury almost invariably brings in a verdict of insanity. First of all, we should allow moral feeling to decide the matter and compare the impression made on us by the news that an acquaintance of ours had committed a crime, such as murder, cruelty, fraud, or theft, with that made by the report of his voluntary death. Whereas the former report arouses lively indignation, the greatest resentment, and a demand for punishment or revenge, the latter will move us to sorrow and sympathy often mingled with a certain admiration for his courage rather than with the moral condemnation that accompanies a bad action. Who has not had acquaintances, friends, and relations who have voluntarily departed from the world? And should we all regard these with abhorrence as criminals? *Nego ac pernego!*[1] I am rather of the opinion that the clergy should be challenged once and for all to tell us with what right they stigmatize as a *crime* an action that has been committed by many who were honored and beloved by us; for they do so from the pulpit and in their writings without being able to point to any biblical authority and in fact without having any valid philosophical arguments, and they refuse an honorable burial to those who voluntarily depart from the world. But here it should be stipulated that we want *reasons* and shall not accept in their place mere empty phrases or words of abuse. If criminal law condemns suicide, that is not an ecclesiastically valid reason and is, moreover, definitely ridiculous; for what punishment can frighten the man who seeks death? If we punish the *attempt* to commit suicide, then we are simply punishing the want of skill whereby it failed.

Even the ancients were far from regarding the matter in that light. Pliny (*Historia naturalis*, lib. 28, c. 1; vol. 4, p. 351 *ed. Bip.*) says: *Vitam quidem non adeo expetendam censemus, ut quoque modo trahenda sit. Quisquis es talis, aeque moriere, etiam cum obscoenus vixeris, aut nefandus. Quapropter hoc primum quisque in remediis animi sui habeat: ex omnibus bonis, quae homini tribuit natura, nullum melius esse tempestiva morte: idque in ea optimum, quod illam sibi quisque praestare poterit.*[2] He also says (lib. 2, c. 7; vol. 1, p. 125): *ne Deum quidem posse omnia. Namque nec sibi potest mortem consciscere, si velit, quod homini dedit optimum in tantis vitae poenis, etc.*[3] In Massilia and on the island of Ceos, the

---

1. I say no, certainly not.—TR.
2. We are of the opinion that one should not love life so much as to prolong it at all costs. Whoever you may be, you who desire this will likewise die, even though you may have lived a (good or) vicious and criminal life. Therefore may everyone above all keep as a remedy for his soul the fact that, of all the blessings conferred by nature on man, none is better than an opportune death; and the best thing is that everyone can procure for himself such a death.—TR.
3. Not even God is capable of everything. For even if he wanted to, he cannot come to a decision about his own death. Yet with so much suffering in life, such a death is the best gift he has granted to man.—TR.

cup of hemlock was even publicly handed to the man who could
state convincing reasons for quitting life (Valerius Maximus, lib.
2, c. 6, sections 7 and 8).[4] And how many heroes and sages of
antiquity have not ended their lives by a voluntary death! It is true
that Aristotle says (*Nicomachean Ethics,* v. 15) suicide is a wrong
against the State, although not against one's own person. Yet in
his exposition of the ethics of the Peripatetics, Stobaeus quotes the
sentence (*Eclogae ethicae,* lib. 2, c. 7, vol. 3, p. 286): *Vitam autem
relinquendam esse bonis in nimiis quidem miseriis, pravis vero in
nimium quoque secundis*[5] And similarly on page 312: *Ideoque et
uxorem ducturum, et liberos procreaturum, et ad civitatem ac-
cessurum etc. atque omnino virtutem colendo tum vitam serva-
turum, tum iterum, cogente necessitate, relicturum, etc.*[6]

We find suicide extolled as a noble and heroic action even by the
Stoics, as can be proved from hundreds of passages, the most vigorous of which are from Seneca. Further with the Hindus, it is well-
known that suicide often occurs as a religious action, particularly
as widow burning, self-destruction under the wheels of the Jugger-
naut Car, self-sacrifice to the crocodiles of the Ganges or the sacred
temple tanks, and otherwise. It is precisely the same at the theater,
that mirror of life; for example, in the celebrated Chinese play
L'Orphelin de la Chine (translated by Saint-Julien, 1834), we see
almost all the noble characters end in suicide without there being
any suggestion or its occurring to the spectator that they had committed a crime. In fact, at bottom on our own stage it is not otherwise, for example, Palmira in *Mahomet,* Mortimer in *Maria Stuart,*
Othello, Countess Terzky. And Sophocles says:

God will release me when I myself wish it.[7]

Is Hamlet's monologue the meditation of a crime? He merely states

4. On the island of Ceos it was the custom for *old people to die voluntarily.*
See Valerius Maximus, lib. 2, c. 6. Heraclides Ponticus, *Fragmenta de rebus publicis,*
lib. 9 Aelianus, *Variae historiae,* 3: 37. Strabo, lib. 10, c. 5, section 6, ed. Kramer.
5. That the good must quit life when their misfortune is too great, but the
bad also when their good fortune is too great.—TR.
6. Therefore a man must marry, have children, devote himself to the service
of the State, and generally preserve his life in the cultivation of skill and ability,
but again quit it under the compulsion of necessity.—TR.
7. Not Sophocles, but Euripides, *Bacchae,* 498.—TR.

that, if we were sure of being absolutely annihilated by death, we would undoubtedly choose it in view of the state of the world. "Ay, there's the rub."[8] But the reasons against suicide that are advanced by the clergy of the monotheistic, i.e., Jewish, religions and by the philosophers who accommodate themselves to them, are feeble sophisms that can easily be refuted. (See my essay *On the Basis of Ethics*, section 5.) The most thorough refutation of them has been furnished by Hume in his essay *On Suicide*, which first appeared after his death and was at once suppressed in England by the disgraceful bigotry and scandalous power of the parsons. And so only a few copies were sold secretly and at a high price, and for the preservation of this and another essay by that great man we are indebted to the Basel reprint: *Essays on Suicide and the Immortality of the Soul*, by the late David Hume, Basel, 1799, sold by James Decker, 124 pp.; 8vo. But that a purely philosophical essay, coldly and rationally refuting the current reasons against suicide and coming from one of the leading thinkers and authors of England, had to be secretly smuggled through that country like a forbidden thing until it found refuge abroad, brings great discredit on the English nation. At the same time, it shows what kind of a conscience the Church has on this point. I have expounded in my chief work, volume 1, section 69, the only valid moral reason against suicide. It lies in the fact that suicide is opposed to the attainment of the highest moral goal since it substitutes for the real salvation from this world of woe and misery one that is merely apparent. But it is still a very long way from this aberration to a crime, such as the Christian clergy would like to stamp it.

In its innermost core, Christianity bears the truth that suffering (the Cross) is the real purpose of life; and therefore as suicide opposes such purpose, Christianity rejects it, whereas antiquity, from a lower point of view, approved and even honored it. That reason against suicide is, however, ascetic and therefore applies only to an ethical standpoint much higher than that which European moral philosophers have ever occupied. But if we descend from that very high point, there is no longer any valid moral reason for condemning suicide. It seems, therefore, that the extraordinarily

8. *Hamlet*, act 3, sc. 1—TR.

lively zeal of the clergy of the monotheistic religions against suicide,[9] a zeal that is not supported either by the Bible or by valid grounds, must have a hidden foundation. Might it not be that the voluntary giving up of life is a poor compliment to him who said, *everything was very good*.[10] So once again, it is the customary and orthodox optimism of these religions that denounces suicide in order not to be denounced by it.

158

On the whole, we shall find that, as soon as a point is reached where the terrors of life outweigh those of death, man puts an end to his life. The resistance of the latter is nevertheless considerable; they stand, so to speak, as guardians at the gate of the exit. Perhaps there is no one alive who would not already have made an end of his life if such an end were something purely negative, a sudden cessation of existence. But it is something positive, namely, the destruction of the body, and this frightens people back just because the body is the phenomenon of the will-to-live.

However, the struggle with those guardians is not, as a rule, *so* difficult as it may seem from a distance and indeed in consequence of the antagonism between mental and bodily sufferings. Thus if physically we suffer very severely or continuously, we become indifferent to all other troubles; only our recovery is uppermost in our thoughts. In the same way, severe mental suffering makes us indifferent to physical; we treat it with contempt. In fact, if physical suffering should predominate, this is a wholesome diversion, a pause in the mental suffering. It is precisely this that makes suicide easier, since the physical pain associated with this loses all importance in the eyes of one who is tormented by an excessive amount of mental suffering. This becomes particularly noticeable in those who are driven to suicide through a purely morbid deep depression. It does not cost such men any self-restraint at all; they need not make a resolute rush at it, but, as soon as the warder appointed

9. On this point all are unanimous. According to Rousseau, *Oeuvres*, vol. 4, p. 275, Augustine and Lactantius were the first to declare suicide to be a sin, but took their argument from Plato's *Phaedo* (139), since shown to be as trite as it is utterly groundless, that we are on duty or are slaves of the gods.
10. (And God saw) everything (that he had made, and behold, it) was very good. (Genesis 1:31.)—Tr.

to look after them leaves them for two minutes, they quickly put an end to their life.

159

If in heavy horrible dreams anxiety reaches its highest degree, it causes us to wake up, whereby all those monstrous horrors of the night vanish. The same thing happens in the dream of life when the highest degree of anxiety forces us to break it off.

160

Suicide can also be regarded as an experiment, a question we put to nature and try to make her answer, namely, what change the existence and knowledge of man undergo through death. But it is an awkward experiment, for it abolishes the identity of the consciousness that would have to listen to the answer.

Translated by E. F. J. Payne

6

On the Fundamental View of Idealism

In endless space countless luminous spheres, round each of which some dozen smaller illuminated ones revolve, hot at the core and covered over with a hard cold crust; on this crust a moldy film has produced living and knowing beings; this is empirical truth, the real, the world. Yet for a being who thinks, it is a precarious position to stand on one of those numberless spheres freely floating in boundless space, without knowing whence or whither, and to be only one of innumerable similar beings that throng, press, and toil, restlessly and rapidly arising and passing away in beginningless and endless time. Here there is nothing permanent but matter alone, and the recurrence of the same varied organic forms by means of certain ways and channels that inevitably exist as they do. All that empirical science can teach is only the more precise nature and rule of these events. But at last the philosophy of modern times, especially through Berkeley and Kant, has called to mind that all this in the first instance is only *phenomenon of the brain*, and is encumbered by so many great and different *subjective* conditions that its supposed absolute reality vanishes, and leaves room for an entirely different world-order that lies at the root of that phenomenon, in other words, is related to it as is the thing-in-itself to the mere appearance.

"The world is my representation" is, like the axioms of Euclid, a proposition that everyone must recognize as true as soon as he understands it, although it is not a proposition that everyone

The world is mine, not Fate's.

Let the best man win, but only fatalists are losers.

understands as soon as he hears it. To have brought this proposition to consciousness and to have connected it with the problem of the relation of the ideal to the real, in other words, of the world in the head to the world outside the head, constitutes, together with the problem of moral freedom, the distinctive characteristic of the philosophy of the moderns. For only after men had tried their hand for thousands of years at merely *objective* philosophizing did they discover that, among the many things that make the world so puzzling and precarious, the first and foremost is that, however immeasurable and massive it may be, its existence hangs nevertheless on a single thread; and this thread is the actual consciousness in which it exists. This condition, with which the existence of the world is irrevocably encumbered, marks it with the stamp of *ideality,* in spite of all *empirical* reality, and consequently with the stamp of the mere *phenomenon.* Thus the world must be recognized, from one aspect at least, as akin to a dream, indeed as capable of being put in the same class with a dream. For the same brain function that conjures up during sleep a perfectly objective, perceptible, and indeed palpable world must have just as large a share in the presentation of the objective world of wakefulness. Though different as regards their matter, the two worlds are nevertheless obviously molded from one form. This form is the intellect, the brain function. Descartes was probably the first to attain the degree of reflection demanded by that fundamental truth; consequently, he made that truth the starting point of his philosophy, although provisionally only in the form of skeptical doubt. By his taking *cogito ergo sum*[1] as the only thing certain, and provisionally regarding the existence of the world as problematical, the essential and only correct starting point, and at the same time the true point of support, of all philosophy was really found. This point, indeed, is essentially and of necessity the *subjective, our own consciousness.* For this alone is and remains that which is immediate; everything else, be it what it may, is first mediated and conditioned by consciousness, and therefore dependent on it. It is thus rightly considered that the philosophy of the moderns starts from Descartes as its father. Not long afterwards, Berkeley went farther along this path, and arrived at *idealism* proper; in other words, at

1. I think, therefore I am.—Tʀ.

the knowledge that what is extended in space, and hence the objective, material world in general, exists as such simply and solely in our *representation*, and that it is false and indeed absurd to attribute to it, *as such*, an existence outside all representation and independent of the knowing subject, and so to assume a matter positively and absolutely existing in itself. But this very correct and deep insight really constitutes the whole of Berkeley's philosophy; in it he had exhausted himself.

Accordingly, true philosophy must at all costs be *idealistic;* indeed, it must be so merely to be honest. For nothing is more certain than that no one ever came out of himself in order to identify himself immediately with things different from him; but everything of which he has certain, sure, and hence immediate knowledge, lies within his consciousness. Beyond this consciousness, therefore, there can be no *immediate* certainty; but the first principles of a science must have such a certainty. It is quite appropriate to the empirical standpoint of all the other sciences to assume the objective world as positively and actually existing; it is not appropriate to the standpoint of philosophy, which has to go back to what is primary and original. *Consciousness* alone is immediately given, hence the basis of philosophy is limited to the facts of consciousness; in other words, philosophy is essentially *idealistic*. Realism, which commends itself to the crude understanding by appearing to be founded on fact, starts precisely from an arbitrary assumption, and is in consequence an empty castle in the air, since it skips or denies the first fact of all, namely, that all that we know lies within consciousness. For that the *objective existence* of things is conditioned by a representer of them, and that consequently the objective world exists only as *representation*, is no hypothesis, still less a peremptory pronouncement, or even a paradox put forward for the sake of a debate or argument. On the contrary, it is the surest and simplest truth, and a knowledge of it is rendered more difficult only by the fact that it is indeed too simple, and that not everyone has sufficient power of reflection to go back to the first elements of his consciousness of things. There can never be an existence that is objective absolutely and in itself; such an existence, indeed, is positively inconceivable. For the objective, as such, always and essentially has its existence in the consciousness of a subject; it is therefore the representation of this subject, and consequently is conditioned by the subject, and moreover by the subject's forms of representation, which belongs to the subject and not to the object.

That the *objective world would exist* even if there existed no knowing being at all, naturally seems at the first onset to be sure and certain, because it can be thought in the abstract, without the contradiction that it carries within itself coming to light. But if we try to *realize* this abstract thought, in other words, to reduce it to representations of perception, from which alone (like everything abstract) it can have content and truth; and if accordingly we attempt to *imagine an objective world without a knowing subject,* then we become aware that what we are imagining at that moment is in truth the opposite of what we intended, namely, nothing but just the process in the intellect of a knowing being who perceives an objective world, that is to say, precisely what we had sought to exclude. For this perceptible and real world is obviously a phenomenon of the brain; and so in the assumption that the world as such might exist independently of all brains there lies a contradiction.

The principal objection to the inevitable and essential *ideality of every object,* the objection that arises distinctly or indistinctly in everyone, is certainly as follows: even my own person is object for another, and is therefore that other's representation, and yet I know certainly that I should exist even without that other representing me in his mind. But all other objects also stand in the same relation to his intellect as *I* stand; consequently, they too would exist without his representing them in his mind. The answer to this is as follows: that other being, whose object I am now considering my person to be, is not absolutely *the subject,* but is in the first instance a knowing individual. Therefore, if he too did *not* exist, in fact, even if there existed in general no other knowing being except myself, this would still by no means be the elimination of the *subject* in whose representation alone all objects exist. For I myself am in fact that *subject,* just as is every knowing being. Consequently, in the case here assumed, my person would certainly still exist, but again as representation, namely, in my own knowledge. For even by myself it is always known only indirectly, never directly, since all existence as representation is an indirect existence. Thus as *object,* in other words, as extended, filling space, and acting, I know my body only in the perception of my brain. This perception is brought about through the senses, and on their

This doesn't exclude the possibility that what we think is there is what actually is there objectively; that human beings have the ability to discover reality. Common sense is only wrong when it jumps to conclusions

data the perceiving understanding carries out its function of passing from the effect to the cause. In this way, by the eye seeing the body, or the hands touching it, the understanding constructs the spatial figure that presents itself in space as my body. In no way, however, are there given to me directly, in some general feeling of the body or in inner self-consciousness, any extension, shape, and activity that would coincide with my inner being itself, and that inner being accordingly requires no other being in whose knowledge it would manifest itself, in order so to exist. On the contrary, that general feeling, just like self-consciousness, exists directly only in relation to the *will*, namely, as comfortable or uncomfortable, and as active in the acts of will, which exhibit themselves for external perception as actions of the body. It follows from this that the existence of my person or of my body *as an extended and acting thing* always persupposes a knowing being different from it, since it is essentially an existence in the apprehension, in the representation, and hence an existence *for another being*. In fact, it is a phenomenon of the brain, no matter whether the brain in which it exhibits itself belongs to my own person or to another's. In the first case, one's own person is then split up into the knowing and the known, into object and subject, and here, as everywhere, these two face each other inseparable and irreconcilable. Therefore, if my own person, in order to exist as such, always requires a knower, this will apply at any rate just as much to all other objects; and to vindicate for these an existence independent of knowledge and of the subject of knowledge was the aim of the above objection.

[margin handwritten note: non sequitur]

However, it is evident that the existence conditioned through a knowing being is simply and solely existence in *space*, and hence that of a thing extended and acting. This alone is always a known thing, and consequently an existence *for another being*. At the same time, everything that exists in this way may still have an *existence for itself*, for which it requires no subject. This existence by itself, however, cannot be extension and activity (together space-occupation), but is necessarily another kind of being, namely, that of a *thing-in-itself*, which, purely as such, can never be *object*. This, therefore, is the answer to the principal objection stated above, and accordingly this objection does not overthrow the fundamental truth that the objectively present and existing world can exist only in the representation, and so only for a subject.

[bottom handwritten note: Discoverer's Fallacy: Like Plotinus, he's onto something, but misinterprets his own intuition. Similar too is their belief that the beyond is superior. The Will is a tool to be used, not a chain to be broken]

It is also to be noted here that even Kant, at any rate so long as he remained consistent, cannot have thought of any *objects* among his things-in-themselves. For this follows already from the fact that he proved space as well as time to be a mere form of our intuition or perception, which in consequence does not belong to the things-in-themselves. What is not in space or in time cannot be *object;* therefore the being or existence of *things-in-themselves* can no longer be *objective,* but only of quite a different kind, namely, a metaphysical being or existence. Consequently, there is already to be found in that Kantian principle also the proposition that the objective world exists only as *representation.*

In spite of all that may be said, nothing is so persistently and constantly misunderstood as *idealism,* since it is interpreted as meaning that the *empirical* reality of the external world is denied. On this rests the constant return of the appeal to common sense, which appears in many different turns and guises, for example, as *"fundamental conviction"* in the Scottish school, or as Jacobi's *faith or belief* in the reality of the external world. The external world by no means gives itself, as Jacobi explains, merely on credit; nor is it accepted by us on faith and trust. It gives itself as what it is, and performs directly what it promises. It must be remembered that Jacobi set up such a credit system of the world, and was lucky enough to impose it on a few professors of philosophy, who for thirty years went on philosophizing about it extensively and at their ease; and that it was this same Jacobi who once denounced Lessing as a Spinozist, and later Schelling as an atheist, and received from the latter the well-known and well-merited reprimand. In accordance with such zeal, by reducing the external world to a matter of faith, he wanted merely to open a little door for faith in general, and to prepare the credit for what was afterwards actually to be offered on credit; just as if, to introduce paper money, we tried to appeal to the fact that the value of the ringing coin depended merely on the stamp the State put on it. In his philosopheme on the reality of the external world assumed on faith, Jacobi is precisely the "transcendental realist playing the part of the empirical idealist," whom Kant censured in the *Critique of Pure Reason,* first edition, page 369.

True idealism, on the other hand, is not the empirical, but the transcendental. It leaves the *empirical* reality of the world untouched, but adheres to the fact that all *object*, and hence the empirically real in general, is conditioned by the *subject* in a two-fold manner. In the first place it is conditioned *materially*, or as *object* in general, since an objective existence is conceivable only in face of a subject and as the representation of this subject. In the second place, it is conditioned *formally*, since the *mode and manner* of the object's existence, in other words, of its being represented (space, time, causality), proceed from the subject, and are predisposed in the subject. Therefore immediately connected with simple or *Berkeleian* idealism, which concerns the *object in general*, is *Kantian* idealism, which concerns the specially given *mode and manner* of objective existence. This proves that the whole of the material world with its bodies in space, extended and, by means of time, having causal relations with one another, and everything attached to this—all this is not something existing *independently* of our mind, but something that has its fundamental presuppositions in our brain functions, *by means of* which and *in* which alone is *such* an objective order of things possible. For time, space, and causality, on which all those real and objective events rest, are themselves nothing more than functions of the brain; so that, therefore, this unchangeable *order* of things, affording the criterion and the clue to their empirical *reality*, itself comes first from the brain, and has its credentials from that alone. Kant has discussed this thoroughly and in detail; though he does not mention the brain, but says "the faculty of knowledge." He has even attempted to prove that that objective order in time, space, causality, matter, and so on, on which all the events of the real world ultimately rest, cannot even be *conceived*, when closely considered, as a self-existing order, i.e., an order of things-in-themselves, or as something absolutely objective and positively existing; for if we attempt to think it out to the end, it leads to contradictions. To demonstrate this was the purpose of the antinomies; in the appendix to my work,[2] however, I have demonstrated the failure of the attempt. On the other hand, the Kantian teaching, even without the antinomies, leads to the insight that things and their whole mode and manner of existence are inseparably associated with our consciousness of them. Therefore he who has clearly grasped this soon

[margin note: So a scene exists only in a camera, and is represented by a photograph or film]

2. Criticism of the Kantian Philosophy at the end of volume 1.—TR.

reaches the conviction that the assumption that things exist as such, even outside and independently of our consciousness, is really absurd. Thus are we so deeply immersed in time, space, causality, and in the whole regular course of experience resting on these; we (and in fact even the animals) are so completely at home, and know how to find our way in experience from the very beginning. This would not be possible if our intellect were one thing and things another; but it can be explained only from the fact that the two constitute a whole; that the intellect itself creates that order, and exists only for things, but that things also exist only for it.

But even apart from the deep insight and discernment revealed only by the Kantian philosophy, the inadmissible character of the assumption of absolute *realism*, clung to so obstinately, can indeed be directly demonstrated, or at any rate felt, by the mere elucidation of its meaning through considerations such as the following. According to realism, the world is supposed to exist, as we know it, independently of this knowledge. Now let us once remove from it all knowing beings, and thus leave behind only inorganic and vegetable nature. Rock, tree, and brook are there, and the blue sky; sun, moon, and stars illuminate this world, as before, only of course to no purpose, since there exists no eye to see such things. But then let us subsequently put into the world a knowing being. That world then presents itself *once more* in his brain, and repeats itself inside that brain exactly as it was previously outside it. Thus to the *first* world a *second* has been added, which, although completed separated from the first, resembles it to a nicety. Now the *subjective* world of this perception is constituted in *subjective* known space exactly as the *objective* world is in *objective*, infinite space. But the subjective world still has an advantage over the objective, namely, the knowledge that that external space is infinite; in fact, it can state beforehand most minutely and accurately the full conformity to law of all the relations in that space that are possible and not yet actual, and it does not need to examine them first. It can state just as much about the course of time, as also about the relation of cause and effect that governs the changes in outer space. I think that, on closer consideration, all this proves absurd enough, and thus leads to the conviction that that absolutely *objective* world outside the head, independent of it and *prior* to all knowledge, which we at first imagined we had conceived, was really no other than the second world already known *subjectively,* the world of the representation, and that it is alone that we are actually capable of conceiving. Accordingly the assumption is automatically forced on us that the world, as we know it, exists only for our knowledge, and consequently in the *representation* alone, and not once again outside that representation.[3*] In keeping with this assumption, then, the thing-in-itself, in other words, that which exists independently of our knowledge and of all knowledge, is to be regarded as something quite different from the *representation* and all its attributes, and hence from objectivity in general. What this is, will afterwards be the theme of our second book.

On the other hand, the controversy about the reality of the external world, considered in section 5 of our first volume, rests on the assumption, just criticized, of an objective and a subjective world both in *space,* and on the impossibility, arising in the case of this presupposition, of a transition, a bridge, between the two. On this controversy I have to make the following remarks.

Subjective and objective do not form a continuum. That of which we are immediately conscious is bounded by the skin, or rather by the extreme ends of the nerves proceeding from the cerebral system. Beyond this lies a world of which we have no other knowledge than that gained through pictures in our mind. Now the question is whether and to what extent a world existing independently of us corresponds to these pictures. The relation between the two could be brought about only by means of the law of causality, for this law alone leads from something given to something quite different from it. This law itself, however, has first of all to substantiate its validity. Now it must be either of *objective* or of *subjective* origin; but in either case it lies on one bank or the other, and therefore cannot serve as a bridge. If, as Locke and Hume assumed,

3*. Here I specially recommend the passage in Lichtenberg's *Vermischte Schriften* (Göttingen, 1801, vol. 2, page 12 *seq.*): "Euler says in his letters on various subjects of natural science (vol. 2, p. 228), that it would thunder and lighten just as well, even if there existed no human being whom the lightning could strike. It is a very common expression, but I must confess that it has never been easy for me to grasp it completely. It always seems to me as if the concept of *being* were something borrowed from our thinking, and that if there are no longer any sentient and thinking creatures, then also there *is* nothing more."

In this chapter, footnotes marked with an asterisk represent additions made by Schopenhauer in his interleaved copy of the third edition between its appearance in 1859 and his death in 1860.—Tr.

If it were our creation, it would behave the way we wanted it to, especially since it would exist only in our minds. The subjective representation would have no free will it is *a posteriori,* and hence drawn from experience, it is of *objective* origin; it then itself belongs to the external world in question, and therefore cannot vouch for the reality of that world. For then, according to Locke's method, the law of causality would be demonstrated from experience, and the reality of experience from the law of causality. If, on the other hand, it is given *a priori,* as Kant more correctly taught, then it is of *subjective* origin; and so it is clear that with it we always remain in the *subjective.* For the only thing actually given *empirically* in the case of perception is the occurrence of a sensation in the organ of sense. The assumption that this sensation, even only in general, must have a *cause* rests on a law that is rooted in the form of our knowledge, in other words, in the functions of our brain. The origin of this law is therefore just as subjective as is that sensation itself. The *cause* of the given sensation, assumed as a result of this law, immediately manifests itself in perception as *object,* having space and time as the form of its appearance. But again, even *these* forms themselves are of entirely subjective origin, for they are the mode and manner of our faculty of perception. That transition from the sensation to its cause, which, as I have repeatedly shown, lies at the foundation of all sense perception, is certainly sufficient for indicating to us the empirical presence in space and time of an empirical object, and is therefore fully satisfactory for practical life. But it is by no means sufficient for giving us information about the existence and real inner nature of the phenomena that arise for us in such a way, or rather of their intelligible substratum. Therefore, the fact that, on the occasion of certain sensations occurring in my organs of sense, there arises in my head a *perception* of things extended in space, permanent in time, and causally operative, by no means justifies me in assuming that such things also exist in themselves, in other words, that they exist with such properties absolutely belonging to them, independently of my head and outside it. This is the correct conclusion of the *Kantian* philosophy. It is connected with an earlier result of Locke that is just as correct, and very much easier to understand. Thus, although, as is allowed by Locke's teaching, external things are positively assumed to be the causes of the sensations, there cannot be any *resemblance* at all between the *sensation,* in which the *effect* consists, and the objective *nature* or *quality* of the *cause* that gives rise to this sensation. For the sensation, as organic function, is above all determined by the very artificial and complicated nature of our sense organs; thus it is merely stimulated by the external cause, but is then perfected entirely in accordance with its own laws, and hence is wholly subjective. Locke's philosophy was the criticism of the functions of sense; but Kant has furnished the criticism of the functions of the brain. But to all this we still have to add the result of Berkeley, which has been revised by me, namely, that every *object*, whatever its origin, is, *as object*, already conditioned by the subject, and thus is essentially only the subject's *representation*. The aim of realism is just the object without subject; but it is impossible even to conceive such an object clearly.

From the whole of this discussion it follows with certainty and distinctness that it is absolutely impossible to arrive at a comprehension of the *inner nature* of things on the path of mere *knowledge* and *representation*, since this knowledge always comes to things *from without*, and must therefore remain eternally *outside* them. This purpose could be attained only by our finding *ourselves* in the inside of things, so that this inside would be known to us directly. My second book considers to what extent this is actually the case. However, so long as we stop, as in this first book we do, at objective comprehension, and hence at *knowledge*, the world is and remains for us a mere *representation*, since no path is here possible that leads beyond this. *A couch potato who didn't even need*

But in addition to this, adherence to the *idealistic* point of view *TV* is a necessary counterpoise to the *materialistic*. Thus the contro- *to* versy over the real and the ideal can also be regarded as one con- *be* cerning the existence of *matter*. For it is ultimately the reality or *invented* ideality of matter that is the point in question. Is matter as such *yet.* present merely in our representation, or is it also independent thereof? In the latter case, it would be the thing-in-itself; and he who assumes a matter existing in itself must also consistently be a materialist, in other words, must make matter the principle of explanation of all things. On the other hand, he who denies it to be a thing-in-itself is *eo ipso* an idealist. Among the moderns only Locke has asserted positively and straightforwardly the reality of matter; therefore his teaching, through the instrumentality of Condillac, led to the sensualism and materialism of the French. Berkeley alone has denied matter positively and without modifications. Therefore the complete antithesis is that of idealism and material-

Even God is subservient to Man. Practical theists treat Him that way. "Ask and it shall be given," and if it isn't given, the average believer thinks it probably would've turned out harmful and not that it was a

ism, represented in its extremes by Berkeley and the French materialists (Holbach). Fichte is not to be mentioned here; he deserves
no place among real philosophers, those elect of mankind who
with deep earnestness seek not their own affairs, but the *truth*,
They must therefore not be confused with those who under this
pretext have only their personal advancement in view. Fichte is
the father of *sham philosophy*, of the *underhand* method that by
ambiguity in the use of words, incomprehensible talk, and sophisms, tries to deceive, to impress by an air of importance, and thus
to befool those eager to learn. After this method had been applied
by Schelling, it reached its height, as is well-known, in Hegel, with
whom it ripened into real charlatanism. But whoever in all seriousness even mentions that Fichte along with Kant shows that he
has no notion of what Kant is. On the other hand, materialism
also has its justification. It is just as true that the knower is a
product of matter as that matter is a mere representation of the
knower; but it is also just as one-sided. For materialism is the
philosophy of the subject who forgets to take account of himself.
Therefore, against the assertion that I am a mere modification of
matter, it must also be asserted that all matter exists merely in my
representation, and this assertion is no less right. An as yet obscure
knowledge of these relations appears to have evoked the Platonic
saying, *materia mendacium verax.*[4]

Realism, as I have said, necessarily leads to *materialism*. For
while empirical perception gives us things-in-themselves, as they
exist independently of our knowledge, experience also gives us the
order of things-in-themselves, in other words, the true and only
world-order. But this way leads to the assumption that there is only
one thing-in-itself, namely, matter, of which everything else is a
modification; for the course of nature is the absolute and only
world order. To avoid these consequences, *spiritualism* was set up
along with *realism*, so long as the latter was in undisputed authority; thus the assumption was made of a second substance, outside
and along with matter, namely, an *immaterial substance*. This dual-
ism and *spiritualism*, devoid equally of experience, proofs, and
comprehensibility, was denied by Spinoza, and shown to be false
by Kant, who ventured to do this because at the same time he

4. Matter is a lie, and yet true.—Tr.

established *idealism* in its rights. For with *realism, materialism,* as the counterpoise to which *spiritualism* had been devised, falls to the ground of its own accord, since matter and the course of nature then become mere *phenomenon,* conditioned by the intellect; for the phenomenon has its existence only in the *representation* of the intellect. Accordingly, *spiritualism* is the specious and false safeguard against *materialism;* but the real and true safeguard is *idealism.* By making the objective world dependent *on us,* idealism gives the necessary counterpoise to the dependence *on* the objective world in which *we* are placed by the course of nature. The world, from which I part at death, is, on the other hand, only my representation. The center of gravity of existence falls back into the *subject.* What is proved is not, as in spiritualism, the knower's independence of matter, but the dependence of all matter on the knower. Of course, this is not so easy to understand and so convenient to handle as is spiritualism with its two substances; but *what is noble is difficult.*

In opposition to the *subjective* starting point, namely, "the world is my representation," there certainly is at the moment with equal justification the *objective* starting point, namely, "the world is matter," or "matter alone positively exists" (as it alone is not liable to becoming and to passing away), or "all that exists is matter." This is the starting point of Democritus, Leucippus, and Epicurus. More closely considered, however, starting from the *subject* retains a real advantage; it has the advantage of one perfectly justified step, for consciousness alone is what is *immediate.* We skip this, however, when we go straight to matter and make that our starting point. On the other hand, it would be possible to construct the world from matter and its properties, if these were correctly, completely, and exhaustively known (and many of them we still lack). For everything that has come into existence has become actual through *causes,* which were able to operate and come together only in consequence of the *fundamental forces of matter.* But these must be capable of complete demonstration at least *objectively,* even if we shall never get to know them *subjectively.* But such an explanation and construction of the world would always have as its foundation not only the assumption of an existence-in-itself of matter (whereas in truth such existence is conditioned by the subject), but it would also have to let all the *original properties* in this matter remain in force, and yet be absolutely inexplicable, that is, be *qualitates occultae* (See sections 26, 27 of the first volume.) For matter is only the bearer of these forces, just as the law of causality is only the regulator of their phenomena. Consequently, such an explanation of the world would still be only relative and conditioned, really the work of a *physical science* that at every step longed for a *metaphysic*. On the other hand, even the subjective starting point and axiom, "the world is my representation," has something inadequate about it, firstly inasmuch as it is one-sided, for the world is much more besides this (namely, thing-in-itself, will); in fact, being representation is to a certain extent accidental to it; secondly also inasmuch as it expresses merely the object's being conditioned by the subject without at the same time stating that the subject as such is also conditioned by the object. For the proposition that "the subject would nevertheless be a knowing being, even if it had no object, in other words, no representation at all" is just as false as is the proposition of the crude understanding to the effect that "the world, the object, would still exist, even if there were no subject." A consciousness without object is no consciousness at all. A thinking subject has *concepts* for its object; a sensuously perceiving subject has objects with the qualities corresponding to its organization. Now if we deprive the *subject* of all the particular determinations and forms of its knowing, all the properties in the *object* also disappear, and nothing but *matter without form and quality* is left. This matter can occur in experience as little as can the subject without the forms of its knowledge, yet it remains opposed to the bare subject as such, as its reflex, which can only disappear simultaneously with it. Although materialism imagines that it postulates nothing more than this matter—atoms, for instance—yet it unconsciously adds not only the subject, but also space, time, and causality, which depend on special determinations of the subject.

The world as representation, the objective world, has thus, so to speak, two poles, namely, the knowing subject plain and simple without the forms of its knowing, and crude matter without form and quality. Both are absolutely unknowable; the subject, because it is that which knows; matter, because without form and quality it cannot be perceived. Yet both are the fundamental conditions of all empirical perception. Thus the knowing subject, merely as such, which is likewise a presupposition of all experience, stands in oppo-

We would never even think we know reality if this concocted Kantian nonsense were true.

sition, as its clear counterpart, to crude, formless, quite dead (i.e., will-less) matter. This matter is not given in any experience, but is presupposed in every experience. This subject is not in time, for time is only the more direct form of all its representing. Matter, standing in opposition to the subject, is accordingly eternal, imperishable, endures through all time; but properly speaking it is not extended, since extension gives form, and hence it is not spatial. Everything else is involved in a constant arising and passing away, whereas these two constitute the static poles of the world as representation. We can therefore regard the permanence of matter as the reflex of the timelessness of the pure subject, that is simply taken to be the condition of every object. Both belong to the phenomenon, not to the thing-in-itself; but they are the framework of the phenomenon. Both are discovered only through abstraction; they are not given immediately, pure and by themselves.

The fundamental mistake of all systems is the failure to recognize this truth, namely, that *the intellect and matter are correlatives,* in other words, the one exists only for the other; both stand and fall together; the one is only the other's reflex. They are in fact really one and the same thing, considered from two opposite points of view; and this one thing—here I am anticipating—is the phenomenon of the will or of the thing-in-itself. Consequently, both are secondary, and therefore the origin of the world is not to be looked for in either of them. But in consequence of their failure to recognize this, all systems (with the possible exception of Spinoza's) have sought the origin of all things in one of those two. Thus some of them suppose an *intellect,* as positively the first thing; and accordingly they allow a *representation* in this of things and of the world to precede their real existence; consequently they distinguish the real world from the world as representation, which is false. Therefore, *matter* now appears as that by which the two are distinguished, namely, as a thing-in-itself. Hence arises the difficulty of producing this matter, so that, when added to the mere representation of the world, it may impart reality thereto. That original intellect must either find it already in existence. Or the intellect produces matter out of nothing, an assumption that our understanding combats, for this understanding is capable of grasping only changes in matter, not an arising or passing away of that matter. At bottom, this rests on the very fact that matter is the essential correlative of the understanding. The systems opposed to these, which make the other of the two correlatives, namely, matter, the absolutely first thing, suppose a matter that exists without being represented by a subject; and, as is sufficiently clear from all that has been said above, this is a direct contradiction, for in the existence of matter we always think only of its being represented by a subject. But then there arises for them the difficulty of bringing to this matter, which alone is their absolutely first thing, the intellect that is ultimately to know it from experience. In section 7 of the first volume I have spoken of this weak side of materialism. With me, on the other hand, matter and intellect are inseparable correlatives, existing for each other, and therefore only relatively. Matter is the representation of the intellect; the intellect is that in the representation of which alone matter exists. Both together constitute the *world as representation,* which is precisely Kant's *phenomenon,* and consequently something secondary. What is primary is that which appears, namely, the *thing-in-itself,* which we shall afterwards learn to recognize as the *will.* In itself this is neither the representer nor the represented, but is quite different from its mode of appearance.

As an impressive conclusion to this important and difficult discussion, I will now personify those two abstractions, and introduce them into a dialogue, after the manner of *Prabodha Chandro Daya.*[5] We may also compare it with a similar dialogue between matter and form in Raymond Lull's *Duodecim Pricipia Philosophiae,* c. 1 and 2.

The Subject

I am, and besides me there is nothing. For the world is my representation.

Matter

Presumptuous folly! *I* am, and besides me there is nothing: For the world is my fleeting form. You are a mere result of a part of this form, and quite accidental.

---

5. More correctly *Prabodha-candra-udaya,* "the rising of the moon of knowledge," an allegorical drama in six acts by Krishna Misra (about A.D. 1200) in which philosophical concepts appear as persons.—TR.

The Subject

What silly conceit! Neither you nor your form would exist without me; you are conditioned through me. Whoever thinks me away, and then believes he can still think of you, is involved in a gross delusion; for your existence outside my representation is a direct contradiction, a wooden-iron. *You are,* simply means you are represented by me. My representation is the locality of your existence; I am therefore its first condition.

Matter

Fortunately the boldness of your assertion will soon be refuted in a real way, and not by mere words. A few more moments, and you—actually are no more; with all your boasting and bragging, you have sunk into nothing, floated past like a shadow, and suffered the fate of every one of my fleeting forms. But I, I remain intact and undiminished from millennium to millennium, throughout endless time, and behold unmoved the play of my changing forms.

The Subject

This endless time, to live through which is your boast, is, like the endless space you fill, present merely in my representation; in fact, it is the mere form of my representation that I carry already prepared within me, and in which you manifest yourself. It receives you, and in this way do you first of all exist. But the annihilation with which you threaten me does not touch me, otherwise you also would be annihilated. On the contrary, it concerns merely the individual that for a short time is my bearer, and that, like everything else, is my representation.

Matter

Even if I grant you this, and go so far as to regard your existence, which is inseparably linked to that of these fleeting individuals, as something existing by itself, it nevertheless remains dependent on mine. For you are subject only insofar as you have an object; and that object is I. I am its kernel and content, that which is permanent in it, that which holds it together, without which it would be as incoherent and as wavering and unsubstantial as the dreams and fancies of your individuals, that have borrowed even their fictitious content from me.

The Subject

You do well to refrain from disputing my existence on account of its being linked to individuals; for just as inseparably as I am tied to these, so are you tied to form, your sister, and you have never yet appeared without her. No eye has yet seen either you or me naked and isolated; for we are both only abstractions. At bottom it is *one* entity that perceives itself and is perceived by itself, but its being-in-itself cannot consist either in perceiving or in being perceived, as these are divided between us.

Both

So we are inseparably connected as necessary parts of one whole, which includes us both and exists through us both. Only a misunderstanding can set up the two of us as enemies in opposition to each other, and lead to the false conclusion that the one contests the existence of the other, with which its own existence stands and falls.

This whole, including both, is the world as representation, or the phenomenon. After this is taken away, there remains only the purely metaphysical, the thing-in-itself, which in the second book we shall recognize as the will.

Translated by E. F. J. Payne

PART 2

7

On the Will in Nature

I have lived to enjoy the pleasure of being able, after nineteen years, to put the finishing touches of improvement to this small work, a pleasure that has been the greater, since the work is of special importance to my philosophy. For, starting from the purely empirical, from the observations of impartial investigators of nature who pursue the line of their special science, I reach here directly the real core of my metaphysics; I indicate its points of contact with the natural sciences, and thus to a certain extent furnish the arithmetical proof of my fundamental dogma. In precisely this way such a dogma gains more detailed and special proofs, and is also more clearly, easily, and properly understood than anywhere else.

The improvements given to this new edition are confined almost entirely to additional remarks, since nothing of note in the first edition has been omitted; on the contrary, numerous, and in some instances important, additions have been inserted.

But also in general it is a good sign that the book trade has called for a new edition of this work, because it indicates generally a serious interest in philosophy, and confirms the fact that the need for a real progress in it is at the present time felt to be more urgent than ever. But this is due to two circumstances. The first is the unparalleled zeal and energy shown in all branches of natural science. As this is applied, for the most part, by people who have learned nothing else, it threatens to lead to a crass and stupid materialism whose *primarily* objectionable feature is not the moral bestiality of the ultimate results, but the incredible want of understanding of first principles; for even vital force is denied, and organic nature is degraded to a chance play of chemical forces.[1*] It must be made clear to such gentlemen of the crucible and retort that mere chemistry enables a man to become an apothecary, not a philosopher. It should also be made equally clear to certain other investigators of nature of a like mentality that one can be an accomplished zoologist and have at one's fingertips all the sixty species of monkeys and yet be on the whole an ignoramus, to be classed with the crowd, if one has learned nothing else except perhaps his catechism. But this is a case that often occurs in these days, for people proclaim themselves as enlighteners of the world who have learned their chemistry, physics, mineralogy, zoology, or physiology, but nothing else on earth: to this they add their only other knowledge, namely, what still sticks to them from the teachings of the catechism they learned in their years at school. Now if for them these two elements are not in harmony, they at once become scoffers of religion, and are soon turned into shallow and absurd materialists.[2*] Perhaps at school they once heard of the existence of a Plato and an Aristotle, of a Locke, and especially of a Kant. But as these men handled neither crucibles and retorts, nor stuffed monkeys, these people did not deem them worthy of further acquaintance. Calmly throwing out of the window the intellectual labor of two thousand years, they treat the public to a philosophy that is concocted from their own rich store of mental resources and based on the catechism on the one hand, and on crucibles and retorts or the catalogue of monkeys, on the other. They ought to be told bluntly that they are ignorant fellows who still have a great deal to learn before they can have anything to say on the matter. And, generally, any dogmatizing at random on the soul, God, the beginning of the world, atoms, and the like with naive realism of

1*. And it has been possible for this infatuation to reach such a degree that men quite seriously imagine they have found in wretched *chemical affinities* the key to the riddle of the essence and existence of this marvelous and mysterious world! Indeed, compared with the delusion of our *physiological* chemists, that of the alchemists was a mere trifle, because they were looking for the philosophers' stone and hoped only to make gold.

[In this chapter, footnotes marked with an asterisk represent additions made by Schopenhauer in his interleaved copy of the second edition between its appearance in 1854 and his death in 1860.]

2*. *Aut catechismus, aut materialismus* (either catechism or materialism is their motto).

a child, as if the *Critique of Pure Reason* had been written on the moon and no copy of it had come down to earth, belongs simply to the common crowd. Send him to the servants' hall where he may dispose of his wisdom.[3*]

The other circumstance calling for a real progress in philosophy is the steady growth of unbelief, in spite of all the hypocritical disguises and all the semblance of life of the church. This unbelief necessarily and inevitably goes hand in hand with the ever-growing expansion of all kinds of empirical and historical knowledge. It threatens to reject not only the form, but also the spirit and sense of Christianity (a spirit having a much wider reach than has Christianity itself), and to hand humanity over to a moral materialism that is even more dangerous than the chemical one just mentioned. Here nothing plays more into the hands of this unbelief than orthodox Tartuffian hypocrisy, which at the moment impudently flaunts itself everwhere. Still holding in their hands their gratuities, its clumsy disciples preach with such unction and emphasis that their voices reach even learned critical periodicals edited by academies and universities, and physiological as well as philosophical books. Being quite out of place here, such voices injure their own cause by stirring up indignation.[4*] In these circumstances, therefore, it is gratifying to see the public reveal an interest in philosophy.

Nevertheless, I have to convey a sad piece of news to the professors of philosophy. Their Caspar Hauser (according to Dorguth) whom they had so carefully secluded and so securely walled in from light and air for nearly forty years that not a sound could betray his existence to the world—their Caspar Hauser, I say, has escaped! He has escaped and is running around the world; some even imagine he is a prince. Or to speak plainly, what they feared more than anything else has nevertheless come to pass. For more than a generation they were fortunate enough to avert this misfortune by acting with united effort and rare steadfastness by means

---

3*. There he will also find men who are fond of flinging forth foreign words they have picked up and do not understand; and this he does when, for example, he likes to talk of *"Idealism"* without knowing what it means; thus he often uses it instead of spiritualism (which as realism is the opposite of idealism). This and similar *quid pro quos* can be seen a hundred times in books and in critical and scholarly periodicals.

4*. It should everywhere be pointed out to them that no one believes in their faith.

of such profound silence, unanimous secreting, and ignoring as had never previously occurred. What I mean is that people have begun to read my works and will not again refrain from so doing. *Legor et legar*[5]: and it cannot be altered. This is really terrible and extremely inconvenient; indeed, it is a positive misfortune, not to say calamity. Is this, then, the reward for such faithful and intimate reticence, for holding together so firmly and unanimously? Poor simpletons! What becomes of Horace's promise: *Est et fideli tuta silentio / Merces?*[6] For they have certainly not been sparing in faithful reticence; on the contrary, this is just their strong point wherever they suspect merit; and against this it is actually the cleverest artifice; for what no one knows as if it did not exist. But whether the *merces*[7] will remain quite so *tuta*[8] now seem somewhat doubtful, unless *merces* is interpreted in a *bad* sense; and of course this can be supported even by good classical authorities. These gentlemen had rightly seen that the only method to be used against my works was to conceal them from the public by maintaining a profound silence about them, whereas much noise was made at the birth of every misshapen offspring of the philosophy of the professors— just as the voice of the newborn Zeus was once rendered inaudible by the uproarious clamor and noise of the Corybantes. But this method is played out, and the secret has been betrayed: the public has discovered me. The rage of the professors of philosophy is great but impotent; for now that the only effective means, applied with success for so long, is exhausted, no amount of bawling at me can stop my influence, and in vain do they take up this or that attitude. Of course they have succeeded insofar as the generation that was really contemporary to my philosophy went to the grave without any information of it. But this was a mere postponement, for time, as always, has kept its word.

Now there are two reasons why my philosophy is so hated by the gentlemen of the "philosophical trade" (they themselves have the incredible naïveté thus to call it).[9] The first is that my works ruin the public's taste for empty tissues of phrases, for meaningless

5. People read me and will read me.—Tr.
6. Positive reward certainly comes to faithful silence.—Tr.
7. "Reward."—Tr.
8. "Certain."—Tr.
9. See *Göttingen gelehrte Anzeige* of 1853, p. 1.

word accumulations that are piled on top of one another. For hollow, superficial, and slowly tormenting twaddle, for Christian dogmatics appearing in the disguise of the most wearisome metaphysics, for the lowest and most systematized philistinism representing ethics, accompanied even by instructions on dancing and card playing: in short, a taste for that entire method of petticoat philosophy that has already scared so many forever from all philosophy.

The second reason is that the gentlemen of the "philosophical trade" simply dare not approve of my philosophy, and thus cannot use it for the benefit of the "trade"—a fact that they even heartily regret, for my wealth would prove admirably useful to their own bitter poverty. But my philosophy can never find favor in their eyes, not even if it contained the greatest treasures of human wisdom ever unearthed, for it lacks all speculative theology as well as rational psychology, and these, just these, are the breath of life to those gentlemen, the *conditio sine qua non*[10] of their existence, for above all things in heaven and on earth, they want to hold their official posts, and these demand, above all things in heaven and on earth, speculative theology and rational psychology: *extra haec non datur salus.*[11] Theology shall and must be, no matter whence it comes. Moses and the prophets must be right in the end; this is the highest principle of philosophy; and in addition, there must be rational psychology, as is right and proper. Now there is nothing like this to be gotten from either Kant or me. Yes indeed, as we all know, the most cogent theological arguments are smashed, like a glass thrown at a wall, when they come up against Kant's criticism of all speculative theology, and of rational psychology not a shred remains whole in his hands! And now neither speculative theology nor rational psychology any longer appears in me, as is only consistent and honest with one who is the dauntless continuer of Kant's philosophy.[12]* On the other hand, the philosophy of the chair has the task ultimately of expounding the fundamental truths of the catechism under a veil of very abstract, abstruse, and difficult formulas and phrases, which are for this reason tedious and tor-

10. Indispensable condition.—Tr.
11. Apart from these no salvation can be found.—Tr.
12*. In philosophy nothing is given by revelations; and so above all a philosopher is bound to be an unbeliever.

menting. In the end, such truths always reveal themselves as the kernel of the matter, however confused, strange, intricate, and eccentric it may at first sight appear to be. Such a proceeding may have its uses, although to me it is unknown. I know only this much, that in philosophy, in other words, the inquiry after truth, I mean the truth *par excellence* by which are understood the most sublime and important disclosures dearer to the heart of the human race than anything else in the world, no step forward, not even an inch, will ever be made by such maneuvers. On the contrary, the way is thus barred to such inquiry, and for this reason I long ago saw in university philosophy the antagonist of the real and genuine. Now if in such circumstances there once appears a philosophy with honest intentions and one quite seriously bent on the truth and nothing but the truth, are not the gentlemen of the "philosophical trade" bound to feel as would stage knights clad in pasteboard if one clad in real armor suddenly appeared in their midst and made the light stage floor shake under his heavy gait? Such a philosophy, therefore, *must* be bad and false, and consequently imposes on the gentlemen of the "trade" the painful necessity of playing the part of one who, in order to appear to be what he is not, dare not allow others to pass for what they are. But from all this there now unfolds the amusing spectacle that we enjoy when these gentlemen, now that ignoring me has unfortunately come to an end after forty years, begin to measure me with their own puny standard and, from the heights of their wisdom, pass judgment on me as if by virtue of their office they were fully competent so to do; but they are most amusing when they try to assume toward me the attitude of respectable people.

Their hatred of Kant, although less openly expressed, is not much less than their hatred of me, just because he has undermined, and indeed in the opinion of all who understand seriousness, irretrievably ruined speculative theology as well as rational psychology, the *gagne-pain*[13] of these gentlemen. And why should the gentlemen not hate him who has rendered their "philosophical trade" so difficult that they are hardly able to see how they can creditably get by? Kant and I are therefore bad, and the gentlemen take absolutely no notice of us. For nearly forty years they have

13. Bread winning.—Tr.

deemed me not even worthy of a glance, and now from the heights of their wisdom they look down on Kant with pity and smile at his errors. This is a very wise and profitable policy; for they are then able entirely at their ease to discuss God and the soul in volume after volume as if these were well-known personalities with whom they are intimately acquainted, and to talk deeply and learnedly about the relation of the former to the world and of the latter of the body, as if there did not exist anywhere in the world a *Critique of Pure Reason.* Just throw aside the *Critique of Pure Reason,* and everything will then go on splendidly! Now for this purpose they have been trying for many years to push Kant gradually and gently to one side, to regard him as out of date, in fact to turn up their noses at him. In this business one encourages the other, and they are now becoming bolder than ever.[14*] There is no opposition to fear from their own colleagues, since all have the same aims and mission, and form a numerous company whose ingenious members, *coram popule,* bow and scrape to each other on all sides. Things have thus gradually come to such a pass that the most miserable compilers of compendia have the impertinence to treat Kant's great and immortal discoveries as antiquated errors.

I break a seventeen-year silence[15] in order to point out to the few who are in advance of the times and have given their attention to my philosophy some corroborations it has obtained from unprejudiced empiricists who are not familiar with it. Their path was directed to mere knowledge of experience, and at the end of it they were able to discover just what my teaching propounded as the metaphysical from which experience in general is to be explained. This circumstance is the more encouraging, as it distinguishes my system from all previous ones, in that all of them, not even excepting the most recent by Kant, still leave a wide gap between their results and experience. They are far from coming down directly to it, and from being in contact with it. Thus my metaphysics proves

14*. One always states that the other is right.

15. So I wrote in 1835 when I first composed the present work. That is to say, I had published nothing since the year 1818, before the end of which *The World as Will and Representation* had appeared. For a Latin version of my essay *On Vision and Colors* (published in 1816), which I wrote for foreign readers and incorporated in the third volume of the *Scriptores ophthaimologics minores,* edited in 1830 by J. Radius, cannot be regarded as breaking that silence.

to be the only one that actually has an extreme point in common with the physical sciences, a point up to which those sciences use their own means in coming to meet it, so that they really connect and agree with it. Moreover, this is not effected by twisting and turning the empirical sciences to make them fit metaphysics, or by secretely abstracting metaphysics from them in advance, and then, after the manner of Schelling, finding a priori what it had learned a posteriori. On the contrary, my metaphysics and the sciences meet of their own accord and without collusion at the same point. Thus, unlike all those previous systems, mine does not float in air far above all reality and experience, but comes right down to this firm ground of actuality where the physical sciences again take up the learner.

The empirical corroborations of others here now to be mentioned all concern the core and main point of my teaching, its metaphysics proper. Thus they are concerned with the paradoxical, fundamental truth that what Kant set as the *thing-in-itself* over against mere *appearance*, more definitely called by me *representation* [*Vorstellung*], and regarded as absolutely unknowable, that this *thing-in-itself*, I say, this substratum of all appearances and consequently of the whole of nature, is nothing but what we know immediately and very intimately and find within ourselves as *will*. Accordingly, far from being inseparable from, and even a mere result of *knowledge*, as all previous philosophers assumed, this *will* is fundamentally different from, and wholly independent of knowledge, which is quite secondary and of later origin. Consequently, the will can exist and manifest itself even without knowledge, as is actually the case in the whole of nature from the animal kingdom downward. As the one and only thing-in-itself, that which alone is truly real, the only original and metaphysical thing in a world in which everything else is only appearance, in other words, mere representation, this will endows all things, whatever they be, with the power by virtue whereof they are able to exist and act. Accordingly, not only the voluntary actions of animals, but also the organic mechanism of their living bodies, even the shape and constitution thereof, also the vegetation of plants, and finally even in the inorganic kingdom crystallization, and generally every original force manifesting itself in physical and chemical appearances, in fact gravity itself—all these in themselves and outside the appearance, which merely means outside our head and its representation, are absolutely identical with what we find in ourselves as *will*. Of this *will* we have the most immediate and intimate knowledge that is at all possible. Further, the individual manifestations of this will are set in motion by motives in the case of knowing, i.e., animal beings, but no less by stimuli in the organic life of animals and plants, and finally by mere causes in the narrowest sense of the word in the case of inorganic nature; such distinctions concern only the appearance. On the other hand, knowledge and its substratum, the intellect, is a merely secondary phenomenon, entirely different from the will and accompanying only the higher stages of the will's objectification, and not essential to the will itself. It is dependent on the will's appearance in the animal organism, and is therefore physical, not metaphysical like the will itself. Consequently, absence of will can never be inferred from an absence of knowledge; on the contrary, the will can be demonstrated even in all those appearances of nature where there is no knowledge, of vegetable as well as inorganic nature. Therefore, will is not conditioned by knowledge, as was hitherto assumed without exception, although knowledge is conditioned by will.

Now this fundamental truth, even today sounding so paradoxical, is that part of my teaching that in all its main points has obtained from the empirical sciences, which steer as far as possible away from all metaphysics, many corroborations. These have been forcibly elicited by the power of truth, but coming from such a quarter are most surprising. Indeed, they came to light only after the publication of my work, and yet quite independently of it in the course of many years. Now it is an advantage in two respects that it is precisely this fundamental dogma of my teaching that has met with those corroborations: first because it is the principal idea that conditions all the other parts of my philosophy; and secondly because only for it could there be corroborations from sciences that are foreign to, and entirely independent of, philosophy. For though it is true that the last seventeen years, during which I have been constantly occupied with my doctrine, have brought me numerous verifications even for its other parts, such as ethics, aesthetics, and dianoiology; but these by their nature pass from the soil of actuality, from which they have sprung, directly to that of philosophy itself. Therefore, they cannot bear the character of extraneous evidence, and because they have been collected by me, they cannot be as cogent, unequivocal, and convincing as those concerning *metaphysics* proper, which are furnished primarily by the correlative thereof, namely, *physics* (this word taken in the wide sense of the ancients). Physics itself, and therefore natural science generally, pursues its own paths in all its branches; it must ultimately reach a point where its explanations come to an end. This point is just the *metaphysical,* perceived by science merely as its boundary beyond which it cannot go. Science stops here, and now hands over its subject to metaphysics. Thus Kant was right in saying "it is evident that the primary sources of the effects of nature must by all means be a subject of metaphysics." (*Von der wahren Schätzung der lebendigen Kräfte,* section 51). Therefore, this something, inaccessible and unknown to physics, at which its investigations end and which is afterwards taken for granted by its explanations, is usually designated by it with such terms as natural force, vital force, creative force, and the like, which say no more than x, y, z. Now in particular propitious instances, unusually sharp and observant investigators succeed in casting, as it were, a furtive glance behind the curtain that defines the boundary of the domain of natural science. They manage to feel the boundary not merely as such, but to some extent succeed in perceiving even its nature, and thus peep into the realm of metaphysics that lies beyond it. The physics, so favored now expressly and positively, describes the boundary thus explored as that which has been stated to be the true inner essence and ultimate principle of all things by a system of metaphysics wholly unknown to it at the time and takes its grounds and reasons from an entirely different realm. Besides, this system recognizes all things only as appearances, i.e., representations. Therefore, the two bodies of investigators must really feel like miners in the bowels of the earth who drive two galleries toward each other from two widely separated points, and who, having long worked from both directions in subterranean darkness and relied only on compass and spirit level, at last experience the longed-for joy of hearing each other's hammer blows. For those investigators now know that they have reached the point of contact between physics and metaphysics—a point for so long sought in vain, for these two were always as hard to bring together as are heaven and earth—and that a reconciliation of the two sciences has been initiated and their point of connection found. But the philosophical system that witnesses this triumph thereby obtains so firm and satisfactory external proof of its truth and correctness that none greater is possible. Compared with such a corroboration, which can be regarded as an arithmetical proof, the interest or indifference of an age is of no importance at all, expecially when we consider what in the meantime has been the subject of such interest, and find it like what has been achieved since Kant's time. The eyes of the public are at last being opened to the game that has been played in Germany for the last forty years in the name of philosophy; and such will continue to be the case. The day of reckoning has come, and it will be seen whether the endless scribbling and quibbling since Kant has brought to light any truth. This spares me the necessity of discussing unworthy subjects here, especially as the requirements of my purpose can be more briefly and agreeably achieved by an anecdote. When during the carnival, Dante was lost in the crowd of masks, the duke of Medici gave orders for a search to be made. Those commissioned to look for him doubted whether it was possible to find him, for he too was wearing a mask. And so the duke gave them a question that they were to put to anyone wearing a mask and in any way resembling Dante. The question was: "Who recognizes what is good?" After receiving many silly replies, they finally received from one mask: "He who recognizes what is bad," by this they recognized Dante.[16] What is meant here by this is that I have found no cause for allowing myself to be discouraged by the absence of my contemporaries' sympathy, since at the same time I had in mind the object of such sympathy. Posterity will see from their works who the individuals were, but from the reception accorded to them, it will merely see who the contemporaries were. My teaching makes no claim at all to be called the "philosophy of the present time," a name for which one has attempted to compete with the delightful adepts of Hegelian mystification. But it does claim to be called the philosophy of the time to come, of that time that will no longer be satisfied with meaningless verbiage, hollow phrases, and playful parallelisms, but will demand from philosophy real substance and

16. Baltasar Gracián, *El Criticón*, 3:9, who may be responsible for the anachronism.

serious disclosures. On the contrary, such a time will exempt philosophy from the unjust and preposterous demand of having to be a paraphrase of the existing religion of the country. "For it is very absurd to expect enlightenment from reason, and yet to prescribe in advance to it which side it must necessarily take," Kant, *Critique of Pure Reason* (5th ed., p. 775 [A 747, B 775]). It is sad to live in so degenerate an age that such a self-evident truth still has to be established first through the authority of a great man. But it is ridiculous to expect great things from a philosophy that is tied to a chain, and it is quite amusing to see how such a philosophy with solemn seriousness goes to work to achieve great things, while everyone knows in advance the brief meaning of the long speech.[17] But the more keen-sighted maintain that under the cloak of philosophy they mostly detected disguised theology, which then holds forth and in its own way instructs the student who is thirsting for the truth, and which recalls a favorite scene from the great poet. Others, however, who think they have looked even more closely into the matter, assert that what is hidden under that cloak is neither theology nor philosophy, but merely a poor half-starved wretch who, while pretending with the most solemn countenance and profound earnestness to look for lofty and sublime truth, is really in search of nothing but a morsel of bread for himself and the young family of the future. He could, of course, with less trouble and more honor achieve this in other ways; yet at this price he is prepared to do what is demanded of him, if need be, to deduce a priori, in fact where necessary, to have an intellectual intuition even of the devil and his grandmother. Here the extremely comic effect is certainly attained to a rare degree by the contrast between the loftiness of the ostensible purpose and the lowliness of the actual one. Nevertheless, it remains desirable for the pure and sacred soil of philosophy to be purged of such tradesmen, just as formerly the temple at Jerusalem was purged of vendors and money changers. Thus until those better times come, may the philosophical public apply its attention and interest as it has done hitherto. May it continue, as hitherto, alongside Kant—that great mind that

17. Schiller's *Der langen Rede kurzer Sinn.*—TR.

nature succeeded in producing but once, and that has cast a light on its own depths—let each time Fichte be named as another of that kind invariably; and all this without even one voice crying out, *Hercules and the ape!* May also Hegel's philosphy of absolute nonsense (three-quarters cash and one-quarter crazy notions) continue, as hitherto, to pass for unfathomably profound wisdom, without anyone proposing as a motto to his works the words of Shakespeare: "Such stuff as madmen tongue and brain not,"[18] and, as an emblem at the head of these works, a cuttle fish creating a cloud of obscurity around itself so that no one sees what it is, with the legend, *mea-caligine-tutus.*[19] Finally, may each day bring us, as hitherto, new systems made up of nothing but words and phrases for the use of universities, along with a learned jargon, in which one can talk for days and days without ever saying anything, and may these delights never be disturbed by that Arabic proverb: "Indeed I hear the clacking of the mill, but do not see the flour." For all this is now in keeping with the times and must run its course, just as in every age something analogous exists that more or less noisily occupies contemporaries and then dies away and disappears so completely and without a trace that the next generation is no longer able to say what it was. Truth can wait, for it has a long life before it. What is genuine and seriously meant makes its way and attains its end always slowly; indeed, almost as by a miracle; for when it appears it usually meets with a cool and even unfavorable reception, and this for exactly the same reason that, when it has obtained full recognition and reached posterity, an incalculably great number of people subsequently accept it solely on authority in order not to compromise themselves. But the number of those who sincerely appreciate it always remains almost as small as at the beginning. These few, however, are able to hold it in esteem, since they themselves are held in high repute. They pass it from hand to hand throughout the centuries over the heads of the incompetent masses. So difficult is the existence of humanity's best inheritance. If, on the other hand, truth in order to be true had to ask permission from those who have at heart quite different things,

18. *Cymbeline*, 5:4.—Tr.
19. Fortified by my own obscurity.—Tr.

then indeed one might despair of its cause, for then the answer might often be the witches' watchword: "Fair is foul, and foul is fair."[20] Fortunately, however, this is not the case. Truth does not depend on any favor or disfavor, and does not have to ask anyone's permission; it stands on its own feet; time is its ally; its power is irresistible; its life indestructible.

Translated by E. F. J. Payne

20. Shakespeare, *Macbeth*, 1:1.—Tr.

8
On Genius

What is properly denoted by the name genius is the predominant capacity for the kind of knowledge described in the two previous chapters, from which all genuine works of the arts, of poetry, and even of philosophy, spring. Accordingly, as this has for its object the (Platonic) *Ideas*, these being apprehended, however, not in the abstract but only *in perception*, the true nature of genius must lie in the completeness and energy of the knowledge of *perception*. In accordance with this, we hear described most decidedly as works of genius those that start from, and appeal to, perception, hence those of the plastic and pictorial arts, and then those of poetry that brings about its perceptions through the imagination. Here too the difference between genius and mere talent becomes marked. Talent is a merit to be found in the greater versatility and acuteness of discursive rather than of intuitive knowledge. The person endowed with talent thinks more rapidly and accurately than do the rest; on the other hand, the genius perceives a world different from them all, though only by looking more deeply into the world that lies before them also, since it presents itself in his mind more objectively, consequently more purely and distinctly.

By its destiny, the intellect is merely the medium of motives; and so it apprehends originally in things nothing but their relations to the will, the direct, the indirect, the possible. In the case of the animals, where it remains almost entirely at the direct relations, the matter is on that account most apparent. That which has no reference to their will does not exist for them. For this reason we occasionally see with surprise that even clever animals do not at all notice something conspicuous in itself; for instance, they express no surprise at obvious alterations in our person or environment. In the case of the normal person, the indirect, in fact the possible, relations to the will are added, and the sum of these constitutes the whole of useful knowledge; but even here knowledge remains confined to *relations*. Therefore an entirely pure and objective picture of things is not reached in the normal mind, because its power of perception at once becomes tired and inactive, as soon as this is not spurred on and set in motion by the will. For it has not enough energy to apprehend the world purely objectively from its own elasticity and *without a purpose*. On the other hand, where this happens, where the brain's power of forming representations has such a surplus that a pure, distinct, objective picture of the external world exhibits itself *without a purpose* as something useless for the intentions of the will, which is even disturbing in the higher degrees, and can even become injurious to them—then there already exists at least the natural disposition for that abnormality. This is denoted by the name of *genius*, which indicates that something foreign to the will, i.e., to the I or ego proper, a *genius* added from outside so to speak, seems to become active here. To speak without metaphor, however, genius consists in the knowing faculty having received a considerably more powerful development than is required by the *service of the will*, for which alone it originally came into being. Therefore, strictly speaking, physiology could to a certain extent class such a surplus of brain activity, and with this of the brain itself, among the *monstra per excessum*, which, as we know, are coordinated by it with the *monstra per defectum* and the *monstra per situm mutatum*.[1] Genius, therefore, consists in an abnormal excess of intellect that can find its use only by being employed on the universal of existence. In this way it then applies itself to the service of the whole human race, just as does the normal intellect to that of the individual. To make the matter really intelligible, we might say that, if the normal person consists of two-thirds will and one-third intellect, the genius, on the contrary, has two-thirds intellect and one-third will. This could again be illus-

1. Deformities through excess, through defect, and through wrong position.—TR.

trated by a chemical simile; the base and the acid of a neutral salt are distinguished by the fact that in each of the two the radical has a ratio to oxygen that is the inverse of that in the other. Thus the base or the alkali is what it is because in it the radical predominates with reference to the oxygen, and the acid is what it is because in it the oxygen predominates. Now in just the same way are the normal person and the genius related as regards will and intellect. From this arises a fundamental difference between them, visible already in their whole nature and activity, but that really comes to light in their achievements. We might still add as a distinction that, whereas that total contrast between the chemical materials establishes the strongest affinity and attraction to each other, in the case of the human race it is rather the opposite that is usually seen.

The first manifestation occasioned by such a surplus of the power of knowledge shows itself for the most part in the really original and fundamentally essential knowledge, i.e., knowledge of *perception,* and brings about the repetition of this in a picture or image; hence arise the painter and the sculptor. Accordingly, with these the path from the apprehension of genius to the artistic production is the shortest; therefore the form in which genius and its activity are exhibited in them is the simplest, and its description the easiest. Yet it is just here that the source is seen from which all genuine productions in every art, even poetry and philosophy, have their origin, though in these cases the process is not so simple.

Let us here recall the result obtained in the first book, that all perception is intellectual, and not merely of the senses. If we now add to this the explanation given here, and at the same time fairly take into consideration that the philosophy of the eighteenth century denoted the perceiving faculty of knowledge by the name "lower powers of the soul," we shall not find it so utterly absurd, or so worthy of the bitter scorn with which Jean-Paul mentions it in his *Vorschule der Aesthetik,* that Adelung, having to speak the language of this time, placed genius in "a marked strength of the lower powers of the soul." However great the merits possessed by this admirable man's above-mentioned work, I must nevertheless remark that, wherever a theoretical discussion and instruction in general are the end in view, the method of presentation that indulges in displays of wit and strides along in mere similes cannot be appropriate. *No wonder he loves Kant.*

But it is *perception* above all to which the real and true nature of things discloses and reveals itself, although still in a limited way. All concepts, all things that are thought, are indeed only abstractions, and consequently partial representations from perception, and have arisen merely through our thinking something away. All profound knowledge, even wisdom proper, is rooted in the *perceptive* apprehension of things. We have considered this fully in the supplements to the first book. A *perceptive* apprehension has always been the process of generation in which every genuine work of art, every immortal idea, received the spark of life. All original and primary thinking takes place figuratively. On the other hand, from *concepts* arise the works of mere talent, merely rational ideas, imitations, and generally everything calculated only for the present need and for contemporary events.

But if our perception were always tied to the real presence of things, its material would be entirely under the dominion of chance, which rarely produces things at the right time, seldom arranges them appropriately, and often presents them to us in very defective copies. For this reason *imagination* is needed, in order to complete, arrange, amplify, fix, retain, and repeat at pleasure all the significant pictures of life, according as the aims of a profoundly penetrating knowledge and of the significant work by which it is to be communicated may require. On this rests the high value of imagination as an indispensable instrument of genius. For only by virtue of imagination can genius present to itself each object or event in a vivid image, according to the requirements of the connection of its painting, poetry, or thinking, and thus always draw fresh nourishment from the primary source of all knowledge, perception. The man gifted with imagination is able, so to speak, to call up spirits revealing to him at the right time truths that the bare reality of things exhibits only feebly, rarely, and often at the wrong time. Therefore the man without imagination is related to him as the mussel fastened to its rock, compelled to wait for what chance brings it, is to the freely moving or even winged animal. For such a man knows no other perception than the actual perception of the senses; until it comes, he nibbles at concepts and abstractions that are nevertheless only shells and husks, not the kernel of knowledge. He will never achieve anything great, unless it be in arithmetic and mathematics. The works of the plastic and pictorial arts and of

You can hear something correctly and react as if you heard the exact opposite – it's more than mishearing

poetry, likewise the achievements of mimicry, can also be regarded as the means by which those who have no imagination may make up for this defect as far as possible, and those gifted with imagination may facilitate the use of it.

Accordingly, although the peculiar and essential kind of knowledge of genius is that of *perception*, particular things do not by any means constitute its real object; this is rather the (Platonic) Ideas expressing themselves therein, as the apprehension of them was analyzed in chapter 29. Always to see the universal in the particular is precisely the fundamental characteristic of genius, whereas the normal man recognizes in the particular only the particular as such; for only as such does it belong to reality, which alone has interest for him, has reference to his *will*. The degree in which everyone not so much conceives as actually perceives in the particular thing only the particular, or something more or less universal up to the most universal of the species, is the measure of his approach to genius. In accordance with this, the real object of genius is only the essential nature of things in general, the universal in them, the totality. The investigation of individual phenomena is the field of the talents, in the modern sciences, whose object in reality is always only the relations of things to one another.

What was shown at length in the previous chapter, namely, that the apprehension of the *Ideas* is conditioned by the fact that the knower is the *pure subject* of knowledge, and that the will vanishes entirely from consciousness, is here present to our minds. The pleasure we enjoy in many of Goethe's songs that bring the landscape before our eyes, or in Jean-Paul's descriptions of nature, rests on our thus participating in the objectivity of those minds, that is to say, in the purity with which in them the world as representation had been separated from the world as will, and had been as it were entirely detached therefrom. The kind of knowledge of the genius is essentially purified of all willing and of references to the will; and it also follows from this that the works of genius do not result from intention or arbitrary choice, but that genius is here guided by a kind of instinctive necessity. What is called the awakening of genius, the hour of inspiration, the moment of rapture or exaltation, is nothing but the intellect's becoming free, when, relieved for a while from its service under the will, it does not sink into inactivity or apathy, but is active for a short time, entirely alone and of

because He has no right to twist his own philosophy w/of his personal problem with the Will

No genius without the Will, and very little insight

its own accord. The intellect is then of the greatest purity, and becomes the clear mirror of the world; for, wholly separated from its origin, that is, from the will, it is now the world as representation itself concentrated in *one* consciousness. At such moments is the soul of immortal works, so to speak, begotten. On the other hand, in the case of all intentional reflection the intellect is not free, for the will in fact guides it, and prescribes its theme.

The stamp of commonness, the expression of vulgarity, impressed on the great majority of faces, really consists in this, that there becomes visible in them the strict subordination of their knowing to their willing, the firm chain linking the two together, and the impossibility that follows from this of apprehending things save in reference to the will and its aims. On the other hand, the expression of genius, which constitutes the evident family likeness of all highly gifted men, lies in our distinctly reading in it the intellect's liberation, manumission, from the service of the will, the predominance of knowing over willing. Because all suffering proceeds from willing, while knowing on the other hand is in and by itself painless and serene, this gives to their lofty brows and to their clear, perceptive glance, which are not subject to the service of the will and its needs, the appearance of great, as it were supernatural, unearthly serenity. At times this breaks through, and is quite consistent with the melancholy of the other features of the face, especially the mouth; in this connection it can be aptly described by the motto of Giordano Bruno: *In tristitia hilaris, in hilaritate tristis.*[2] *Nazi robots freed themselves from their wills too*

This is true again. Logic proves what you want to prove. It has a hidden flexibility The will that is the root of the intellect is opposed to every activity of the intellect that is directed to anything other than its own aims. Therefore the intellect is capable of a purely objective and profound apprehension of the external world only when it has detached itself, for a while at any rate, from this its root. So long as it still remains bound to the will, it is quite incapable of any activity from its own resources; it sleeps in stupor, whenever the will (the interest) does not awaken it and set it in motion. If this happens, however, it is then very suitable for recognizing the relations of things according to the interest of the will. This is done by the prudent mind that must also be always awakened, in other

2. Cheerful in sadness, sad in cheerfulness.—TR.

words, by a mind that is vividly aroused by willing; but, on this very account, it is incapable of comprehending the purely objective nature of things. For willing and aims make it so one-sided, that it sees in things only what refers to these, and the rest partly disappears, partly enters consciousness in an adulterated form. For example, a traveler who is anxious and in a hurry, will see the Rhine and its banks only as a dash or stroke, and the bridge over it only as a line intersecting that stroke. In the head of the man filled with his own aims, the world appears just as a beautiful landscape does on the plan of a battlefield. These, of course, are extremes taken for the sake of clarity; but even every slight excitement of the will will have as its consequence a slight, yet always analogous, falsification of knowledge. The world can appear in its true color and form, in its complete and correct significance, only when the intellect, freed from willing, moves freely over objects, and yet is energetically active without being spurred on by the will. This is certainly contrary to the nature and destiny of the intellect; thus it is to a certain extent unnatural, and for this reason exceedingly rare. But it is precisely in this that the true nature of *genius* lies; and in this alone does that state occur in a high degree and for some time, whereas in the rest it appears only approximately and exceptionally. I take it in the sense here discussed, when Jean-Paul (*Vorschule der Aesthetik,* section 12) puts the essence of genius in *reflectiveness.* Thus the normal person is immersed in the whirl and tumult of life, to which he belongs through his will; his intellect is filled with the things and events of life, but he does not in the least become aware of these things and of life in their objective significance; just as the merchant on the Amsterdam exchange hears and understands perfectly what his neighbor says, but does not hear at all the continual humming of the whole exchange, which is like the roaring of the sea, and which astonishes the distant observer. On the other hand, the intellect of the genius is detached from the will and so from the person, and what concerns these does not conceal from him the world and things themselves; on the contrary, he becomes distinctly conscious of them, and apprehends them in objective perception in and by themselves; in this sense he is *reflective.*

It is this *reflectiveness* that enables the painter to reproduce faithfully on canvas the nature he has before his eyes, and the poet accurately to call up again by means of abstract concepts the perceptive present by expressing it, and thus bringing it to distinct consciousness; likewise to express in words everything that others merely feel. The animal lives without any reflectiveness. It has consciousness, that is to say, it knows itself and its weal and woe, and in addition the objects that occasion these. Its knowledge, however, always remains subjective; it never becomes objective. Everything occuring therein seems to the animal to be a matter of course, and can therefore never become for it the matter to be dealt with (object of description) or the problem (object of meditation). Its consciousness is therefore entirely *immanent*. The consciousness of the common type of man is of course not of the same kind, but yet is of a kindred nature, since his apprehension of things and of the world is also chiefly subjective, and remains predominantly immanent. It apprehends the things in the world, but not the world; its own actions and sufferings, but not itself. Now as the distinctness of consciousness is enhanced in infinite gradations, reflectiveness appears more and more; in this way it gradually comes about that occasionally, though rarely and again with extremely different degrees of distinctness, the question passes through the mind like a flash: "What is all this?" or: "*How* is it really constituted?" If the first question attains to great distinctness and is continuously present, it will make the philosopher; and in just the same way the other question will make the artist or the poet. Therefore the high calling of these two has its root in the reflectiveness that springs primarily from the distinctness with which they are conscious of the world and of themselves, and thus come to reflect on these. But the whole process springs from the fact that, through its preponderance, the intellect frees itself for a time from the will to which it was originally subject.

These considerations concerning genius are connected as supplements to the exposition, contained in chapter 22, of the *ever wider separation between the will and the intellect* that is observable in the whole range of beings. This reaches its highest degree precisely in genius, where it attains to the complete detachment of the intellect from its root, the will, so that here the intellect becomes wholly free, whereby the *world as representation* first of all attains to complete objectification.

Now a few more remarks concerning the individuality of genius.

Even this self-misinterpretation is more valid than the computer-sick cognitive scientists, who think we're all just complicated robots.

According to Cicero (*Tusc.*, 1:33), Aristotle already remarked *omnes ingeniosos melancholicos esse;*[3] this undoubtedly refers to the passage in Aristotle's *Problemata,* 30:1. Goethe also says:

> My poetic fire was very low
> So long as I encountered good;
> Whereas it was all aflame,
> When I fled from imminent evil.
> The delicate verse like a rainbow
> Is drawn only on a dark ground,
> Hence the poet's genius relishes
> The element of melancholy.

This is explained by the fact that, as the will constantly reasserts its original mastery over the intellect, the latter withdraws more easily from such mastery in unfavorable personal circumstances, because it readily turns from adverse circumstances in order to divert itself to a certain extent. It then directs itself with all the greater energy to the foreign external world, and thus more easily becomes purely objective. Favorable personal circumstances have the opposite effect. On the whole, however, the melancholy accompanying genius rests on the fact that, the brighter the intellect enlightening the will-to-live, the more distinctly does it perceive the wretchedness of its condition. The gloomy disposition of highly gifted minds, so frequently observed, has its emblem in Mont Blanc, whose summit is often hidden in the clouds. But when on occasion, especially in the early morning, the veil of clouds is rent, and the mountain, red in the sunlight, looks down on Chamonix from its celestial height above the clouds, it is then a sight at which the heart of everyone is most deeply stirred. So also does the genius, who is often melancholy, display at times that characteristic serenity already described, which is possible in him alone, and springs from the most perfect objectivity of the mind. It floats like a radiant gleam of light on his lofty brow; *in tristitia hilaris, in hilaritate tristis.*[4]

All bunglers are what they are ultimately because their intellect, still too firmly tied to the will, becomes active only under the will's spur, and therefore remains entirely in its service. Accordingly they

---

3. All men of genius are melancholy.—TR.
4. Cheerful in sadness, sad in cheerfulness.—TR.

are capable of none other than personal aims. In keeping with this they produce bad paintings, dull and spiritless poems, shallow, absurd, and very often dishonest philosophemes, when, that is, it is of importance to them to recommend themselves to higher authorities through pious dishonesty. Thus all their thoughts and actions are personal; and so they succeed at most in appropriating as mannerisms what is external, accidental, and arbitrary in the geniune works of others. They seize the shell instead of the kernel, and yet imagine they have reached everything, indeed have surpassed those works. If the failure becomes obvious, many hope nevertheless to attain success in the end through their goodwill. But it is precisely this goodwill that makes it impossible, since this leads only to personal ends; with these, however, neither art, nor poetry, nor philosophy can ever be taken seriously. Therefore the expression that they stand in their own light is quite peculiarly applicable to such men. They have no idea that it is only the intellect, torn from the mastery of the will and from all its projects and thus freely active, that makes one capable of genuine productions, because it alone imparts true seriousness; and for them this is a good thing, otherwise they would jump into the water. In *morality* the *goodwill* is everything, but in *art* it is nothing; for, as the word [*Kunst*] already indicates, *ability* [*Können*] alone is of any consequence. Ultimately it is all a question of where the man's real *seriousness* is to be found. In the case of almost all, it is to be found exclusively in their own well-being and that of their families. They are therefore in a position to promote this and nothing else, since no resolution, no arbitrary and intentional effort, imparts, or makes up for, or more correctly furnishes, true, profound seriousness proper. For it always remains where nature has placed it; but without it everything can be only half performed. For the same reason, therefore, individuals of genius often give very little attention of their own welfare. Just as a leaden pendulum always brings a body back into the position required by the center of gravity determined by such a pendulum, so man's true seriousness always draws the force and attention of his intellect back to *where it lies;* everything else is pursued by him *without true seriousness.* Therefore only extremely rare and abnormal men, whose true seriousness lies not in the personal and practical, but in the objective and theoretical, are in a position to apprehend the essential element

We must purge intellectualism of everything
that leads to a lack of common sense, social
clumsiness, absent-mindedness, etc. Our enemies
seek to alienate us from the majority. We should

of things and of the world, and hence the highest truths, and in some way to reproduce them. For such a seriousness of the individual, falling outside him in the *objective,* is something foreign to human nature, something unnatural, properly speaking supernatural. But only through it is a man *great;* and accordingly, what he produces or creates is then ascribed to a *genius* different from him, which takes possession of him. For such a man, his painting, poetry, or thinking is an *end;* for the other it is a *means.* These others look in it for *their own interest* and, as a rule, know quite well how to promote it, for they insinuate themselves into the favor of contemporaries, and are ready to serve their wants and whims. They therefore usually live in happy circumstances; whereas the genius often exists under very wretched conditions. For he sacrifices his personal welfare to the *objective* end; he simply cannot do otherwise, because there lies his seriousness. They act conversely; therefore they are *small,* but he is *great.* His work, accordingly, is for all times and ages, but its recognition usually begins only with posterity; *they* live and die with their time. In general, he alone is *great* who in his work, be it practical or theoretical, *seeks not his own interest,* but pursues only an *objective* end. However, he is such even when in the practical this aim or end is misunderstood, and even when, in consequence of this, it should be a crime. What makes him *great* in all circumstances is the fact that *he does not seek himself and his own interest.* On the other hand, all action or effort directed to personal ends or aims is *small,* since he who is moved to activity in this way knows and finds himself only in his own evanescent and trifling person. On the other hand, he who is *great* recognizes himself in all and thus in the whole; he does not live, like others, only in the microcosm, but still more in the macrocosm. For this reason, the whole concerns him, and he tries to grasp it, in order to present it, or explain it, or act on it in practice. For to him it is not strange; he feels that it concerns him. On account of this extension of his sphere, he is called *great.* Accordingly, that sublime predicate belongs by right only to the true hero in any sense and to the genius; it signifies that, contrary to human nature, they have not sought their own interest, and have lived not for themselves, but for all. Now just as the great majority must obviously be *always* small, and can *never* be great, the converse is not possible, namely that a person should be great in every way, that is to say, constantly and at every moment:

> For man is made of common clay,
> And custom he calls his nurse.
> [Schiller]

Thus every great man must nevertheless often be only the individual, have in view only *himself;* and this means he must be *small.* On this rests the very true remark that no man is a hero to his valet, not on the fact that the valet does not know how to appreciate the hero; Goethe in the *Elective Affinities* (vol. 2, chap. 5) serves this up as an idea that occurred to Ottilie.

Genius is its own reward; for the best that one is, one must necessarily be for oneself. "Whoever is born *with* a talent, *to* a talent, finds his fairest existence therein," says Goethe. When we look back at a great man of former times, we do not think, "How lucky he is to be still admired by us all!" but, "How lucky he must have been in the immediate enjoyment of a mind, with the remaining traces of which centuries regale themselves!" Not in fame, but in that by which it is attained, lies the value, and in the production of immortal children lies the pleasure. Therefore those who attempt to demonstrate the vanity of posthumous fame from the fact that he who acquires it has no experience of it, is to be compared to the wiseacre who very sagely tried to demonstrate the utter uselessness of a heap of oyster shells to a man casting envious glances at one in his neighbor's yard.

In accordance with the description we have given of the true nature of genius, it is contrary to nature insofar as it consists in the intellect, whose real destiny is the service of the will, emancipating itself from that service in order to be active on its own account. Accordingly, genius is an intellect that has become unfaithful to its destiny; on this rest the *disadvantages* connected with it. We now prepare the way for a consideration of these by comparing genius with the less-decided preponderance of the intellect.

The intellect of the normal man, strictly bound to the service of his will, and thus in reality occupied only with the reception and taking up of motives, may be regarded as the complex system of wires with which each of these puppets is set in motion on the stage of the world theater. From this springs the dry, grave seriousness of most people, which is surpassed only by that of the animals, which never laugh. On the other hand, the genius, with his unfettered intellect, could be compared to a living person playing among the *Hitler* large puppets of the famous Milan puppet show. This person would be the only one among them who would perceive everything, and would therefore gladly quit the stage for a while in order to enjoy the play from the boxes; this is the reflectiveness of genius. But even the extremely intelligent and rational man, whom we might almost call wise, is very different from the genius; and indeed he is so because his intellect retains a *practical* tendency. It is concerned with the choice of the best of all ends and means; it therefore remains in the service of the will, and accordingly is occupied really and truly in conformity with nature. The firm, practical seriousness of life, described by the Romans as *gravitas,* presupposes that the intellect does *not* forsake the service of the will, in order to wander away after what does not concern this. It therefore does not admit of that separation of the will and the intellect that is the condition of genius. The able, indeed the eminent man, fitted for great achievements in the practical sphere, is as he is precisely through objects that keenly rouse his will, and spur it on to the restless investigation of their connections and relations. Thus his intellect has grown up firmly connected with his will. On the other hand, there floats before the mind of the genius, in its objective apprehension, the phenomenon of the world as something foreign to him, as an object of contemplation, expelling his willing from consciousness. On this point hinges the difference between the capacity for *deeds* and that for *works.* The latter demands an objectivity and depth of knowledge that presuppose the complete separation of the intellect from the will. The former, on the other hand, demands the application of knowledge, presence of mind, and resoluteness, and these require that the intellect shall constantly carry out the service of the will. Where the bond between intellect and will is loosened, the intellect, diverted from its natural destiny, will neglect the service of the will. For example, even in the emergency of the moment, it will still maintain its emancipation, and possibly will have no choice but to apprehend the environment, according to the picturesque impression thereof, from which the present danger threatens the individual. On the other hand, the intellect of the

man of reason and understanding is always at its post, is directed
to the circumstances and their requirements. Therefore such a man
will in all cases determine and carry out what is appropriate to the
matter. Consequently he will certainly not run into those eccentric-
ities, personal slips, and even follies, to which the genius is exposed.
The genius does this because his intellect does not remain exclusively the guide and guardian of his will, but is engrossed more or
less in what is purely objective. In the contrast between Tasso and
Antonio, Goethe has given us an illustration of the opposition in
which the two entirely different kinds of capacity, here described
in the abstract, stand to each other. The frequently observed kin-
ship of genius with madness rests chiefly on that very separation
of the intellect from the will, essential to genius yet contrary to
nature. But this separation itself is not in any way to be ascribed
to the fact that genius is accompanied by less intensity of the will,
for it is rather conditioned by a vehement and passionate character;
on the contrary, it is to be explained from the fact that the practically eminent man, the man of deeds, has merely the whole, full
measure of intellect required for an energetic will, whereas most
men lack even this. Genius, however, consists in a wholly abnormal, actual excess of intellect, such as is not required for the service
of any will. For this reason, the men of genuine works are a thousand times rarer than the men of deeds. It is just that abnormal
excess of intellect by virtue of which it obtains the decided preponderance, emancipates itself from the will, and, forgetful of its origin, is freely active from its own force and elasticity. It is from this
that the creations of genius result.

Further, genius consists in the working of the free intellect, that
is, of the intellect emancipated from the service of the will; and a
consequence of this very fact is that the productions of genius serve
no useful purpose. The work of genius may be music, philosophy,
painting, or poetry; it is nothing for use or profit. To be useless and
unprofitable is one of the characteristics of the works of genius; it
is their patent of nobility. All other human works exist only for the
maintenance or relief of our existence; only those here discussed do
not; they alone exist for their own sake, and are to be regarded in
this sense as the flower or the net profit of existence. Our heart is
therefore gladdened at the enjoyment of them, for we rise out of
the heavy earthly atmosphere of need and want. Moreover, analo-

gous to this, we rarely see the beautiful united with the useful. Tall and fine trees bear no fruit; fruit trees are small, ugly, and stunted. The double garden rose is not fruitful, but the small, wild, almost scentless rose is. The most beautiful buildings are not the useful ones; a temple is not a dwelling house. A person of high, rare mental gifts, compelled to attend to a merely useful piece of business for which the most ordinary person would be fitted, is like a valuable vase decorated with the most beautiful painting, which is used as a kitchen-pot; and to compare useful men with men of genius is like comparing bricks with diamonds.

Translated by E. F. J. Payne

9

On the Inner Nature of Art

Not merely philosophy but also the fine arts work at bottom toward the solution of the problem of existence. For in every mind that once gives itself up to the purely objective contemplation of the world, a desire has been awakened, however concealed and unconscious, to comprehend the true nature of things, of life, and of existence. For this alone is of interest to the intellect as such, in other words, to the subject of knowing that has become free from the aims of the will and is therefore pure; just as for the subject, knowing as mere individual, only the aims and ends of the will have interest. For this reason the result of every purely objective, and so of every artistic, apprehension of things is an expression more of the true nature of life and of existence, more an answer to the question, "What is life?" Every genuine and successful work of art answers this question in its own way quite calmly and serenely. But all the arts speak only the naive and childlike language of *perception,* not the abstract and serious language of *reflection;* their answer is thus a fleeting image, not a permanent universal knowledge. Thus for *perception,* every work of art answers that question, every painting, every statue, every poem, every scene on the stage. Music also answers it, more profoundly indeed than do all the others, since in a language intelligible with absolute directness, yet not capable of translation into that of our faculty of reason, it expresses the innermost nature of all life and existence. Thus all the other arts together hold before the questioner an image or picture of perception and say: "Look here; this is life!" However correct their answer may be, it will yet always afford only a temporary, not a complete and final satisfaction. For they always give only a fragment, an example instead of the rule, not the whole that can be given only in the universality of the *concept*. Therefore it is the task of philosophy to give for the concept, and hence for reflection and in the abstract, a reply to that question, which on that very account is permanent and satisfactory for all time. Moreover we see here on what the relationship between philsophy and _the fine arts rests, and can conclude from this to what extent the capacity for the two, though very different in its tendency and in secondary matters, is yet radically the same.

Accordingly, every work of art really endeavors to show us life and things as they are in reality; but these cannot be grasped directly by everyone through the mist of objective and subjective contingencies. Art takes away this mist.

The works of poets, sculptors, and pictorial or graphic artists generally contain an acknowledged treasure of profound wisdom, just because the wisdom of the nature of things themselves speaks from them. They interpret the utterances of things merely by elucidation and purer repetition. Therefore everyone who reads the poem or contemplates the work of art must of course contribute from his own resources toward bringing that wisdom to light. Consequently, he grasps only so much of the work as his capacity and culture allow, just as every sailor in a deep sea lets down the sounding lead as far as the length of its line will reach. Everyone has to stand before a picture as before a prince, waiting to see whether it will speak and what it will say to him; and, as with the prince, so he himself must not address it, for then he would hear only himself. It follows from all this that all wisdom is certainly contained in the works of the pictorial or graphic arts, yet only *virtualiter* or *implicite*. Philosophy, on the other hand, endeavors to furnish the same wisdom *actualiter* and *explicite;* in this sense philosophy is related to these arts as wine is to grapes. What it promises to supply would be, so to speak, a clear gain already realized, a firm and abiding possession, whereas that which comes from the achievements and works of art is only one that is always to be produced afresh. But for this it makes discouraging demands, hard to fulfill not merely for those who are to produce its works, but also for those who are to enjoy them. Therefore its public remains small, while that of the arts is large.

The above-mentioned cooperation of the beholder, required for the enjoyment of a work of art, rests partly on the fact that every work of art can act only through the medium of the imagination. It must therefore excite the imagination, which can never be left out of the question and remain inactive. This is a condition of aesthetic effect, and therefore a fundamental law of all the fine arts. But it follows from this that not everything can be given directly to the senses through the work of art, but only as much as is required to lead the imagination on to the right path. Something, and indeed the final thing, must always be left over for it to do. Even the author must always leave something over for the reader to think; for Voltaire has very rightly said: *Le secret d'être ennuyeux, c'est de tout dire.*[1] But in addition to this, the very best in art is too spiritual to be given directly to the senses; it must be born in the beholder's imagination, though it must be begotten by the work of art. It is due to this that the sketches of great masters are often more effective than their finished paintings. Of course another advantage contributes to this, namely, that they are completed at one stroke in the moment of conception, whereas the finished painting is brought about only through continued effort by means of clever deliberation and persistent premeditation, for the inspiration cannot last until the painting is completed. From the fundamental aesthetic law we are considering, it can also be explained why *wax figures* can never produce an aesthetic effect, and are therefore not real works of fine art, although it is precisely in them that the imitation of nature can reach the highest degree. For they leave nothing over for the imagination. Thus sculpture gives the mere form without the color; painting gives the color, but the mere appearance of the form; therefore both appeal to the imagination of the beholder. The wax figure, on the contrary, gives everything, form and color at the same time; from this arises the appearance of reality, and the imagination is left out of account. On the other hand, *poetry* appeals indeed to the imagination alone, and makes it active by means of mere words.

An arbitrary playing with the means of art without proper knowledge of the end is in every art the fundamental characteristic

1. The secret of being dull and tedious consists in our saying everything.—TR.

of bungling. Such bungling shows itself in the supports that carry nothing, in the purposeless volutes, prominences, and projections of bad architecture, in the meaningless runs and figures together with the aimless noise of bad music, in the jingling rhymes of verses with little or no meaning, and so on.

It follows from the previous chapter and from my whole view of art that its object is to facilitate knowledge of the *ideas* of the world (in the Platonic sense, the only one that I recognize for the word *idea*). But the *ideas* are essentially something of perception, and therefore, in its fuller determinations, something inexhaustible. The communication of such a thing can therefore take place only on the path of perception, which is that of art. Therefore, whoever is imbued with the apprehension of an *idea* is justified when he chooses art as the medium of his communication. The mere *concept*, on the other hand, is something completely determinable, hence something to be exhausted, something distinctly thought, which can be, according to its whole content, communicated coldly and dispassionately by words. Now to wish to communicate such a thing through *a work of art* is a very useless indirect course; in fact, it belongs to that playing with the means of art without knowledge of the end that I have just censured. Therefore, a work of art, the conception of which has resulted from mere, distinct concepts, is always ungenuine. If, when considering a work of plastic art, or reading a poem, or listening to a piece of music (which aims at describing something definite), we see the distinct, limited, cold, dispassionate concept glimmer and finally appear through all the rich resources of art, the concept that was the kernel of this work, the whole conception of the work having therefore consisted only in clearly thinking this concept, and accordingly being completely exhausted by its communication, then we feel disgust and indignation, for we see ourselves deceived and cheated of our interest and attention. We are entirely satisfied by the impression of a work of art only when it leaves behind something that, in spite of all our reflection on it, we cannot bring down to the distinctiveness of a concept. The mark of that hybrid origin from mere concepts is that the author of a work of art should have been able, before setting about it, to state in distinct words what he intended to present; for then it would have been possible to attain his whole end through these words themselves. It is therefore an undertaking as unworthy as it is absurd when, as has often been attempted at the present day, one tries to reduce a poem of Shakespeare or Goethe to an abstract truth, the communication whereof would have been the aim of the poem. Naturally the artist should think when arranging his work, but only *that* idea that was *perceived* before it was thought has suggestive and stimulating force when it is communicated, and thereby becomes immortal and imperishable. Hence we will not refrain from remarking that the work done at one stroke, like the previously mentioned sketches of painters, perfected in the inspiration of the first conception and drawn unconsciously as it were; likewise the melody that comes entirely without reflection and wholly as if by inspiration; finally also the lyrical poem proper, the mere song, in which the deeply felt mood of the present and the impression of the surroundings flow forth as if involuntarily in words, whose metre and rhyme are realized automatically—that all these, I say, have the great merit of being the pure work of the rapture of the moment, of the inspiration, of the free impulse of genius, without any admixture of deliberation and reflection. They are therefore delightful and enjoyable through and through, without shell and kernel, and their effect is much more infallible than is that of the greatest works of art of slow and deliberate execution. In all these, e.g., in great historical paintings, long epic poems, great operas, and so on, reflection, intention, and deliberate selection play an important part. Understanding, technical skill, and routine must fill up here the gaps left by the conception and inspiration of genius, and all kinds of neccssary subsidiary work must run through the really only genuine and brilliant parts as their cement. This explains why all such works, with the sole exception of the most perfect materpieces of the very greatest masters (such as *Hamlet, Faust,* the opera *Don Juan,* for example), inevitably contain an admixture of something insipid and tedious that restricts the enjoyment of them to some extent. Proofs of this are the *Messiad, Gerusalemme Liberata,* even *Paradise Lost* and the *Aeneid;* and Horace makes the bold remark: *Quandoque dormitat bonus Homerus.*[2] But that this is the case is a consequence of the limitation of human powers in general.

The mother of the useful arts is necessity; that of the fine arts

---

2. [I am mortified] whenever the great Homer sleeps. (*Ars Poetica,* 359.)—TR.

superfluity and abundance. As their father, the former have understanding, the latter genius, which is itself a kind of superfluity, that
of the power of knowledge beyond the measure required for the
service of the will.

Translated by E. F. J. Payne

10
On History

In the passage of the first volume referred to below I have shown in detail that more is achieved for knowledge of the true nature of mankind by poetry than by history, and I have shown why this is so, inasmuch as more real instruction is to be expected from the former than from the latter. Aristotle also has admitted this, for he says: (*Poetry is more philosophical and valuable than history.* (*Poetics, c. 9*). But I will state my ideas on the value of history, so as to avoid causing any misunderstanding about it.

In every class and species of things the facts are innumerable, the individual beings infinite in number, and the multiplicity and variety of their differences beyond our reach. With one look at all this, the curious and inquisitive mind is in a whirl; however much it investigates, it sees itself condemned to ignorance. But then comes *science;* it separates out the innumerable many, collects them under generic concepts, and these in turn under specific concepts, and so opens the way to a knowledge of the general and the particular. This knowledge comprehends the innumerable individuals, since it holds good of all without our having to consider each one by itself. In this way it promises satisfaction to the inquiring mind. All the sciences then put themselves together and over the real world of individual things that they have parceled out among themselves. But philosophy excels them all as the most universal, and thus the most important, knowledge, promising information for which the others have only prepared the way. *History* alone cannot properly enter into this series, since it cannot boast of the same advantage as the others, for it lacks the fundamental characteristic of science, the subordination of what is known; instead of this it boasts of the mere coordination of what is known. Therefore there is no system of history, as there is of every other branch of knowledge; accordingly, it is rational knowledge indeed, but, not a science. For nowhere does it know the particular by means of the universal, but it must comprehend the particular directly, and continue to creep along the ground of experience, so to speak. The real sciences, on the other hand, excel it, since they have attained to comprehensive concepts by means of which they command and control the particular, and, at any rate within certain limits, foresee the possibility of things within their province, so that they can be reassured even about what is still to come. As the sciences are systems of concepts, they always speak of species; history speaks of individuals. History would accordingly be a science of individual things, which implies a contradiction. It follows also from the first statement that the sciences all speak of that which always is; history, on the other hand, speaks of that which is only once, and then no more. Further, as history has to do with the absolutely particular and with individuals, which by their nature are inexhaustible, it knows everything only imperfectly and partially. At the same time, it must allow itself to be taught by the triviality of every new day that which as yet it did not know at all. If it should be objected that in history subordination of the particular under the universal also takes place, since the periods of time, the governments, and the other main and political changes, in short, everything to be found in historical tables, are the universal to which the special is subordinated, this would rest on a false understanding of the concept of the universal. For the universal here referred to is in history merely *subjective,* that is to say, its generality springs merely from the inadequacy of the individual *knowledge* of things; it is not *objective,* in other words, a concept in which the things would actually be thought together. Even the most universal in history is in itself only something individual and particular is, namely, a long epoch or a principal event. Hence the particular is related to this as the part to the whole, but not as the case to the rule, as occurs, on the other hand, in all the sciences proper, because they furnish concepts, not mere facts. Therefore, through correct knowledge of the universal, we can in these sciences determine with certainty the particular case that arises. For example, if I know the laws of the triangle in general, I can accordingly also state what must be the properties of the triangle before me. What holds good of all mammals, for example, that they have double ventricles of the heart, exactly seven cervical vertebrae, lungs, diaphragm, bladder, five senses, and so on, I can assert also of the strange bat that has just been caught, before it is dissected. But this is not the case in history, where the universal is not an objective universal of concepts, but merely a subjective universal of my knowledge, that can be called universal only insofar as it is superficial. Thus I may know in general about the Thirty Years' War, namely, that it was a religious war waged in the seventeenth century; but this general knowledge does not enable me to state anything more detailed about its course. The same contrast also holds good in the fact that, in the actual sciences, it is the special and the individual that is the most certain, for it rests on immediate apprehension; universal truths, on the other hand, are first abstracted from it, and therefore something can more readily be erroneously assumed in these. Conversely, in history the most universal is the most certain; for example, the periods of time, the succession of kings, revolutions, wars, and treaties of peace; on the other hand, the particular of the events and of their connection is more uncertain, and becomes always more so the deeper we go into details. History is therefore the more interesting the more special it is, but also the less trustworthy; and thus it approximates in all respects to a work of fiction. For the rest, he will best be able to judge what importance is to be attached to the boasted pragmatism of history, who remembers that at times it was only after twenty years that he understood the events of his own life in their true connection, although the data for these were completely before him, so difficult is the combination of the action of motives under the constant interference of chance and the concealment of intentions. Now insofar as history always has for its object only the particular, the individual fact, and regards this as the exclusively real, it is the direct opposite and counterpart of philosophy, which considers things from the most universal point of view, and has the universal as its express object. In every particular this universal remains identical; thus in the former philosophy always sees only the latter, and recognizes as inessential the change in its phenomenal appearance: *The philosopher is a friend of the universal.* Whereas history teaches us that at each time something different has been, philosophy endeavors to assist us to the insight that at all times exactly the same was, is, and will be. In truth, the essence of human life, as of nature everywhere, exists complete in every present time, and therefore requires only depth of comprehension in order to be exhaustively known. History, however, hopes to make up for depth by length and breadth; every present time is for it only a fragment that must be supplemented by the past. But the length of the past is infinite, and joined to it again is an infinite future. On this rests the opposition between philosophical and historical minds; the former want to fathom and find out, the latter try to narrate to the end. History shows on every side only the same thing under different forms; but he who does not recognize such a thing in one or a few forms, will hardly attain to a knowledge of it by running through all the forms. The chapters of the history of nations are at bottom different only through the names and dates; the really essential content is everywhere the same.

Therefore, insofar as the material of art is the *idea,* and the material of science the *concept,* we see both occupied with that which always exists at all times in the same way, but not with something that now is and then is not, which now is thus and then otherwise. For this reason, both are concerned with what Plato posited exclusively as the object of actual rational knowledge. The material of history, on the other hand, is the individual thing in its individuality and contingency; this thing exists once, and then exists no more for ever. The material of history is the transient complexities of a human world moving like clouds in the wind, which are often entirely transformed by the most trifling accident. From this point of view, the material of history appears to us as scarcely an object worthy of the serious and arduous consideration of the human mind. Just because it is so transitory, the human mind should select for its consideration that which is destined never to pass away.

Finally, as regards the attempt specially introduced by the Hegelian pseudophilosophy that is everywhere so pernicious and stupefying to the mind, the attempt, namely, to comprehend the history of the world as a planned whole, or, as they call it, "to construct it organically," a crude and shallow *realism* is actually at the root of this. Such realism regards the *phenomenon* as the *being-in-itself* of the world, and imagines that it is a question of this phenomenon and of its forms and events. It is still secretly supported in this by certain, mythological, fundamental views that it tacitly assumes; otherwise it might be asked for what spectator such a comedy was really being enacted. For since only the individual, not the human race, has actual, immediate unity of consciousness, the unity of this race's course of life is a mere fiction. Moreover, as in nature only the species are real and the genera mere abstractions, so in the human race only the individuals and their course of life are real, the nations and their lives being mere abstractions. Finally, constructive histories, guided by a shallow optimism, always ultimately end in a comfortable, substantial, fat state with a well-regulated constitution, good justice and police, useful arts and industries, and at most intellectual perfection, since this is in fact the only possible perfection, for that which is moral remains essentially unaltered. But according to the testimony of our innermost consciousness, it is the moral element on which everything depends; and this lies only in the individual as the tendency of his will. In reality, only the life course of each individual has unity, connection, and true significance; it is to be regarded as an instruction, and the significance of this is a moral one. Only the events of our *inner* life, insofar as they concern the *will,* have true reality and are actual occurrences, since the will alone is the thing-in-itself. In every microcosm lies the macrocosm, and the latter contains nothing more than is contained in the former. Plurality is phenomenon, and external events are mere configurations of the phenomenal world; they therefore have neither reality nor significance directly, but only indirectly, through their relation to the will of the individuals. Accordingly, the attempt to explain and expound them is like the attempt to see groups of persons and animals in the forms of clouds. What history relates is in fact only the long, heavy, and confused dream of mankind.

The Hegelians, who regard the philsophy of history as even the main purpose of all philosophy, should be referred to Plato, who untiringly repeats that the object of philosophy is the unchangeable and ever permanent, not that which now is thus and then otherwise. All who set up such constructions of the course of the world, or, as they call it, of history, have not grasped the principal truth of all philosophy, that what is is at all times the same, that all becoming and arising are only apparent, that the ideas alone are permanent, that time is ideal. This is what Plato means, this is what Kant means. Accordingly, we should try to understand what *exists,* what actually *is,* today and always, in other words, to know the *ideas* (in Plato's sense). On the other hand, fools imagine that something is supposed to come into existence. They therefore concede to history a principal place in their philosophy, and construct this on an assumed plan of the world, according to which everything is managed for the best. This is then supposed to appear *finaliter,* and will be a great and glorious thing. Accordingly, they take the world to be perfectly real, and set its purpose in miserable earthly happiness. Even when it is greatly cherished by man and favored by fate, such happiness is yet a hollow, deceptive, frail, and wretched thing, out of which neither constitutions, legal systems, steam engines, nor telegraphs can ever make anything that is essentially better. Accordingly, the aforesaid philosophers and glorifiers of history are simple realists, and also optimists and eudaemonists, and consequently shallow fellows and philistines incarnate. In addition, they are really bad Christians, for the true spirit and kernel of Christianity, as of Brahmanism and Buddhism also, is the knowledge of the vanity of all earthly happiness, complete contempt for it, and the turning away to an existence of quite a different, indeed an opposite, kind. This, I say, is the spirit and purpose of Christianity, the true "humor of the matter"; but it is not, as they imagine, monotheism. Therefore, atheistic Buddhism is much more closely akin to Christianity than are optimistic Judaism and its variety, Islam.

Therefore, a real philosophy of history should not consider, as do all these, what is always *becoming* and never *is* (to use Plato's language), and regard this as the real nature of things. On the contrary, it should keep in view what always is, and never becomes or passes away. Thus it does not consist in our raising the temporal aims of men to eternal and absolute aims, and then constructing with ingenuity and imagination their progress to these through every intricacy and perplexity. It consists in the insight that history is untruthful not only in its arrangement, but also in its very nature, since, speaking of mere individuals and particular events, it always pretends to relate something different, whereas from beginning to end it constantly repeats only the same thing under a different name and in a different cloak. The true philosophy of history thus consists in the insight that, in spite of all these endless changes and their chaos and confusion, we yet always have before us only the same, identical, unchangeable essence, acting in the same way to-day as it did yesterday and always. The true philosophy of history should therefore recognize the identical in all events, of ancient as of modern times, of the East as of the West, and should see every-where the same humanity, in spite of all difference in the special circumstances, in costume and customs. This identical element, per-sisting under every change, consists in the fundamental qualities of the human heart and head, many bad, few good. The motto of history in general should run: *Eadem, sed aliter.*[1] If we have read Herodotus, we have already studied enough history from a philo-sophical point of view. For everything that constitutes the subse-quent history of the world is already there, namely, the efforts, actions, sufferings, and fate of the human race, as it results from the aforesaid qualities and from its physical earthly lot.

If, in what has been said so far, we have recognized that history, considered as a means of knowing the true nature of mankind, is inferior to poetry; and again, that it is not a science in the proper sense; and finally, that the attempt to construct it as a whole with beginning, middle, and end, together with a connection fraught with meaning, is vain and is based on misunderstanding; then it would appear as though we wished to deny it all value, unless we showed in what its value consists. Actually, however, there remains for it, after this conquest of art and rejection by science, a province that is quite peculiar and different from both, and in which it exists most honorably.

What the faculty of reason is to the individual, history is to the human race. By virtue of this faculty, man is not, like the animal, restricted to the narrow present of perception, but knows also the incomparably more extended past with which it is connected, and out of which it has emerged. But only in this way does he have a proper understanding of the present itself, and can he also draw conclusions as to the future. On the other hand, the animal, whose knowledge, devoid of reflection, is restricted to perception, and therefore to the present, moves about among persons ignorant, dull, stupid, helpless, and dependent, even when tamed. Now

1. The same, but otherwise.—Tr.

analogous to this is a nation that does not know its own history, and is restricted to the present time of the generation now living. It therefore does not understand itself and its own present, because it is unable to refer this to a past, and to explain it from such a past; still less can it anticipate the future. Only through history does a nation become completely conscious of itself. Accordingly, history is to be regarded as the rational self-consciousness of the human race; it is to the race what the reflected and connected consciousness, conditioned by the faculty of reason, is to the individual. Through lack of such a consciousness, the animal remains confined to the narrow present of perception. Every gap in history is therefore like a gap in a person's recollecting self-consciousness; and before a monument of extreme antiquity that has outlived its own knowledge and information, as, for example, the pyramids, the temples and palaces of Yucatan, we stand as senseless and stupid as an animal does in the presence of human actions in which it is involved as a servant, or as a man before an old cipher of his own to which he has forgotten the key; in fact, as a somnambulist does who in the morning finds in front of him what he did in his sleep. In this sense, therefore, history is to be regarded as the faculty of reason, or the reflected consciousness of the human race; and it takes the place of a self-consciousness directly common to the whole race; so that only by virtue of history does this actually become a whole, a humanity. This is the true value of history, and accordingly the universal and predominant interest in it rests mainly on its being a personal concern of the human race. Now what *language* is for the reasoning faculty of individuals, as an indispensable condition for its use, *writing* is for the reasoning faculty of the whole race that is indicated here; for only with writing does the actual existence of this faculty of reason begin, just as the existence of the individual's reason first begins with language. Thus writing serves to restore to unity the consciousness of the human race, which is incessantly interrupted by death, and is accordingly piecemeal and fragmentary; so that the idea that arose in the ancestor is thought out to the end by his remote descendant. Writing remedies the breaking up of the human race and its consciousness into an immense number of ephemeral individuals, and thus bids defiance to irresistibly hurrying time, in whose hands goes oblivion. Written as well as *stone* monuments are to be regarded as an attempt to achieve this; to some extent the latter are older than the former. For who will believe that those who, at incalculable cost, set in motion the human powers of many thousands throughout many years, in order to erect pyramids, monoliths, rock tombs, obelisks, temples, and palaces, which still stand after thousands of years, could have had in view only themselves, the short span of their own life, too short to enable them to see the end of the construction, or even the ostensible purpose that the uncultured state of the masses required them to use as a pretext? Obviously the real purpose was to speak to their latest descendants, to enter into relationship with these, and thus to restore to unity the consciousness of mankind. The buildings of the Hindus, Egyptians, even of the Greeks and Romans, were calculated to last for several thousand years, because, through higher culture, their horizon was broader. On the other hand, the buildings of the Middle Ages and of modern times were intended to last a few centuries at most. This is due also to the fact that more confidence was placed in writing, after its use had become more general, and even more after the art of printing had been born from its womb. Yet even in the buildings of more recent times we see the urge to speak to posterity; it is therefore scandalous when they are destroyed or disfigured, to let them serve base, utilitarian purposes. Written monuments have less to fear from the elements, but more from barbarians, than have stone monuments; they achieve much more. The Egyptians sought to unite both kinds by covering their stone monuments with hieroglyphs; indeed, they added paintings in case the hieroglyphs should no longer be understood.

Translated by E. F. J. Payne

11

On the Metaphysics of Music

The outcome of my discussion of the real significance of this wonderful art, which is given in the passage of volume 1 referred to below, and is here present in the mind of the reader, was that there is indeed of necessity no resemblance between its productions and the world as representation, i.e., nature, but that there must be a distinct *parallelism,* which was then also demonstrated. I have still to add some fuller particulars of this parallelism that are worth noting. The four voices or parts of all harmony, that is, bass, tenor, alto, and soprano, or fundamental note, third, fifth, and octave, correspond to the four grades in the series of existences, hence to the mineral, plant, and animal kingdoms, and to man. This obtains an additional and striking confirmation in the fundamental rule of music, which states that the bass should remain at a much greater interval below the three upper voices or parts than these have between themselves, so that it may never approach nearer to them than an octave at most, but often remains even further below them. Accordingly, the correct triad has its place in the third octave from the fundamental note. In keeping with this, the effect of *extended* harmony, where the bass remains at a distance from the other parts, is much more powerful and beautiful than that of close harmony, where the bass is moved up nearer to them. Such close harmony is introduced only on account of the limited range of the instruments. This whole rule, however, is by no means arbitrary, but has its root in the natural origin of the tonal system, namely, insofar as the shortest harmonic intervals, which sound in unison by means of the secondary vibrations, are the octave and its fifth. In this rule we recognize the musical analogue of the fundamental disposition of nature, by virtue of which organic beings are much more closely related among themselves than they are to the inanimate, inorganic mass of the mineral kingdom. Between this and them are placed the most decided boundary and the widest gulf in the whole of nature. The high voice, singing the melody, is of course at the same time an integral part of the harmony, and in this is connected even with the deepest ground bass. This may be regarded as the analogue of the fact that *the same* matter that in a human organism is the supporter of the idea of man must nevertheless at the same time manifest and support the ideas of gravity and of chemical properties, hence the ideas of the lowest grades of the will's objectification.

Because music does not, like all the other arts, exhibit the *ideas* or grades of the will's objectification, but directly the *will itself,* we can also explain that it acts directly on the will, i.e., the feelings, passions, and emotions of the hearer, so that it quickly raises these or even alters them.

Far from being a mere aid to poetry, music is certainly an independent art; in fact, it is the most powerful of all the arts, and therefore attains its ends entirely from its own resources. Just as certainly, it does not require the words of a song or the action of an opera. Music as such knows only the tones or notes, not the causes that produce them. Accordingly, even the *vox humana* is for it originally and essentially nothing but a modified tone, just like that of an instrument; and like every other tone, it has the characteristic advantages and disadvantages that are a consequence of the instrument producing it. Now in this case it is an accidental circumstance that this very instrument serves in a different way as the organ of speech for the communication of concepts, and incidentally, of course, music can make use of this circumstance in order to enter into a relationship with poetry. But it must never make this the main thing, and be entirely concerned only with the expression of what are often, indeed essentially, silly and insipid verses (as Diderot gives us to understand in *Le Neveu de Rameau*). The words are and remain for the music a foreign extra of secondary value, as the effect of the tones is incomparably more powerful, more infallible, and more rapid than that of the words. If these are incorporated in the music, therefore, they must of course occupy only an entirely subordinate position, and adapt themselves completely to it. But the relation assumes the opposite aspect in regard to the given poetry, and hence to the song or libretto of an opera, to which a piece of music is added. For in these the musical art at once shows its power and superior capacity, since it gives the most profound, ultimate, and secret information on the feeling expressed in the words, or the action presented in the opera. It expresses their real and true nature, and makes us acquainted with the innermost soul of the events and occurrences, the mere cloak and body of which are presented on the stage. With regard to this superiority of music, and insofar as it stands to the text and the action in the relation of universal to particular, of rule to example, it might perhaps appear more suitable for the text to be written for the music than for the music to be composed for the text. With the usual method, however, the words and actions of the text lead the composer to the affections of the will that underlie them, and call up in him the feelings to be expressed; consequently they act as a means for exciting his musical imagination. Moreover, that the addition of poetry to music is so welcome, and a song with intelligible words give such profound joy, is due to the fact that our most direct and most indirect methods of knowledge are here stimulated simultaneously and in union. Thus the most direct is that for which music expresses the stirrings of the will itself, but the most indirect that of the concepts denoted by words. With the language of the feelings, our faculty of reason does not willingly sit in complete idleness. From its own resources, music is certainly able to express every movement of the will, every feeling; but through the addition of the words, we receive also their objects, the motives that give rise to that feeling. The music of an opera, as presented in the score, has a wholly independent, separate, and as it were abstract existence by itself, to which the incidents and characters of the piece are foreign, and which follows its own unchangeable rules; it can therefore be completely effective even without the text. But as this music was composed with respect to the drama, it is, so to speak, the soul of this, since, in its connection with the incidents, characters, and words, it becomes the expression of the inner significance of all those incidents, and of their ultimate and secret necessity that rests on this significance. Unless the spectator is a mere gaper, his pleasure really depends on an obscure feeling of this. Yet in opera, music shows its heterogeneous nature and its superior intrinsic virtue by its complete indifference to everything material in the incidents; and in consequence of this, it expresses the storm of the passions and the pathos of the feelings everywhere in the same way, and accompanies these with the same pomp of its tones, whether Agamemnon and Achilles or the dissensions of an ordinary family furnish the material of the piece. For only the passions, the movements of the will, exist for it, and, like God, it sees only the heart. It never assimilates the material, and therefore, when it accompanies even the most ludicrous and extravagant farces of comic opera, it still preserves its essential beauty, purity, and sublimity; and its fusion with those incidents cannot drag it down from its height to which everything ludicrous is really foreign. Thus the deep and serious significance of our existence hangs over the farce and the endless miseries of human life, and does not leave it for a moment.

Now if we cast a glance at purely instrumental music, a symphony of Beethoven presents us with the greatest confusion that yet has the most perfect order as its foundation; with the most vehement conflict that is transformed the next moment into the most beautiful harmony. It is *rerum concordia discors,*[1] a true and complete picture of the nature of the world, which rolls on in the boundless confusion of innumerable forms, and maintains itself by constant destruction. But at the same time, all the human passions and emotions speak from this symphony; joy, grief, love, hatred, terror, hope, and so on in innumerable shades, yet all, as it were, only in the abstract and without any particularization; it is their mere form without the material, like a mere spirit world without matter. We certainly have an inclination to realize it while we listen, to clothe it in the imagination with flesh and bone, and to see in it all the different scenes of life and nature. On the whole, however, this does not promote an understanding or enjoyment of it, but rather gives it a strange and arbitrary addition. It is therefore better to interpret it purely and in its immediacy.

After considering music, in the foregoing remarks as well as in the text, from the metaphysical aspect only, and thus with regard to the inner significance of its achievements, it is appropriate for

---

1. The discordant concord of the world.—Tr.

me to subject to a general consideration the means by which, acting on our mind, it brings these about, and consequently to show the connection of that metaphysical aspect of music with the physical, which has been adequately investigated and is well-known. I start from the theory, generally known and by no means overthrown by recent objections, that all harmony of the tones rests on the coincidence of the vibrations. When two tones sound simultaneously, this coincidence occurs perhaps at every second, or third, or fourth vibration, according to which they are the octave, the fifth, or the fourth of one another, and so on. Thus, so long as the vibrations of two tones have a rational relation to one another, expressible in small numbers, they can be taken together in our apprehension through their constantly recurring coincidence; the tones are blended and are thus in harmony. On the other hand, if that relation is an irrational one, or one expressible only in large numbers, no intelligible coincidence of the vibrations occurs, but *obstrepunt sibi perpetuo*,[2] an in this way they resist being taken together in our apprehension, and accordingly are called a dissonance. As a result of this theory, music is a means of making intelligible rational and irrational numerical relations, not, like arithmetic, with the aid of the concept, but by bringing them to a knowledge that is quite direct and simultaneously affects the senses. The connection of the metaphysical significance of music with this its physical and arithmetical basis rests on the fact that what resists our *apprehension*, namely, the irrational relation or dissonance, becomes the natural image of what resists our *will*; and, conversely, the consonance or the rational relation, by easily adapting itself to our *apprehension*, becomes the image of the satisfaction of the *will*. Now as that rational and irrational element in the numerical relations of the vibrations admits of innumerable degrees, nuances, sequences, and variations, music by means of it becomes the material in which all movements of the human heart, i.e., of the will, movements whose essential nature is always satisfaction and dissatisfaction, although in innumerable degrees, can be faithfully portrayed and reproduced in all their finest shades and modifications; and this takes place by means of the invention of the melody. Thus we here see the movements of the will tinted with the province of

---

2. They clamor incessantly against one another.—TR.

the mere *representation* that is the exclusive scene of the achievements of all the fine arts. For these positively demand that the *will itself* be left out of account, and that we behave in every way as purely *knowing* beings. Therefore the affections of the will itself, and hence actual pain and actual pleasure, must not be excited, but only their substitutes, that which is in conformity with the *intellect* as a *picture or image* of the will's satisfaction, and that which more or less opposes it as a *picture or image* of greater or lesser pain. Only in this way does music never cause us actual suffering, but still remains pleasant even in its most painful chords; and we like to hear in its language the secret history of our will and of all its stirrings and strivings with their many different delays, postponements, hindrances, and afflictions, even in the most sorrowful melodies. On the other hand, where in real life and its terrors our *will itself* is that which is roused and tormented, we are then not concerned with tones and their numerical relations; on the contrary, we ourselves are now the vibrating string that is stretched and plucked.

Further, since, in consequence of the underlying physical theory, the really musical quality of the notes is to be found in the proportion of the rapidity of their vibrations, but not in their relative strength, the musical ear always prefers to follow in harmony the highest note, not the strongest. Therefore, even in the most powerful orchestral accompaniment, the soprano stands out, and thus obtains a natural right to deliver the melody. At the same time this is supported by the great flexibility of the soprano, which depends on the same rapidity of the vibrations, as is seen in the ornate passages and movements. In this way the soprano becomes the suitable representative of the enhanced sensibility that is susceptible to the slightest impression and determinable through this, and consequently of the most highly developed consciousness that stands at the highest stage of the scale of beings. From opposite causes, the contrast to the soprano is formed by the bass, which moves heavily, rises and falls only by large intervals, thirds, fourths, and fifths, and is guided here by fixed rules in each of its steps. It is therefore the natural representative of the inorganic kingdom of nature, which is devoid of feeling, is inaccessible to fine impressions, and is determinable only according to universal laws. It can never rise by *one* tone, e.g., from a fourth to a fifth, for this produces in the upper voices or parts the incorrect fifth or octave sequence. Therefore, originally and in its own nature, the bass can never present the melody. But if the melody is assigned to it, this is done by means of counterpoint, in other words, it is a bass *transposed*, that is to say, one of the upper voices or parts is lowered and disguised as a bass. It then really requires a second fundamental bass for its accompaniment. This unnaturalness of a melody in the bass is the reason why bass airs with full accompaniment never afford us the pure and perfect delight of the soprano air. In the connection of the harmony, the soprano air alone is natural. Incidentally, such a melodious bass, forcibly obtained by transposition, might be compared, in the sense of our metaphysics of music, to a block of marble on which the human form has been impressed. For this reason it is wonderfully appropriate to the stone guest in *Don Juan*.

But we will now go somewhat nearer to the root of the *genesis* of melody. This can be effected by analyzing melody into its constituent parts; and in any case, this will afford us the pleasure that arises from our once bringing to abstract and distinct consciousness things of which everyone is aware in the concrete, whereby they gain the appearance of novelty.

Melody consists of two elements, a rhythmical and a harmonious; the former can also be described as the quantitative element, the latter as the qualitative, since the first concerns the duration of the notes, the second their pitch and depth. In writing music, the former belongs to the perpendicular lines, the latter to the horizontal. Purely arithmetical relations, hence those of time, are the basis of both; in the one case, the relative duration of the notes, in the other, the relative rapidity of their vibrations. The rhythmical element is the most essential, for by itself alone and without the other element it can present a kind of melody, as is done, for example, on the drum; yet complete melody requires both elements. Thus it consists in an alternating *discord* and *reconciliation* of them, as I shall show in a moment; but as the harmonious element has been discussed in what has been said already, I will consider somewhat more closely the rhythmical element.

Rhythm is in time what *symmetry* is in space, namely, division into equal parts corresponding to one another, and first into larger parts that are again divisible into smaller parts subordinate to the former. In the series of arts furnished by me, *architecture* and *music* form the two extremes. Moreover, they are the most heterogeneous, in fact the true antipodes, according to their inner nature, their power, the range of their spheres, and their significance. This contrast extends even to the form of their appearance, since architecture is in *space* alone, without any reference to time, and music is in *time* alone without any reference to space.[3] From this springs their sole analogy, namely, that as in architecture it is *symmetry* that arranges and holds together, in music it is *rhythm;* and thus we also have confirmation here that *les extrêmes se touchent.*[4] As the ultimate constituent elements of a building are the exactly similar stones, so the ultimate constituent elements of a piece of music are the exactly similar measures of time. But through arsis and thesis, or in general through the numerical fraction denoting the time, these are divided into equal parts that may perhaps be compared to the dimensions of the stone. The musical period consists of several bars, and also has two equal halves, one rising, aspiring, often going to the dominant, and one sinking, calming, and finding again the fundamental note. Two or even several periods constitute a part that is often doubled, likewise symmetrically, by the sign of repetition. From two parts we get a smaller piece of music, or only a movement of a larger piece; and thus a concerto or sonata usually consists of three movements, a symphony of four, and a mass of five. We therefore see the piece of music combined and rounded off as a whole by symmetrical distribution and repeated division, down to the beats and their fractions with general subordination, superordination, and coordination of its members, exactly as a building is by its symmetry; only that what with the latter is exclusively in space is with the former exclusively in time. The mere feeling of this analogy has occasioned the bold witticism, often repeated in the last thirty years, that architecture is frozen music. The origin of this can be traced to Goethe, for, according to Eckermann's *Conversations,* vol. 2, p. 88, he said: "Among my papers

---

3. It would be a false objection to say that sculpture and painting are also merely in space; for their works are connected with time, not directly of course, but indirectly, since they depict life, movement, action. It would be just as false to say that poetry, as speech, belongs only to time. This is also true only indirectly of the words; its material is everything that exists, hence the spatial.

4. Extremes meet.—TR.

I have found a sheet on which I call architecture a congealed music, and actually there is something in it; the mood arising from architecture approximates to the effect of music." He probably uttered that witticism much earlier in the conversation, and in that case we know quite well that there was never a lack of people to glean what he dropped, in order to go about subsequently dressed up in it. For the rest, whatever Goethe may have said, the analogy of music with architecture, which I refer to its sole ground, namely, the analogy of rhythm with symmetry, accordingly extends only to the outer form, and by no means to the inner nature of the two arts, which is vastly different. Indeed, it would be ridiculous to try to put the most limited and feeble of all the arts on an equal footing in essential respects with the most extensive and effective. As an amplification of the analogy pointed out it might also be added that when music, in a sudden urge for independence, so to speak, seizes the opportunity of a pause, in order to free itself from the control of rhythm, to launch out into the free fancy of an ornate cadenza, such a piece of music, divested of rhythm, is analogous to the ruin divested of symmetry. Accordingly, in the daring language of that witticism, such a ruin may be called a frozen cadenza.

After this discussion of *rhythm*, I have now to show how the true nature of melody consists in the constantly renewed *discord and reconciliation* of its rhythmical with its harmonious element. Its harmonious element has as its assumption the fundamental note, just as the rhythmical element has the measure of time, and it consists in a deviation from this through all the notes of the scale, until, by longer or shorter detours, it reaches a harmonious stage, often the dominant or subdominant that affords it an incomplete satisfaction. But then there follows on an equally long path its return to the fundamental note, with which appears complete satisfaction. But the two must now take place in such a way that reaching the aforesaid stage and finding the fundamental note once more coincide with certain favorite points of time in the *rhythm*, as otherwise it does not work. Therefore, just as the harmonious sequence of sounds requires certain *notes*, first of all the tonic, then the dominant, and so on, so rhythm on its part requires certain *points of time*, certain numbered bars, and certain parts of these bars, which are called heavy or good beats, or the accented parts of the bar, as opposed to the light or bad beats, or unaccented parts of the bar. The *discord* of those two fundamental elements consists in the fact that, by the demand of the one being satisfied, that of the other is not. But *reconciliation* consists in the two being satisfied simultaneously and at once. Thus the wandering of the sequence of notes, until the attainment of a more or less harmonious stage, must hit upon this only after a definite number of bars, but then on a *good* part of the bar, whereby this becomes for it a certain point of rest. In just the same way, the return to the tonic must again find this after an equal number of bars, and likewise on a *good* part of the bar, whereby complete satisfaction then occurs. So long as this required coincidence of the satisfactions of the two elements is not attained, the rhythm, on the one hand, may follow its regular course, and on the other hand the required notes occur often enough; yet they will remain entirely without that effect through which the melody originates. The following extremely simple example may serve to illustrate this:

Here the harmonious sequence of notes strikes the tonic right at the end of the first bar, but does not thereby obtain any satisfaction, because the rhythm is conceived in the worst part of the bar. Immediately afterwards in the second bar, the rhythm has the good part of the bar, but the sequence of notes has arrived at the seventh. Here, therefore, the two elements of the melody are entirely *disunited,* and we feel disquieted. In the second half of the period everything is reversed, and in the last note they are *reconciled.* This kind of proceeding can be demonstrated in every melody, though generally in a much more extended form. Now the constant *discord and reconciliation* of its two elements that occurs here is, metaphysically considered, the copy of the origination of new desires, and then of their satisfaction. Precisely in this way, the music penetrates our hearts by flattery, so that it always holds out to us the complete satisfaction of our desires. More closely considered, we see in this procedure of the melody a condition to a certain extent *inward* (the harmonious) meet with an *outward* condition (the rhythmical) as if by an *accident;* which is of course produced by the composer, and to this extent may be compared to the rhyme in poetry. This, however, is just the copy of the meeting of our desires with the favorable external circumstances independent of them, and is thus the picture of happiness. The effect of the *suspension* also deserves to be considered here. It is a dissonance delaying the final consonance that is with certainty awaited; in this way the longing for it is strengthened, and its appearance affords the greater satisfaction. This is clearly an analogue of the satisfaction of the will that is enhanced through delay. The complete cadence requires the preceding chord of the seventh on the dominant, because the most deeply felt satisfaction and complete relief can follow only the most pressing desire. Therefore music consists generally in a constant succession of chords more or less disquieting, i.e., of chords exciting desire, with chords more or less quieting and satisfying; just as the life of the heart (the will) is a constant succession of greater or lesser disquietude through desire or fear with composure in degrees just as varied. Accordingly the harmonious progress of notes consists of the alternation of dissonance and consonance that conforms to the rules of art. A sequence of merely consonant chords would be satiating, tedious, and empty, like the languor produced by the satisfaction of all desires. Therefore, although dissonances are disquieting and have an almost painful effect, they must be introduced, but only in order to be resolved again into consonances with proper preparation. In fact, in the whole of music there are only two fundamental chords, the dissonant chord of the seventh and the harmonious triad, and all chords that are met with can be referred to these two. This is precisely in keeping with the fact that there are for the will at bottom only dissatisfaction and satisfaction, however many and varied the forms in which these are presented may be. And just as there are two universal and fundamental moods of the mind, serenity, or at any rate vigor, and sadness, or even anguish, so music has two general keys, the major and the minor, corresponding to those moods, and it must always be found in the one or in the other. But it is indeed amazing that there is a sign of pain, namely, the minor, which is neither physically painful nor even conventional, yet is at once pleasing and unmistakable. From this we can estimate how deeply music is rooted in the real nature of things and of man. With northern nations, whose life is subject to hard conditions, especially with the Russians, the minor prevails, even in church music. Allegro in the minor is very frequent in French music, and is characteristic; it is as if a man danced while his shoe pinched him.

I add a couple of secondary observations. Under a change of the tonic or keynote, and with it of the value of all the intervals, in consequence of which the same note figures as the second, the third, the fourth, and so on, the notes of the scale are analogous to actors who have to assume now one role now another, while their person remains the same. The fact that this person is often not exactly suited to that role may be compared to the unavoidable impurity of every harmonic system (mentioned at the end of section 52 of volume 1) that has been produced by the equally hovering temperament.

Perhaps some might take umbrage at the fact that, according to the present metaphysics of music, whereas it so often exalts our minds and seems to speak of worlds different from and better than ours, it nevertheless flatters only the will-to-live, since it depicts the true nature of the will, gives it a glowing account of its success, and at the end expresses its satisfaction and contentment. The following passage from the *Veda* may serve to set at rest such doubts: *And that rapturous that is a kind of delight is called the highest Atman, because wherever there is a desire, this is a part of its delight.* (*Oupnekhat*, vol. 1, p. 405, and again vol. 2, p. 215).

Translated by E. F. J. Payne

12
The World as Will: Second Aspect

The last part of our discussion proclaims itself as the most serious, for it concerns the actions of men, the subject of direct interest to everyone, and one that can be foreign or indifferent to none. Indeed, to refer everything else to action is so characteristic of man's nature that, in every systematic investigation, he will always consider that part of it that relates to action as the result of its whole content, at any rate insofar as this interests him, and he will therefore devote his most serious attention to this part, even if to no other. In this respect, the part of our discussion that follows would, according to the ordinary method of expression, be called practical philosophy in contrast to the theoretical dealt with up to now. In my opinion, however, all philosophy is always theoretical, since it is essential to it always to maintain a purely contemplative attitude, whatever be the immediate object of investigation; to inquire, not to prescribe. But to become practical, to guide conduct, to transform character, are old claims that with mature insight it ought finally to abandon. For here, where it is a question of the worth or worthlessness of existence, of salvation or damnation, not the dead concepts of philosophy decide the matter, but the innermost nature of man himself, the demon that guides him and has not chosen him, but has been chosen by him, as Plato would say; his intelligible character, as Kant puts it. Virtue is as little taught as is genius; indeed, the concept is just as unfruitful for it as it is for art, and in the case of both can be used only as an instrument. We should therefore be just as foolish to expect that our moral systems and ethics would create virtuous, noble, and holy men, as that our aesthetics would produce poets, painters, and musicians.

Philosophy can never do more than interpret and explain what is present and at hand; it can never do more than bring to the distinct, abstract knowledge of the faculty of reason the inner nature of the world that expresses itself intelligibly to everyone in the concrete, that is, as feeling. It does this, however, in every possible relation and connection and from every point of view. Now just as in the three previous books the attempt has been made to achieve the same thing with the generality proper to philosophy, from different points of view, so in the present book man's conduct will be considered in the same way. This side of the world might prove to be the most important of all, not only, as I remarked above, from a subjective, but also from an objective point of view. Here I shall remain absolutely faithful to the method of consideration we have hitherto followed, and shall support myself by assuming what has been stated up to now. Indeed, there is really only one thought that forms the content of this whole work, and as I have developed it hitherto as regards other subjects, I shall now develop it in the conduct of man. I shall thus do the last thing I am able to do for communicating this thought as fully and completely as possible.

The point of view given and the method of treatment announced suggest that in this ethical book no precepts, no doctrine of duty are to be expected; still less will there be set forth a universal moral principle, a universal recipe, so to speak, for producing all the virtues. Also we shall not speak of an *"unconditioned ought,"* since this involves a contradiction, as is explained in the appendix; or of a "law for freedom," which is in the same position. Generally we shall not speak of "ought" at all, for we speak in this way to children and to peoples still in their infancy, but not to those who have appropriated to themselves all the culture of a mature age. It is indeed a palpable contradiction to call the will free and yet to prescribe for it laws by which it is to will. But in the light of our whole view, the will is not only free, but even almighty; from it comes not only its action, but also its world; and as the will is, so does its action appear, so does its world appear; both are its self-knowledge and nothing more. The will determines itself, and therewith its action and its world also; for besides it there is nothing, and these are the will itself. Only thus is the will truly autonomous, and from every other point of view it is heteronomous. Our philosophical attempts can go only so far as to interpret and explain man's action, and the very different and even opposite maxims of which it is the living expression, according to their innermost nature and content. This is done in connection with our previous discussion, and in precisely the same way in which we have attempted hitherto to interpret the remaining phenomena of the world, and to bring their innermost nature to distinct, abstract knowledge. Our philosophy will affirm the same *immanence* here as in all that we have considered hitherto. It will not, in opposition to Kant's great teaching, attempt to use as a jumping pole the forms of the phenomenon, whose general expression is the principle of sufficient reason, in order to leap over the phenomenon itself, which alone gives those forms meaning, and to land in the boundless sphere of empty fictions. This actual world of what is knowable, in which we are and which is in us, remains both the material and the limit of our consideration. It is a world so rich in content that not even the profoundest investigation of which the human mind is capable could exhaust it. Now since the real, knowable world will never fail to afford material and reality to our ethical observations any more than it will to our previous observations, nothing will be less necessary than for us to take refuge in negative concepts devoid of content, and then somehow to make even ourselves believe that we were saying something when we spoke with raised eyebrows about the "absolute," the "infinite," the "supersensuous," and whatever other mere negations of the sort there may be (*Nihil est, nisi negationis nomen, cum obscura notione.* Julian, *Oratio 5.*)[1] Instead of this, we could call it more briefly cloud-cuckoo-land.[2] We shall not need to serve up covered, empty dishes of this sort. Finally, no more here than in the previous books shall we relate histories and give them out as philosophy. For we are of opinion that anyone who imagines that the inner nature of the world can be *historically* comprehended, however finely glossed over it may be, is still infinitely far from a philosophical knowledge

---

1. It is nothing but a mere negation, united with an obscure notion.—TR.
2. From *The Birds* by Aristophanes.—TR.

of the world. But this is the case as soon as a *becoming*, or a *having become*, or a *will become* enters into his view of the inner nature of the world; whenever an earlier or a later has the least significance; and consequently whenever points of beginning and of ending in the world, together with a path between the two, are sought and found, and the philosophizing individual even recognizes his own position on this path. Such *historical philosophizing* in most cases furnishes a cosmogony admitting of many varieties, or else a system of emanations, a doctrine of diminutions, or finally, when driven in despair over the fruitless attempts of those paths to the last path, it furnishes, conversely, a doctrine of a constant becoming, springing up, arising, coming to light out of darkness, out of the obscure ground, primary ground, groundlessness, or some other drivel of this kind. But all this is most briefly disposed of by remarking that a whole eternity, in other words an endless time, has already elapsed up to the present moment, and therefore everything that can or should become must have become already. For all such historical philosophy, whatever airs it may assume, regards *time,* just as though Kant had never existed, as a determination of things-in-themselves, and therefore stops at what Kant calls the phenomenon in opposition to the thing-in-itself, and what Plato calls the becoming never the being in opposition to the being never the becoming, or finally what is called by the Indians the web of Maya. It is just the knowledge belonging to the principle of sufficient reason, with which we never reach the inner nature of things, but endlessly pursue phenomena only, moving without end or aim like a squirrel in its wheel, until in the end we are tired out, and stop still at some arbitrarily chosen point, and then wish to extort respect for this from others as well. The genuine method of considering the world philosophically, in other words, that consideration that acquaints us with the inner nature of the world and thus takes us beyond the phenomenon, is precisely the method that does not ask about the whence, whither, and why of the world, but always and everywhere about the *what* alone. Thus it is the method that considers things not according to any relation, not as becoming and passing away, in short not according to one of the four forms of the principle of sufficient reason. On the contrary, it is precisely what is still left over after we eliminate the whole of this method of consideration that follows the principle of sufficient reason; thus it is the inner nature of the world, always appearing the same in all relations, but itself never amenable to them, in other words the Ideas of the world, that forms the object of our method of philosophy. From such knowledge we get philosophy as well as art; in fact, we shall find in this book that we can also reach that disposition of mind that alone leads to true holiness and to salvation from the world.

The first three books will, it is hoped, have produced the distinct and certain knowledge that the mirror of the will has appeared to it in the world as representation. In this mirror the will knows itself in increasing degrees of distinctness and completeness, the highest of which is man. Man's inner nature, however, receives its complete expression above all through the connected series of his actions. The self-conscious connection of these actions is rendered possible by the faculty of reason, which enables him to survey the whole in the abstract.

The will, considered purely in itself, is devoid of knowledge, and is only a blind, irresistible urge, as we see it appear in inorganic and vegetable nature and in their laws, and also in the vegetative part of our own life. Through the addition of the world as representation, developed for its service, the will obtains knowledge of its own willing and what it wills, namely, that this is nothing but this world, life, precisely as it exists. We have therefore called the phenomenal world the mirror, the objectivity, of the will; and as what the will wills is always life, just because this is nothing but the presentation of that willing for the representation, it is immaterial and a mere pleonasm if, instead of simply saying "the will," we say "the will-to-live."

As the will is the thing-in-itself, the inner content, the essence of the world, but life, the visible world, the phenomenon, is only the mirror of the will, this world will accompany the will as inseparably as a body is accompanied by its shadow; and if will exists, then life, the world, will exist. Therefore life is certain to the will-to-live, and as long as we are filled with the will-to-live we need not be apprehensive for our existence, even at the sight of death. It is true that we see the individual come into being and pass away; but the individual is only phenomenon, exists only for knowledge involved in the principle of sufficient reason, in the *principium individuationis*. Naturally, for this knowledge, the individual re-

A greater will, a deeper source of the will, overcomes this superficial will. It's like physical weakness being overcome by exercise. Or intensity of love for one woman overcoming the promiscuous sex drive rather than abstinence doing that.

ceives his life as a gift, rises out of nothing, and then suffers the loss of this gift through death, and returns to nothing. We, however, wish to consider life philosophically, that is to say, according to its Ideas, and then we shall find that neither the will, the thing-in-itself in all phenomena, nor the subject of knowing, the spectator of all phenomena, is in any way affected by birth and death. Birth and death belong only to the phenomenon of the will, and hence to life; and it is essential to this that it manifest itself in individuals that come into being and pass away, as fleeting phenomena, appearing in the form of time, of that which in itself knows no time, but must be manifested precisely in the way aforesaid in order to objectify its real nature. Birth and death belong equally to life, and hold the balance as mutual conditions of each other, or, if the expression be preferred, as poles of the whole phenomenon of life. The wisest of all mythologies, the Indian, expresses this by giving to the very god who symbolizes destruction and death (just as Brahma, the most sinful and lowest god of the Trimurti, symbolizes generation, origination, and Vishnu preservation), by giving, I say, to Shiva as an attribute not only the necklace of skulls, but also the lingam, that symbol of generation that appears as the counterpart of death. In this way it is intimated that generation and death are essential correlatives that reciprocally neutralize and eliminate each other. It was precisely the same sentiment that prompted the Greeks and Romans to adorn the costly sarcophagi, just as we still see them, with feasts, dances, marriages, hunts, fights between wild beasts, bacchanalia, that is, with presentations of life's most powerful urge. This they present to us not only through such diversions and merriments, but even in sensual groups, to the point of showing us the sexual intercourse between satyrs and goats. The object was obviously to indicate with the greatest emphasis from the death of the mourned individual the immortal life of nature, and thus to intimate, although without abstract knowledge, that the whole of nature is the phenomenon, and also the fulfillment, of the will-to-live. The form of this phenomenon is time, space, and causality, and through these, individuation, which requires that the individual must come into being and pass away. But this no more disturbs the will-to-live, the individual being only a particular example or specimen, so to speak, of the phenomenon of this will, than does the death of an individual injure the whole of nature.

For it is not the individual that nature cares for, but only the species; and in all seriousness she urges the preservation of the species, since she provides for this so lavishly through the immense surplus of the seed and the great strength of the fructifying impulse. The individual, on the contrary, has no value for nature, and can have none, for infinite time, infinite space, and the infinite number of possible individuals therein are her kingdom. Therefore nature is always ready to let the individual fall, and the individual is accordingly not only exposed to destruction in a thousand ways from the most insignificant accidents, but is even destined for this and is led toward it by nature herself, from the moment that individual has served the maintenance of the species. In this way, nature quite openly expresses the great truth that only the Ideas, not individuals, have reality proper, in other words are a complete objectivity of the will. Now man is nature herself, and indeed nature at the highest grade of her self-consciousness, but nature is only the objectified will-to-live; the person who has grasped and retained this point of view may certainly and justly console himself for his own death and for that of his friends by looking back on the immortal life of nature, which he himself is. Consequently, Shiva with the lingam is to be understood in this way, and so are those ancient sarcophagi that with their pictures of glowing life exclaim to the lamenting beholder: *Natura non contristatur.*[3]

That generation and death are to be regarded as something belonging to life, and essential to this phenomenon of the will, arises also from the fact that they both exhibit themselves merely as the higher powers of expression of that in which all the rest of life consists. This is everywhere nothing but a constant change of matter under a fixed permanence of form; and this is precisely the transitoriness of the individuals with the imperishableness of the species. Constant nourishment and renewal differ from generation only in degree, and only in degree does constant excretion differ from death. The former shows itself most simply and distinctly in the plant, which is throughout only the constant repetition of the same impulse of its simplest fiber grouping itself into leaf and branch. It is a systematic aggregate of homogeneous plants supporting one another, and their constant reproduction is its simple

---

3. Nature is not grieved.—Tr.

impulse. It ascends to the complete satisfaction of this impulse by means of the gradation of metamorphosis, finally to the blossom and the fruit, that compendium of its existence and effort in which it attains in a shorter way what is its sole aim. It now produces at one stroke a thousandfold what till then it effected in the particular case, namely, the repetition of itself. Its growth up to the fruit is related to that fruit as writing is to printing. In the case of the animal, it is obviously exactly the same. The process of nourishment is a constant generation; the process of generation is a higher power of nourishment. The pleasure that accompanies procreation is a higher power of the agreeableness of the feeling of life. On the other hand, excretion, the constant exhalation and throwing off of matter, is the same as what at a higher power is death, namely, the opposite of procreation. Now, if here we are always content to retain the form without lamenting the discarded matter, we must behave in the same way when in death the same thing happens at a higher potential and to the whole, as occurs every day and hour in a partial way with excretion. Just as we are indifferent to the one, so we should not recoil at the other. Therefore, from this point of view, it seems just as absurd to desire the continuance of our individuality, which is replaced by other individuals, as to desire the permanence of the matter of our body, which is constantly replaced by fresh matter. It appears just as foolish to embalm corpses as it would be carefully to preserve our excreta. As for the individual consciousness bound to the individual body, it is completely interrupted every day by sleep. Deep sleep, while it lasts, is in no way different from death, into which it constantly passes, for example in the case of freezing to death, differing only as to the future, namely, with regard to the awakening. Death is a sleep in which individuality is forgotten; everything else awakens again, or rather has remained awake.[4]

4. The following remark can also help the person for whom it is not too subtle to understand clearly that the individual is only the phenomenon, not the thing-in-itself. On the one hand, every individual is the subject of knowing, in other words, the supplementary condition of the possibility of the whole objective world, and, on the other, a particular phenomenon of the will, of that will that objectifies itself in each thing. But this double character of our inner being does not rest on a self-existent unity, otherwise it would be possible for us to be conscious of ourselves *in ourselves and independently of the objects of knowing and willing*. Now we simply cannot do this, but as soon as we enter into ourselves in order to attempt it, and

Above all, we must clearly recognize that the form of the phenomenon of the will, and hence the form of life or of reality, is really only the *present,* not the future or the past. Future and past are only in the concept, exist only in the connection and continuity of knowledge insofar as this follows the principle of sufficient reason. No man has lived in the past, and none will ever live in the future; the *present* alone is the form of all life, but it is also life's sure possession that can never be torn from it. The present always exists together with its content; both stand firm without wavering, like the rainbow over the waterfall. For life is sure and certain to the will, and the present is sure and certain to life. Of course, if we think back to the thousands of years that have passed, to the millions of men and women who lived in them, we ask, What were they? What has become of them? But, on the other hand, we need recall only the past of our own life, and vividly renew its scenes in our imagination, and then ask again, What was all this? What has become of it? As it is with our life, so is it with the life of those millions. Or should we suppose that the past took on a new existence by its being sealed through death? Our own past, even the most recent, even the previous day, is only an empty dream of the imagination, and the past of all those millions is the same. What was? What is? The will, whose mirror is life, and will-free knowledge beholding the will clearly in that mirror. He who has not already recognized this, or will not recognize it, must add to the above question as to the fate of past generations this question as well: Why precisely is he, the questioner, so lucky as to possess this precious, perishable, and only real present, while those hundreds of generations of men, even the heroes and sages of former times, have sunk into the night of the past, and have thus become nothing, while he, his insignificant ego, actually exists? Or, more briefly, although strangely: Why is this now, his now, precisely now and *was* not long ago? Since he asks such strange questions, he regards his existence and his time as independent of each other, and the former as projected into the latter. He really assumes two nows,

---

wish for once to know ourselves fully by directing our knowledge inwards, we lose ourselves in a bottomless void; we find ourselves like a hollow glass globe, from the emptiness of which a voice speaks. But the cause of this voice is not to be found in the globe, and since we want to comprehend ourselves, we grasp with a shudder nothing but a wavering and unstable phantom.

one belonging to the object and the other to the subject, and marvels at the happy accident of their coincidence. Actually, however, only the point of contact of the object, the form of which is time, with the subject that has no mode of the principle of sufficient reason as its form, constitutes the present (as is shown in the essay *On the Principle of Sufficient Reason*). But all object is the will, insofar as the will has become representation, and the subject is the necessary correlative of all object; only in the present, however, are there real objects. Past and future contain mere concepts and phantasms; hence the present is the essential form of the phenomenon of the will, and is inseparable from that form. The present alone is that which always exists and stands firm and immovable. That which, empirically apprehended, is the most fleeting of all, manifests itself to the metaphysical glance that sees beyond the forms of empirical perception as that which alone endures, as the *nunc stans* of the scholastics. The source and supporter of its content is the will-to-live, or the thing-in-itself—which we are. That which constantly becomes and passes away, in that it either has been already or is still to come, belongs to the phenomenon as such by virtue of its forms which render coming into being and passing away possible. Accordingly, let us think: *Quid fuit? Quod est. Quid erit? Quod fuit;*[5] and take it in the strict sense of the words, understanding not *simile* but *idem*. For life is certain to the will, and the present is certain to life. Therefore everyone can also say: "I am once for all lord and master of the present, and through all eternity it will accompany me as my shadow; accordingly, I do not wonder where it comes from, and how it is that it is precisely now." We can compare time to an endlessly revolving sphere; the half that is always sinking would be the past, and the half that is always rising would be the future; but at the top, the indivisible point that touches the tangent would be the extensionless present. Just as the tangent does not continue rolling with the sphere, so also the present, the point of contact of the object whose form is time, does not roll on with the subject that has no form, since it does not belong to the knowable, but is the condition of all that is knowable. Or time is like an irresistible stream, and the present like a rock on which the stream breaks, but which it does not carry away. The

---

5. What was? That which is. What will be? That which was.—Tr.

will, as thing-in-itself, is as little subordinate to the principle of sufficient reason as is the subject of knowledge that is ultimately in a certain regard the will itself or its manifestation; and just as life, the will's own phenomenon, is certain to the will, so also is the present, the sole form of actual life. Accordingly, we have not to investigate the past before life or the future after death; rather have we to know the *present* as the only form in which the will manifests itself.[6] It will not run away from the will, nor the will from it. Therefore whoever is satisfied with life as it is, whoever affirms it in every way, can confidently regard it as endless, and can banish the fear of death as a delusion. This delusion inspires him with the foolish dread that he can ever be deprived of the present, and deceives him about a time without a present in it. This is a delusion that in regard to time is like that other in regard to space, in virtue of which everyone imagines the precise position occupied by him on the globe as above, and all the rest as below. In just the same way, everyone connects the present with his own individuality, and imagines that all present becomes extinguished therewith; that past and future are then without a present. But just as on the globe everywhere is above, so the form of all life is the *present;* and to fear death because it robs us of the present is no wiser than to fear that we can slip down from the round globe on the top of which we are now fortunately standing. The form of the present is essential to the objectification of the will. As an extensionless point, it cuts time that extends infinitely in both directions, and stands firm and immovable, like an everlasting midday without a cool evening, just as the actual sun burns without intermission, while only apparently does it sink into the bosom of the night. If, therefore, a person fears death as his annihilation, it is just as if he were to think that the sun can lament in the evening and say: "Woe is me! I am going down into eternal night."[7] Conversely,

---

6. *Scholastici docuerunt quod aeternitas non sit temporis sine fine aut principio successio, sed NUNC STANS; i.e. idem nobis NUNC esse, quod erat NUNC Adamo: i.e. inter NUNC et TUNC nullam esse differentiam.* Hobbes, *Leviathan* [Latin ed., 1841], c. 46. (The scholastics taught that eternity is not a succession without beginning and end, but a permanent *Now;* in other words, that we possess the same *Now* that existed for Adam; that is to say, that there is no difference between the *Now* and the *Then.*—Tr.)

7. In Eckermann's *Gespräche mit Goethe* (second edition, vol. 1, p. 154), Goethe says: "Our spirit is a being of a quite indestructible nature; it acts continu-

whoever is oppressed by the burdens of life, whoever loves life and affirms it, but abhors its torments, and in particular can no longer endure the hard lot that has fallen to just him, cannot hope for deliverance from death, and cannot save himself through suicide. Only by a false illusion does the cool shade of Orcus allure him as a haven of rest. The earth rolls on from day into night; the individual dies; but the sun itself burns without intermission, an eternal noon. Life is certain to the will-to-live; the form of life is the endless present; it matters not how individuals, the phenomena of the idea, arise and pass away in time, like fleeting dreams. Therefore suicide already appears to us to be a vain and therefore foolish action; when we have gone farther in our discussion, it will appear to us in an even less-favorable light. ↓Nature is supernatural Fallacy

Dogmas change and our knowledge is deceptive, but nature does not err; her action is sure and certain, and she does not conceal it. Everything is entirely in nature, and she is entirely in everything. She has her center in every animal; the animal has certainly found its way into existence just as it will certainly find its way out of it. Meanwhile, it lives fearlessly and heedlessly in the presence of annihilation, supported by the consciousness that it is nature herself and is as imperishable as she. Man alone carries about with him in abstract concepts the certainty of his own death, yet this can frighten him only very rarely and at particular moments, when some occasion calls it up to the imagination. Against the mighty voice of nature reflection can do little. In man, as in the animal that does not think, there prevails as a lasting state of mind the certainty, springing from innermost consciousness, that he is nature, the world itself. By virtue of this, no one is noticeably disturbed by the thought of certain and never-distant death, but everyone lives on as though he is bound to live forever. Indeed,

ously from eternity to eternity. It is similar to the sun that seems to set only to our earthly eyes, but that really never sets; it shines on incessantly." Goethe took the simile from me, not I from him. He undoubtedly uses it in this conversation of 1824 in consequence of a (possibly unconscious) reminiscence of the above passage, for it appears in the first edition, p. 401, in the same words as here, and also occurs there again on p. 528, and here at the end of section 65. The first edition was sent to him in December 1818, and in March 1819 he sent me in Naples, where I then was, a letter of congratulation through my sister. He had enclosed a piece of paper on which he had noted the numbers of some pages that had specially pleased him. So he had read my book.

this is true to the extent that it might be said that no one has a really lively conviction of the certainty of his death, as otherwise there could not be a very great difference between his frame of mind and that of the condemned criminal. Everyone recognizes that certainty in the abstract and theoretically, but lays it on one side, like other theoretical truths that are not applicable in practice, without taking it into his vivid consciousness. Whoever carefully considers this peculiarity of the human way of thinking, will see that the psychological methods of explaining it from habit and acquiescence in the inevitable are by no means sufficient, but that the reason for it is the deeper one that we state. The same thing can also explain why at all times and among all peoples dogmas of some kind, dealing with the individual's continued existence after death, exist and are highly esteemed, although the proofs in support of them must always be extremely inadequate, whereas those that support the contrary are bound to be powerful and numerous. This is really in no need of any proof, but is recognized by the healthy understanding as a fact; it is confirmed as such by the confidence that nature no more lies than errs, but openly exhibits her action and her essence, and even expresses these naively. It is only we ourselves who obscure these by erroneous views, in order to explain from them what is agreeable to our limited view.

But we have now brought into clear consciousness the fact that, although the individual phenomenon of the will begins and ends in time, the will itself, as thing-in-itself, is not affected thereby, nor is the correlative of every object, namely, the knowing but never-known subject, and that life is always certain to the will-to-live. This is not to be numbered among those doctrines of immortality. For permanence no more belongs to the will, considered as thing-in-itself, or to the pure subject of knowing, to the eternal eye of the world, than does transitoriness, since passing away and transitoriness are determinations valid in time alone, whereas the will and the pure subject of knowing lie outside time. Therefore the egoism of the individual (this particular phenomenon of the will enlightened by the subject of knowing) can as little extract nourishment and consolation for his wish to assert himself through endless time from the view we express, as he could from the knowledge that, after his death, the rest of the external world will continue to exist in time; but this is only the expression of just the same view considered objectively, and so temporally. For it is true that everyone is transitory only as phenomenon; on the other hand, as thing-in-itself he is timeless, and so endless. But also only as phenomenon is the individual different from the other things of the world; as thing-in-itself, he is the will that appears in everything, and death does away with the illusion that separates his consciousness from that of the rest; this is future existence or immortality. His exemption from death, which belongs to him only as thing-in-itself, coincides for the phenomenon with the continued existence of the rest of the external world.[8] Hence it also comes about that the inward and merely felt consciousness of what we have just raised to distinct knowledge does, as we have said, prevent the thought of death from poisoning the life of the rational being. For such consciousness is the basis of that courage to face life that maintains every living thing and enables it to live on cheerfully, as if there were no death, so long as it is face-to-face with life and is directed thereto. However, the individual is not prevented in this way from being seized with the fear of death, and from trying in every way to escape from it, when it presents itself to him in real life in a particular case, or even only in his imagination, and he then has to face it. For as long as his knowledge was directed to life as such, he was bound to recognize imperishableness in it; and so when death is brought before his eyes, he is bound to recognize it as what it is, namely, the temporal end of the particular temporal phenomenon. What we fear in death is by no means the pain, for that obviously lies on this side of death; moreover, we often take refuge in death from pain, just as, conversely, we sometimes endure the most fearful pain merely in order to escape death for a while, although it would be quick and easy. Therefore we distinguish pain and death as two entirely different evils. What we fear in death is in fact the extinction and end of the individual, which it openly proclaims itself to be, and as the individual is the will-to-live itself in a particular objectification, its whole nature

---

8. In the *Veda* this is expressed by saying that, when a man dies, his visual faculty becomes one with the sun, his smell with the earth, his taste with water, his hearing with the air, his speech with fire, and so on (*Oupnek'hat*, vol. 1, pp. 249 seqq.); as also by the fact that, in a special ceremony, the dying person entrusts his senses and all his faculties one by one to his son, in whom they are then supposed to continue to live. (Ibid., vol. 2, pp. 82 seqq.)

struggles against death. Now when feeling leaves us helpless to such an extent, our faculty of reason can nevertheless appear and for the most part overcome influences adverse to it, since it places us at a higher standpoint from which we now view the whole instead of the particular. Therefore, a philosophical knowledge of the nature of the world that had reached the point we are now considering, but went no farther, could, even at this point of view, overcome the terrors of death according as reflection had power over direct feeling in the given individual. A man who had assimilated firmly into his way of thinking the truths so far advanced, but at the same time had not come to know, through his own experience or through a deeper insight, that constant suffering is essential to all life; who found satisfaction in life and took perfect delight in it; who desired, in spite of calm deliberation, that the course of his life as he had hitherto experienced it should be of endless duration or of constant recurrence; and whose courage to face life was so great that, in return for life's pleasures, he would willingly and gladly put up with all the hardships and miseries to which it is subject; such a man would stand "with firm, strong bones on the well-grounded, enduring earth,"[9] and would have nothing to fear. Armed with the knowledge we confer on him, he would look with indifference at death hastening toward him on the wings of time. He would consider it as a false illusion, an impotent specter, frightening to the weak but having no power over him who knows that he himself is that will of which the whole world is the objectification or copy, to which therefore life and also the present always remain certain and sure. The present is the only real form of the phenomenon of the will. Therefore no endless past or future in which he will not exist can frighten him, for he regards these an an empty mirage and the web of Maya. Thus he would no more have to fear death than the sun would the night. In the *Bhagavad Gita* Krishna puts his young pupil Arjuna in this position, when, seized with grief at the sight of the armies ready for battle (somewhat after the manner of Xerxes), Arjuna loses heart and wishes to give up the fight, to avert the destruction of so many thousands. Krishna brings him to this point of view, and the death of those thousands can no longer hold him back; he gives the

9. From Goethe's *Grenzen der Menschheit* —TR.

sign for battle. This point of view is also expressed by Goethe's *Prometheus,* especially when he says:

> "Here sit I, form men
> In my own image,
> A race that is like me,
> To suffer, to weep,
> To enjoy and to rejoice,
> And to heed you not,
> As I!"

The philosophy of Bruno and that of Spinoza might also bring to this standpoint the person whose conviction was not shaken or weakened by their errors and imperfections. Bruno's philosophy has no real ethics, and the ethics in Spinoza's philosophy does not in the least proceed from the inner nature of his teaching, but is attached to it merely by means of weak and palpable sophisms, though in itself it is praiseworthy and fine. Finally, many men would occupy the standpoint here set forth, if their knowledge kept pace with their willing, in other words if they were in a position, free from every erroneous idea, to become clearly and distinctly themselves. This is for knowledge the viewpoint of the complete *affirmation of the will-to-live.*

The will affirms itself; this means that while in its objectivity, that is to say, in the world and in life, its own inner nature is completely and distinctly given to it as representation, this knowledge does not in any way impede its willing. It means that just this life thus known is now willed as such by the will with knowledge, consciously and deliberately, just as hitherto the will willed it without knowledge and as a blind impulse. The opposite of this, the *denial of the will-to-live,* shows itself when willing ends with that knowledge, since the particular phenomena known then no longer act as *motives* of willing, but the whole knowledge of the inner nature of the world that mirrors the will, knowledge that has grown up through apprehension of the Ideas, becomes the *quieter* of the will, and thus the will freely abolishes itself. It is hoped that these conceptions, quite unfamiliar and difficult to understand in this general expression, will become clear through the discussion, which will shortly follow, of the phenomena, namely, the modes of conduct, in which is expressed affirmation in its different degrees on the one hand, and denial on the other. For both start from *knowledge,* though not from an abstract knowledge expressing itself in words, but from living knowledge expressing itself in deed and conduct alone. Such living knowledge remains independent of the dogmas that here, as abstract knowledge, concern the faculty of reason. To exhibit both and to bring them to the distinct knowledge of the faculty of reason can be my only aim, and not to prescribe or recommend the one or the other, which would be as foolish as it would be pointless. The will in itself is absolutely free and entirely self-determining, and for it there is no law. First of all, however, before we embark on the aforesaid discussion, we must explain and define more precisely this *freedom* and its relation to necessity. Then we must insert a few general remarks, relating to the will and its objects, as regards life, the affirmation and denial whereof are our problem. Through all this, we shall facilitate for ourselves the intended knowledge of the ethical significance of modes of conduct according to their innermost nature.

Since, as I have said, this whole work is only the unfolding of a single thought, it follows therefrom that all its parts have the most intimate connection with one another. Not only does each part stand in a necessary relation to what immediately precedes it, and thus presuppose it as within the reader's memory, as is the case with all philosophies consisting merely of a series of inferences, but every part of the whole work is related to every other part, and presupposes it. For this reason, it is required that the reader should remember not only what has just been said, but also every previous remark, so that he is able to connect it with what he is reading at any moment, however much else there may have been between the two. Plato has also made this exacting demand on his reader through the tortuous and complicated digressions of his dialogues that take up the main idea again only after long episodes; but precisely in this way is it made more clear. With us this demand is necessary, for the analysis of our one and only thought into many aspects is indeed the only means of communicating it, though it is not a form essential to the thought itself, but only an artificial form. The separation of the four principal points of view into four books, and the most careful connection of what is related and homogeneous, help to render the discussion and its comprehension easier. But the subject matter does not by any means admit of an advance in a straight line, like the progress of history, but renders a more complicated discussion necessary. This also makes necessary a repeated study of the book; only thus does the connection of every part with every other become evident, and then all together elucidate one another and become clear.

In all the observations on human conduct hitherto made, we have been preparing for the final discussion, and have greatly facilitated the task of raising to abstract and philosophical clearness, and of demonstrating as a branch of our main idea, the real ethical significance of conduct that in life is described by the words *good* and *bad,* and is thus made perfectly intelligible.

First of all, however, I wish to trace back to their proper meaning these concepts of *good* and *bad,* which are treated by the philosophical writers of our times in a very odd way as simple concepts, that is, as concepts incapable of any analysis. I will do this so that the reader shall not remain involved in some hazy and obscure notion that they contain more than is actually the case, and that they state in and by themselves all that is here necessary. I am able to do this because in ethics I myself am as little disposed to take refuge behind the word *good* as I was earlier to hide behind the words *beautiful* and *true,* in order that, by an added "-ness," supposed nowadays to have a special solemnity, and hence to be of help in various cases, and by a solemn demeanor, I might persuade people that by uttering three such words I had done more than express three concepts that are very wide and abstract, which therefore contain nothing at all, and are of very different origin and significance. Who is there indeed, who has made himself acquainted with the writings of our times, and has not finally become sick of those three words, admirable as are the things to which they originally refer, after he has been made to see a thousand times how those least capable of thinking believe they need only utter these three words with open mouth and the air of infatuated sheep, in order to have spoken great wisdom?

The explanation of the concept *true* is already given in the essay *On the Principle of Sufficient Reason,* chap. 5, sections 29 and following. The content of the concept *beautiful* received for the first time its proper explanation in the whole of our third book. We will now trace the meaning of the concept *good;* this can be done with very little trouble. This concept is essentially relative, and denotes the *fitness or suitableness of an object to any definite effort of the will.* Therefore everything agreeable to the will in any one of its manifestations, and fulfilling the will's purpose, is thought of through the concept *good,* however different in other respects such things may be. We therefore speak of good eating, good roads, good weather, good weapons, good auguries, and so on; in short, we call everything good that is just as we want it to be. Hence a thing can be good to one person, and the very opposite to another. The concept of good is divided into two subspecies, that of the directly present satisfaction of the will in each case, and that of its merely indirect satisfaction concerning the future, in other words, the agreeable and the useful. The concept of the opposite, so long as we are speaking of beings without knowledge, is expressed by the word *bad,* more rarely and abstractly by the word *evil,* which therefore denotes everything that is not agreeable to the striving of the will in each case. Like all other beings that can come into relation with the will, persons who favor, promote, and befriend aims that happen to be desired are called *good,* with the same meaning, and always with the retention of the relative that is seen, for example, in the expression: "This is good for me, but not for you." Those, however, whose character induces them generally not to hinder another's efforts of will as such, but rather to promote them, and who are therefore consistently helpful, benevolent, friendly, and charitable, are called *good,* on account of this relation of their mode of conduct to the will of others in general. In the case of beings with knowledge (animals and human beings), the opposite concept is denoted in German, and has been for about a hundred years in French also, by a word different from that used in the case of beings without knowledge, namely *böse, méchant* (spiteful, malicious, unkind); whereas in almost all other languages this distinction does not occur. *Malus, cattivo, bad,* are used both of human beings and of inanimate things that are opposed to the aims of a definite individual will. Thus, having started entirely from the passive side of the good, the discussion could only later pass to the active side, and investigate the mode of conduct of the man called *good,* in reference no longer to others, but to himself. It could then specially set itself the task of explaining the purely objective esteem produced in others by such conduct, as well as the characteristic contentment with himself obviously engendered in the person, for he purchases this even with sacrifices of another kind. On the other hand, it could also explain the inner pain that accompanies the evil disposition, however many advantages it may bring to the man who cherishes it. Now from this sprang the ethical systems, both the philosophical and those supported by religious teachings. Both always attempt to associate happiness in some way with virtue, the former either by the principle of contradiction, or even by that of sufficient reason, and thus to make happiness either identical with, or the consequence of, virtue, always sophistically; but the latter by asserting the existence of worlds other than the one that can be known to experience.[11] On the other hand, from our discussion, the inner nature of virtue will show itself as a striving in quite the opposite direction to that of happiness, which is that of well-being and life.

It follows from the above remarks that the *good* is according to its concept *something belonging to the relative,* hence every good is essentially relative; for it has its essential nature only in its relation to a desiring will. Accordingly, *absolute good* is a contradiction; highest good, *summum bonum,* signifies the same thing, namely, in reality a final satisfaction of the will, after which no fresh willing would occur; a last motive, the attainment of which

---

11. Incidentally, it should be observed that what gives every positive religious doctrine its great strength, the essential point by which it takes firm possession of souls, is wholly its ethical side; though not directly as such, but as it appears firmly united and interwoven with the rest of the mythical dogma that is characteristic of every religious teaching, and as explicable only through this. So much is this the case that, although the ethical significance of actions cannot possibly be explained in accordance with the principle of sufficient reason, but every myth follows this principle, believers nevertheless consider the ethical significance of conduct and its myth to be quite inseparable, indeed as positively one, and regard every attack on the myth as an attack on right and virtue. This reaches such lengths that, in monotheistic nations, atheism or godlessness has become the synonym for absence of all morality. To priests such confusions of concepts are welcome, and only in consequence of them could that fearful monster, fanaticism, arise and govern not merely single individuals who are exceedingly perverse and wicked, but whole nations, and finally embody itself in the West as the Inquisition, a thing that, to the honor of mankind, has happened only once in its history. According to the latest and most authentic reports, in Madrid alone (while in the rest of Spain there were also many such ecclesiastical dens of murderers) the Inquisition in three hundred years put three hundred thousand human beings to a painful death at the stake, on account of matters of faith. All fanatics and zealots should be at once reminded of this whenever they want to make themselves heard.

would give the will an imperishable satisfaction. According to the discussion so far carried on in this fourth book, such a thing cannot be conceived. The will can just as little through some satisfaction cease to will always afresh, as time can end or begin; for the will there is no permanent fulfillment that completely and forever satisfies its craving. It is the vessel of the Danaides; there is no highest good, no absolute good, for it, but always a temporary good only. However, if we wish to give an honorary, or so to speak an emeritus, position to an old expression that from custom we do not like entirely to discard, we may, metaphorically and figuratively, call the complete self-effacement and denial of the will, true willlessness, which alone stills and silences forever the craving of the will; which alone gives that contentment that cannot again be disturbed; which alone is world redeeming; and which we shall now consider at the conclusion of our whole discussion; the absolute good, the *summum bonum;* and we may regard it as the only radical cure for the disease against which all other good things, such as all fulfilled wishes and all attained happiness, are only palliatives, anodynes. In this sense, the Greek *telos* and also *finis bonorum* meet the case even better. So much for the words *good* and *bad;* now to the matter itself.

If a person is always inclined to do *wrong* the moment the inducement is there and no external power restrains him, we call him *bad.* In accordance with our explanation of wrong, this means that such a man not only affirms the will-to-live as it appears in his own body, but in this affirmation goes so far as to deny the will that appears in other individuals. This is shown by the fact that he demands their powers for the service of his own will, and tries to destroy their existence when they stand in the way of the efforts of his will. The ultimate source of this is a high degree of egoism, the nature of which has already been explained. Two different things are at once clear here; *firstly,* that in such a person an excessively vehement will-to-live, going far beyond the affirmation of his own body, expresses itself; and *secondly,* that this knowledge, devoted entirely to the principle of sufficient reason and involved in the *principium individuationis,* definitely confines itself to the complete difference, established by this latter principle, between his own person and all others. He therefore seeks only his own well-being, and is completely indifferent to that of all others.

On the contrary, their existence is wholly foreign to him, separated from his by a wide gulf; indeed, he really regards them only as masks without any reality. And these two qualities are the fundamental elements of the bad character.

This great intensity of willing is in and by itself and directly a constant source of suffering, firstly because all willing as such springs from want, and hence from suffering. (Therefore, as will be remembered from the third book, the momentary silencing of all willing, which comes about whenever as pure will-less subject of knowing, the correlative of the idea, we are devoted to aesthetic contemplation, is a principal element of pleasure in the beautiful.) Secondly because, through the causal connection of things, most desires must remain unfulfilled, and the will is much more often crossed than satisfied. Consequently, much intense willing always entails much intense suffering. For all suffering is simply nothing but unfulfilled and thwarted willing, and even the pain of the body, when this is injured or destroyed, is as such possible only by the fact that the body is nothing but the will itself become object. Now, for the reason that much intense suffering is inseparable from much intense willing, the facial expression of very bad people already bears the stamp of inward suffering. Even when they have obtained every external happiness, they always look unhappy, whenever they are not transported by momentary exultation, or are not pretending. From this inward torment, absolutely and directly essential to them, there finally results even that delight at the suffering of another that has not sprung from egoism, but is disinterested; this is *wickedness* proper, and rises to the pitch of *cruelty*. For this the suffering of another is no longer a means for attaining the ends of its own will, but an end in itself. The following is a more detailed explanation of this phenomenon. Since man is phenomenon of the will illuminated by the clearest knowledge, he is always measuring and comparing the actual and felt satisfaction of his will with the merely possible satisfaction put before him by knowledge. From this springs envy; every privation is infinitely aggravated by the pleasure of others, and relieved by the knowledge that others also endure the same privation. The evils that are common to all and inseparable from human life do not trouble us much, just as little as do those that belong to the climate and to the whole country. The calling to mind of sufferings greater than our own stills their pain; the sight of another's sufferings alleviates our own. Now a person filled with an extremely intense pressure of will wants with burning eagerness to accumulate everything, in order to slake the thirst of egoism. As is inevitable, he is bound to see that all satisfaction is only apparent, and that the attained object never fulfills the promise held out by the desired object, namely, the final appeasement of the excessive pressure of will. He sees that, with fulfillment, the wish changes only its form, and now torments under another form; indeed, when at last all wishes are exhausted, the pressure of will itself remains, even without any recognized motive, and makes itself known with terrible pain as a feeling of the most frightful desolation and emptiness. If from all this, which with ordinary degrees of willing is felt only in a smaller measure, and produces only the ordinary degree of dejection, there necessarily arise an excessive inner torment, an eternal unrest, an incurable pain in the case of a person who is the phenomenon of the will reaching to extreme wickedness, he then seeks indirectly the alleviation of which he is incapable directly, in other words, he tries to mitigate his own suffering by the sight of another's, and at the same time recognizes this as an expression of his power. The suffering of another becomes for him an end in itself; it is a spectacle over which he gloats; and so arises the phenomenon of cruelty proper, of bloodthirstiness, so often revealed by history in the Neros and Domitians, in the African Deys, in Robespierre and others.

The thirst for revenge is closely related to wickedness. It repays evil with evil, not from regard for the future, which is the character of punishment, but merely on account of what has happened and is past as such, and thus disinterestedly, not as means but as end, in order to gloat over the offender's affliction caused by the avenger himself. What distinguishes revenge from pure wickedness, and to some extent excuses it, is an appearance of right, insofar as the same act that is now revenge, if ordered by law, in other words, according to a previously determined and known rule and in a society that has sanctioned such a rule, would be punishment, and hence justice or right.

Besides the suffering described, and inseparable from wickedness, as having sprung from a single root, namely, a very intense will, there is associated with wickedness another particular pain quite different from this. This pain is felt in the case of every bad action, whether it be mere injustice arising out of egoism, or pure wickedness; and according to the length of its duration it is called the *sting of conscience* or the *pangs of conscience*. Now he who remembers, and has present in his mind, the foregoing contents of this fourth book, especially the truth explained at its beginning, namely, that life itself is always sure and certain to the will-to-live as its mere copy or mirror, and also the discussion on eternal justice, will find that, in accordance with those remarks, the sting of conscience can have no other meaning than the following; in other words, its content, expressed in the abstract, is as follows, in which two parts are distinguished, but again these entirely coincide, and must be thought of as wholly united.

However densely the veil of Maya envelops the mind of the bad person, in other words, however firmly involved he is in the *principium individuationis,* according to which he regards his person as absolutely different from every other and separated from it by a wide gulf, a knowledge to which he adheres with all his might, since it alone suits and supports his egoism, so that knowledge is almost always corrupted by the will, there is nevertheless roused in the innermost depths of his consciousness the secret presentiment that such an order of things is only phenomenon, but that, in themselves, things are quite different. He has a presentiment that, however much time and space separate him from other individuals and the innumerable miseries they suffer, indeed suffer through him; however much time and space present these as quite foreign to him, yet in themselves and apart from the representation and its forms, it is the one will-to-live appearing in them all that, failing to recognize itself here, turns its weapons against itself, and, by seeking increased well-being in one of its phenomena, imposes the greatest suffering on another. He dimly sees that he, the bad person, is precisely this whole will; that in consequence he is not only the tormentor but also the tormented, from whose suffering he is separated and kept free only by a delusive dream, whose form is space and time. But this dream vanishes, and he sees that in reality he must pay for the pleasure with the pain, and that all suffering that he knows only as possible actually concerns him as the will-to-live, since possibility and actuality, near and remote in time and space, are different only for the knowledge of the individual, only by means of the *principium individuationis,* and not in themselves. It is this truth that mythically, in other words, adapted to the principle of sufficient reason, is expressed by the transmigration of souls, and is thus translated into the form of the phenomenon. Nevertheless it has its purest expression, free from all admixture, precisely in that obscurely felt but inconsolable misery called the pangs of conscience. But this also springs from a *second* immediate knowledge closely associated with the first, namely, knowledge of the strength with which the will-to-live affirms itself in the wicked individual, extending as it does far beyond his individual phenomenon to the complete denial of the same will as it appears in individuals foreign to him. Consequently, the wicked man's inward alarm at his own deed, which he tries to conceal from himself, contains that presentiment of the nothingness and mere delusiveness of the *principium individuationis,* and of the distinction established by this principle between him and others. At the same time it contains the knowledge of the vehemence of his own will, of the strength with which he has grasped life and attached himself firmly to it, this very life whose terrible side he sees before him in the misery of those he oppresses, and with which he is nevertheless so firmly entwined that, precisely in this way, the most terrible things come from himself as a means to the fuller affirmation of his own will. He recognizes himself as the concentrated phenomenon of the will-to-live; he feels to what degree he is given up to life, and therewith also to the innumerable sufferings essential to it, for it has infinite time and infinite space to abolish the distinction between possibility and actuality, and to change all the sufferings as yet merely *known* by him into those *felt and experienced* by him. The millions of years of constant rebirth certainly continue merely in conception, just as the whole of the past and future exists only in conception. Occupied time, the form of the phenomenon of the will, is only the present, and time for the individual is always new; he always finds himself as newly sprung into existence. For life is inseparable from the will-to-live, and its form is only the now. Death (the repetition of the comparison must be excused) is like the setting of the sun, which is only apparently engulfed by the night, but actually, itself the source of all light, burns without intermission, brings new days to new worlds, and is always rising and always setting. Beginning and end concern only the individual by means of time, of the form of this phenomenon for the representation. Outside time lie only the will, Kant's thing-in-itself, and its adequate objectivity, namely, Plato's idea. Suicide, therefore, affords no escape; what everyone *wills* in his innermost being, that must he *be;* and what everyone *is,* is just what he *wills.* Therefore, besides the merely felt knowledge of the delusiveness and nothingness of the forms of the representation that separate individuals, it is the self-knowledge of one's own will and of its degree that gives conscience its sting. The course of life brings out the picture of the empirical character, whose original is the intelligible character, and the wicked person is horrified at this picture. It is immaterial whether the picture is produced in large characters, so that the world shares his horror, or in characters so small that he alone sees it; for it directly concerns him alone. The past would be a matter of indifference as mere phenomenon, and could not disturb or alarm the conscience, did not the character feel itself free from all time and incapable of alteration by it, so long as it does not deny itself. For this reason, things that happened long ago still continue to weigh heavily on the conscience. The prayer, "Lead me not into temptation" means "Let me not see who I am." In the strength with which the wicked person affirms life, and which is exhibited to him in the suffering he perpetrates on others, he estimates how far he is from the surrender and denial of that very will, from the only possible deliverance from the world and its miseries. He sees to what extent he belongs to the world, and how firmly he is bound to it. The *known* suffering of others has not been able to move him; he is given up to life and to *felt or experienced* suffering. It remains doubtful whether this will ever break and overcome the vehemence of his will.

This explanation of the significance and inner nature of the *bad,* which as mere feeling, i.e., *not* as distinct, abstract knowledge, is the content of the *pangs of conscience,* will gain even more clarity and completeness from a consideration of the *good* carried out in precisely the same way. This will consider the *good* as a quality of the human will, and finally of complete resignation and holiness that result from this quality, when it has reached the highest degree. For opposites always elucidate each other, and the day simultaneously reveals both itself and the night, as Spinoza has admirably said.

* * *

Morality without argumentation and reasoning, that is, mere moralizing, cannot have any effect, because it does not motivate. But a morality that *does* motivate can do so only by acting on self-love. Now what springs from this has no moral worth. From this it follows that no genuine virtue can be brought about through morality and abstract knowledge in general, but that such virtue must spring from the intuitive knowledge that recognizes in another's individuality the same inner nature as in one's own.

For virtue does indeed result from knowledge, but not from abstract knowledge communicable through words. If this were so, virtue could be taught, and by expressing here in the abstract its real nature and the knowledge at its foundation, we should have ethically improved everyone who comprehended this. But this is by no means the case. On the contrary, we are as little able to produce a virtuous person by ethical discourses or sermons as all the systems of aesthetics from Aristotle's downwards have ever been able to produce a poet. For the concept is unfruitful for the real inner nature of virtue, just as it is for art; and only in a wholly subordinate position can it serve as an instrument in elaborating and preserving what has been ascertained and inferred in other ways. *Velle non discitur.*[12] In fact, abstract dogmas are without influence on virtue, i.e., on goodness of disposition; false dogmas do not disturb it, and true ones hardly support it. Actually it would be a bad business if the principal thing in a man's life, his ethical worth that counts for eternity, depended on something whose attainment was so very much subject to chance as are dogmas, religious teachings, and philosophical arguments. For morality dogmas have merely the value that the man who is virtuous from another kind of knowledge shortly to be discussed has in them a scheme or formula. According to this, he renders to his own faculty of reason an account, for the most part only fictitious, of his non-egoistical actions, the nature of which it, in other words, he himself, does not *comprehend*. With such an account he has been accustomed to rest content.

Dogmas can of course have a powerful influence on *conduct*, on outward actions, and so can custom and example (the latter, be-

---

12. Willing cannot be taught.—Tr.

cause the ordinary man does not trust his judgment, of whose weakness he is conscious, but follows only his own or someone else's experience); but the disposition is not altered in this way.[13] All abstract knowledge gives only motives, but, as was shown above, motives can alter only the direction of the will, never the will itself. But all communicable knowledge can affect the will as motive only; therefore, however the will is guided by dogmas, what a person really and generally wills still always remains the same. He has obtained different ideas merely of the ways in which it is to be attained, and imaginary motives guide him like real ones. Thus, for instance, it is immaterial, as regards his ethical worth, whether he makes donations to the destitute, firmly persuaded that he will receive everything back tenfold in a future life, or spends the same sum on improving an estate that will bear interest, late certainly, but all the more secure and substantial. And the man who, for the sake of orthodoxy, commits the heretic to the flames, is just as much a murderer as the bandit who earns a reward by killing; indeed, as regards inner circumstances, so also is he who massacres the Turks in the Promised Land, if, like the burner of heretics, he really does it because he imagines he will thus earn a place in heaven. For these are anxious only about themselves, about their egoism, just like the bandit, from whom they differ only in the absurdity of their means. As we have already said, the will can be reached from outside only through motives; but these alter merely the way in which it manifests itself, never the will itself. *Velle non discitur.*

In the case of good deeds, however, the doer of which appeals to dogmas, we must always distinguish whether these dogmas are really the motive for them, or whether, as I said above, they are nothing more than the delusive account by which he tries to satisfy his own faculty of reason about a good deed that flows from quite a different source. He performs such a deed because he is *good,* but he does not understand how to explain it properly, since he is not a philosopher, and yet he would like to think something with regard to it. But the distinction is very hard to find, since it lies in the very depths of our inner nature. Therefore we can hardly ever

13. The Church would say they are mere *opera operata,* that are of no avail unless grace gives the faith leading to regeneration; but of this later on.

pronounce a correct moral judgment on the actions of others, and rarely on our own. The deeds and ways of acting of the individual and of a nation can be very much modified by dogmas, example, and custom. In themselves, however, all deeds *(opera operata)* are merely empty figures, and only the disposition that leads to them gives them moral significance. But this disposition can be actually quite the same, in spite of a very different external phenomenon. With an equal degree of wickedness one person can die on the wheel, and another peacefully in the bosom of his family. It can be the same degree of wickedness that expresses itself in one nation in the crude characteristics of murder and cannibalism, and in another finely and delicately in miniature, in court intrigues, oppressions, and subtle machinations of every kind; the inner nature remains the same. It is conceivable that a perfect State, or even perhaps a complete dogma of rewards and punishments after death firmly believed in, might prevent every crime. Politically much would be gained in this way; morally, absolutely nothing; on the contrary, only the mirroring of the will through life would be checked.

Genuine goodness of disposition, disinterested virtue, and pure nobleness of mind, therefore, do not come from abstract knowledge; yet they do come from knowledge. But it is a direct and intuitive knowledge that cannot be reasoned away or arrived at by reasoning; a knowledge that, just because it is not abstract, cannot be communicated, but must dawn on each of us. It therefore finds its real and adequate expression not in words, but simply and solely in deeds, in conduct, in the course of a man's life. We who are here looking for the theory of virtue, and who thus have to express in abstract terms the inner nature of the knowledge lying at its foundation, shall nevertheless be unable to furnish that knowledge itself in this expression, but only the concept of that knowledge. We thus always start from conduct, in which alone it becomes visible, and refer to such conduct as its only adequate expression. We only interpret and explain this expression, in other words, express in the abstract what really takes place in it.

Now before we speak of the *good* proper, in contrast to the *bad* that has been described, we must touch on the mere negation of the bad as an intermediate stage; this is *justice*. We have adequately explained above what right and wrong are; therefore we can briefly say here that the man who voluntarily recognizes and accepts that merely moral boundary between wrong and right, even where no State or other authority guarantees it, and who consequently, according to our explanation, never in the affirmation of his own will goes to the length of denying the will that manifests itself in another individual, is *just*. Therefore, in order to increase his own well-being, he will not inflict suffering on others; that is to say, he will not commit any crime; he will respect the rights and property of everyone. We now see that for such a just man the *principium individuationis* is no longer an absolute partition as it is for the bad; that he does not, like the bad man, affirm merely his own phenomenon of will and deny all others; that others are not for him mere masks, whose inner nature is quite different from his. On the contrary, he shows by his way of acting that he *again recognizes* his own inner being, namely, the will-to-live as thing-in-itself, in the phenomenon of another given to him merely as representation. Thus he finds himself again in that phenomenon up to a certain degree, namely, that of doing no wrong, i.e., of not injuring. Now in precisely this degree he sees through the *principium individuationis*, the veil of Maya. To this extent he treats the inner being outside himself like his own; he does not injure it.

If we examine the innermost nature of this justice, there is to be found in it the intention not to go so far in the affirmation of one's own will as to deny the phenomena of will in others by compelling them to serve one's own will. We shall therefore want to provide for others just as much as we benefit from them. The highest degree of this justice of disposition, which, however, is always associated with goodness proper, the character of this last being no longer merely negative, extends so far that a person questions his right to inherited property, desires to support his body only by his own powers, mental and physical, feels every service rendered by others, every luxury, as a reproach, and finally resorts to voluntary poverty. Thus we see how Pascal would not allow the performance of any more services when he turned to asceticism, although he had servants enough. In spite of his constant bad health, he made his own bed, fetched his own food from the kitchen, and so on. (*Vie de Pascal,* by his sister, p. 19.) Quite in keeping with this, it is reported that many Hindus, even rajas, with great wealth, use it merely to support and maintain their families, their courts, and their establishment of servants, and follow with strict scrupulousness the maxim of eating nothing but what they have sown and reaped with their own hands. Yet at the bottom of this there lies a certain misunderstanding, for just because the individual is rich and powerful, he is able to render such important services to the whole of human society that they counterbalance inherited wealth, for the security of which he is indebted to society. In reality, that excessive justice of such Hindus is more than justice, indeed actual renunciation, denial of the will-to-live, asceticism, about which we shall speak last of all. On the other hand, pure idleness and living through the exertions of others with inherited property, without achieving anything, can indeed be regarded as morally wrong, even though it must remain right according to positive laws.

We have found that voluntary justice has its innermost origin in a certain degree of seeing through the *principium individuationis,* while the unjust man remains entirely involved in this principle. This seeing through can take place not only in the degree required for justice, but also in the higher degree that urges a man to positive benevolence and well-doing, to philanthropy. Moreover, this can happen however strong and energetic the will that appears in such an individual may be in itself. Knowledge can always counterbalance it, can teach a man to resist the temptation to do wrong, and can even produce every degree of goodness, indeed of resignation. Therefore the good man is in no way to be regarded as an originally weaker phenomenon of will than the bad, but it is knowledge that masters in him the blind craving of will. Certainly there are individuals who merely seem to be good-natured on account of the weakness of the will that appears in them; but what they are soon shows itself in the fact that they are not capable of any considerable self-conquest, in order to perform a just or good deed.

Now if, as a rare exception, we come across a man who possesses a considerable income, but uses only a little of it for himself, and gives all the rest to persons in distress, while he himself forgoes many pleasures and comforts, and we try to make clear to ourselves the action of this man, we shall find, quite apart from the dogmas by which he himself will make his action intelligible to his faculty of reason, the simplest general expression and the essential character of his way of acting to be that he *makes less distinction than is usually made between himself and others.* This very distinction is in the eyes of many so great, that the suffering of another is a direct pleasure for the wicked, and a welcome means to their own well-being for the unjust. The merely just person is content not to cause it; and generally most people know and are acquainted with innumerable sufferings of others in their vicinity, but do not decide to alleviate them, because to do so they would have to undergo some privation. Thus a strong distinction seems to prevail in each of all these between his own ego and another's. On the other hand, to the noble person, whom we have in mind, this distinction is not so significant. The *principium individuationis,* the form of the phenomenon, no longer holds him so firmly in its grasp, but the suffering he sees in others touches him almost as closely as does his own. He therefore tries to strike a balance between the two, denies himself pleasures, undergoes privations, in order to alleviate another's suffering. He perceives that the distinction between himself and others, which to the wicked man is so great a gulf, belongs only to a fleeting, deceptive phenomenon. He recognizes immediately, and without reasons or arguments, that the in-itself of his own phenomenon is also that of others, namely, that will-to-live that constitutes the inner nature of everything, and lives in all; in fact, he recognizes that this extends even to the animals and to the whole of nature; he will therefore not cause suffering even to an animal.[14]

He is now just as little able to let others starve, while he himself has enough and to spare, as anyone would one day be on short commons, in order on the following day to have more than he can enjoy. For the veil of Maya has become transparent for the person who performs works of love, and the deception of the *principium*

14. Man's right over the life and power of animals rests on the fact that, since with the enhanced clearness of consciousness suffering increases in like measure, the pain that the animal suffers through death or work is still not so great as that which man would suffer through merely being deprived of the animal's flesh or strength. Therefore in the affirmation of his own existence, man can go so far as to deny the existence of the animal. In this way, the will-to-live as a whole endures less suffering than if the opposite course were adopted. At the same time, this determines the extent to which man may, without wrong, make use of the powers of animals. This limit, however, is often exceeded, especially in the case of beasts of burden, and of hounds used in hunting. The activities of societies for the prevention of cruelty to animals are therefore directed especially against these. In my opinion, that right does not extend to vivisection, particularly of the higher animals. On the other hand, the insect does not suffer through its death as much as man suffers through its sting. The Hindus do not see this.

individuationis has left him. Himself, his will, he recognizes in every creature, and hence in the sufferer also. He is free from the perversity with which the will-to-live, failing to recognize itself, here in one individual enjoys fleeting and delusive pleasures, and there in another individual suffers and starves in return for these. Thus this will inflicts misery and endures misery, not knowing that, like Thyestes, it is eagerly devouring its own flesh. Then it here laments its unmerited suffering, and there commits an outrage without the least fear of Nemesis, always merely because it fails to recognize itself in the phenomenon of another, and thus does not perceive eternal justice, involved as it is in the *principium individuationis*, and so generally in that kind of knowledge that is governed by the principle of sufficient reason. To be cured of this delusion and deception of Maya and to do works of love are one and the same thing; but the latter is the inevitable and infallible symptom of that knowledge.

The opposite of the sting of conscience, whose origin and significance were explained above, is the *good conscience*, the satisfaction we feel after every disinterested deed. It springs from the fact that such a deed, as arising from the direct recognition of our own inner being-in-itself in the phenomenon of another, again affords us the verification of this knowledge, of the knowledge that our true self exists not only in our own person, in this particular phenomenon, but in everything that lives. In this way, the heart feels itself enlarged, just as by egoism it feels contracted. For just as egoism concentrates our interest on the particular phenomenon of our own individuality, and then knowledge always presents us with the innumerable perils that continually threaten this phenomenon, whereby anxiety and care become the keynote of our disposition, so the knowledge that every living thing is just as much our own inner being-in-itself as is our own person, extends our interest to all that lives; and in this way the heart is enlarged. Thus through the reduced interest in our own self, the anxious care for that self is attacked and restricted at its root; hence the calm and confident serenity afforded by a virtuous disposition and a good conscience, and the more distinct appearance of this with every good deed, since this proves to ourselves the depth of that disposition. The egoist feels himself surrounded by strange and hostile phenomena, and all his hope rests on his own well-being. The good person lives in a world of friendly phenomena; the well-being of any of these is his own well-being. Therefore, although the knowledge of the lot of man generally does not make his disposition a cheerful one, the permanent knowledge of his own inner nature in everything that lives nevertheless gives him a certain uniformity and even serenity of disposition. For the interest extended over innumerable phenomena cannot cause such anxiety as that which is concentrated on one phenomenon. The accidents that concern the totality of individuals equalize themselves, while those that befall the individual entail good or bad fortune.

Therefore, although others have laid down moral principles that they gave out as precepts for virtue and laws necessarily to be observed, I cannot do this, as I have said already, because I have no "ought" or law to hold before the eternally free will. On the other hand, in reference to my discussion, what corresponds and is analogous to that undertaking is that purely theoretical truth, and the whole of my argument can be regarded as a mere elaboration thereof, namely, that the will is the in-itself of every phenomenon, but itself as such is free from the forms of that phenomenon, and so from plurality. In reference to conduct, I do not know how this truth can be more worthily expressed than by the formula of the *Veda* already quoted: *Tat tvam asi* (This art thou!). Whoever is able to declare this to himself with clear knowledge and firm inward conviction about every creature with whom he comes in contact, is certain of all virtue and bliss, and is on the direct path to salvation.

Now before I go farther, and show, as the last item in my discussion, how love, whose origin and nature we know to be seeing through the *principium individuationis,* leads to salvation, that is, to the entire surrender of the will-to-live, i.e., of all willing, and also how another path, less smooth yet more frequented, brings man to the same goal, a paradoxical sentence must first be here stated and explained. This is not because it is paradoxical, but because it is true, and is necessary for the completeness of the thought I have to express. It is this: "All love, *caritas,* is compassion or sympathy."

We have seen how, from seeing through the *principium individuationis,* in the lesser degree justice arises, and in the higher degree real goodness of disposition, a goodness that shows itself as pure, i.e., disinterested, affection toward others. Now where this becomes complete, the individuality and fate of others are treated entirely like one's own. It can never go farther, for no reason exists for preferring another's individuality to one's own. Yet the great number of the other individuals whose whole well-being or life is in danger can outweigh the regard for one's own particular well-being. In such a case, the character that has reached the highest goodness and perfect magnanimity will sacrifice its well-being and its life completely for the will-being of many others. So died Codrus, Leonidas, Regulus, Decius Mus, and Arnold von Winkelried; so does everyone die who voluntarily and consciously goes to certain death for his friends, or for his native land. And everyone also stands at this level who willingly takes suffering and death upon himself for the maintenance of what conduces and rightfully belongs to the welfare of all mankind, in other words, for universal, important truths, and for the eradication of great errors. So died Socrates and Giordano Bruno; and so did many a hero of truth meet his death at the stake at the hands of the priests.

Now with reference to the paradox above expressed, I must call to mind the fact that we previously found suffering to be essential to, and inseparable from, life as a whole, and that we saw how every desire springs from a need, a want, a suffering, and that every satisfaction is therefore only a pain removed, not a positive happiness brought. We saw that the joys certainly lie to the desire in stating that they are a positive good, but that in truth they are only of a negative nature, and only the end of an evil. Therefore, whatever goodness, affection, and magnanimity do for others is always only an alleviation of their sufferings; and consequently what can move them to good deeds and to works of affection is always only *knowledge of the suffering of others*, directly intelligible from one's own suffering, and put on a level therewith. It follows from this, however, that pure affection, *caritas*, is of its nature sympathy or compassion. The suffering alleviated by it, to which every unsatisfied desire belongs, may be great or small. We shall therefore have no hesitation in saying that the mere concept is as unfruitful for genuine virtue as it is for genuine art; that all true and pure affection is sympathy or compassion, and all love that is not sympathy is selfishness. All this will be in direct contradiction to Kant, who recognizes all true goodness and all virtue as such, only if they have resulted from abstract reflection, and in fact from the concept of duty and the categorical imperative, and who declares felt sympathy to be weakness, and by no means virtue. Combinations of selfishness and compassion occur frequently; even genuine friendship is always a mixture of selfishness and sympathy. Selfishness lies in the pleasure in the presence of the friend, whose individuality corresponds to our own, and it almost invariably constitutes the greatest part; sympathy shows itself in a sincere participation in the friend's weal and woe, and in the disinterested sacrifices made for the latter. Even Spinoza says: *Benevolentia nihil aliud est, quam cupiditas ex commiseratione orta*[15] (*Ethics*, vol. 3, pr. 27, cor. 3 schol.). As confirmation of our paradoxical sentence, it may be observed that the tone and words of the language and the caresses of pure love entirely coincide with the tone of sympathy or compassion. Incidentally, it may be observed also that sympathy and pure love are expressed in Italian by the same word, *pietà*.

This is also the place to discuss one of the most striking peculiarities of human nature, *weeping*, which, like laughter, belongs to the manifestations that distinguish man from the animal. Weeping is by no means a positive manifestation of pain, for it occurs where pains are least. In my opinion, we never weep directly over pain that is felt, but always only over its repetition in reflection. Thus we pass from the felt pain, even when it is physical, to a mere mental picture or representation of it; we then find our own state so deserving of sympathy that, if another were the sufferer, we are firmly and sincerely convinced that we would be full of sympathy and love to help him. Now we ourselves are the object of our own sincere sympathy; with the most charitable disposition, we ourselves are most in need of help. We feel that we endure more than we could see another endure, and in this peculiarly involved frame of mind, in which the directly felt suffering comes to perception only in a doubly indirect way, pictured as the suffering of another and sympathized with as such, and then suddenly perceived again as directly our own; in such a frame of mind nature finds relief through that curious physical convulsion. Accordingly, *weeping is sympathy with ourselves*, or sympathy thrown back to its

15. Benevolence is nothing but a desire sprung from compassion.

starting point. It is therefore conditioned by the capacity for affection and sympathy, and by the imagination. Therefore people who are either hard-hearted or without imagination do not readily weep; indeed weeping is always regarded as a sign of a certain degree of goodness of character, and it disarms anger. This is because it is felt that whoever is still able to weep must also necessarily be capable of affection, i.e., of sympathy toward others, for this enters in the way described into that mood that leads to weeping. The description that Petrarch gives of the rising of his own tears, naively and truly expressing his feeling, is entirely in accordance with the explanation that has been given:

> I' vo pensando: e nel pensar m'assale
> Una pietà si forte di me stesso,
> Che mi conduce spesso
> Ad alto lagrimar, ch' i' non soleva.[16]

What has been said is also confirmed by the fact that children who have been hurt generally cry only when they are pitied, and hence not on account of the pain, but on account of the conception of it. That we are moved to tears not by our own sufferings, but by those of others, happens in the following way; either in imagination we put ourselves vividly in the sufferer's place, or we see in his fate the lot of the whole of humanity, and consequently above all our own fate. Thus in a very roundabout way, we always weep about ourselves; we feel sympathy with ourselves. This seems also to be a main reason for the universal, and hence natural, weeping in cases of death. It is not the mourner's loss over which he weeps; he would be ashamed of such egoistical tears, instead of sometimes being ashamed of not weeping. In the first place, of course, he weeps over the fate of the deceased; yet he weeps also when for the deceased death was a desirable deliverance after long, grave, and uncurable sufferings. In the main, therefore, he is seized with sympathy over the lot of the whole of mankind that is given over to finiteness. In consequence of this, every life, however ambitious and often rich in deeds, must become extinct and nothing. In this

16. As I wander deep in thought, so strong a *sympathy with myself* comes over me, that I must often weep aloud, a thing I am otherwise not accustomed to do.—Tr.

lot of mankind, however, the mourner sees first of all his own lot, and this the more, the more closely he was related to the deceased, and most of all therefore when the deceased was his father. Although to this father life was a misery through age and sickness, and through his helplessness a heavy burden to the son, the son nevertheless weeps bitterly over the death of his father for the reason already stated.

After this digression on the identity of pure love with sympathy, the turning back of sympathy on to our own individuality having as its symptom the phenomenon of weeping, I take up again the thread of our discussion of the ethical significance of conduct, to show how, from the same source from which all goodness, affection, virtue, and nobility of character spring, there ultimately arises also what I call denial of the will-to-live.

Just as previously we saw hatred and wickedness conditioned by egoism, and this depending on knowledge being entangled in the *principium individuationis,* so we found as the source and essence of justice, and, when carried farther to the highest degrees, of love and magnanimity, that penetration of the *principium individuationis.* This penetration alone, by abolishing the distinction between our own individuality and that of others, makes possible and explains perfect goodness of disposition, extending to the most disinterested love, and the most generous self-sacrifice for others.

Now, if seeing through the *principium individuationis,* if this direct knowledge of the identity of the will in all its phenomena, is present in a high degree of distinctness, it will at once show an influence on the will that goes still farther. If that veil of Maya, the *principium individuationis,* is lifted from the eyes of a man to such an extent that he no longer makes the egoistical distinction between himself and the person of others, but takes as much interest in the sufferings of other individuals as in his own, and thus is not only benevolent and charitable in the highest degree, but even ready to sacrifice his own individuality whenever several others can be saved thereby, then it follows automatically that such a man, recognizing in all beings his own true and innermost self, must also regard the endless sufferings of all that lives as his own, and thus take upon himself the pain of the whole world. No suffering is any longer strange or foreign to him. All the miseries of others, which he sees and is so seldom able to alleviate, all the miseries of which he has indirect knowledge, and even those he recognizes merely as possible, affect his mind just as do his own. It is no longer the changing weal and woe of his person that he has in view, as is the case with the man still involved in egoism, but, as he sees through the *principium individuationis,* everything lies equally near to him. He knows the whole, comprehends its inner nature, and finds it involved in a constant passing away, a vain striving, an inward conflict, and a continual suffering. Wherever he looks, he sees suffering humanity and the suffering animal world, and a world that passes away. Now all this lies just as near to him as only his own person lies to the egoist. Now how could he, with such knowledge of the world, affirm this very life through constant acts of will, and precisely in this way bind himself more and more firmly to it, press himself to it more and more closely? Thus, whoever is still involved in the *principium individuationis,* in egoism, knows only particular things and their relation to his own person, and these then become ever renewed *motives* of his willing. On the other hand, that knowledge of the whole, of the inner nature of the thing-in-itself, which has been described, becomes the *quieter* of all and every willing. The will now turns away from life; it shudders at the pleasures in which it recognizes the affirmation of life. Man attains to the state of voluntary renunciation, resignation, true composure, and complete will-lessness. At times, in the hard experience of our own sufferings or in the vividly recognized suffering of others, knowledge of the vanity and bitterness of life comes close to us who are still enveloped in the veil of Maya. We would like to deprive desires of their sting, close the entry to all suffering, purify and sanctify ourselves by complete and final resignation. But the illusion of the phenomenon soon ensnares us again, and its motives set the will in motion once more; we cannot tear ourselves free. The allurements of hope, the flattery of the present, the sweetness of pleasures, the well-being that falls to the lot of our person amid the lamentations of a suffering world governed by chance and error, all these draw us back to it, and rivet the bonds anew. Therefore Jesus says: "It is easier for a camel to go through the eye of a needle, than for a rich man to enter into the Kingdom of God."[17]

17. Matthew 19:24.—Tr.

If we compare life to a circular path of red-hot coals having a few cool places, a path that we have to run over incessantly, then the man entangled in delusion is comforted by the cool place on which he is just now standing, or which he sees near him, and sets out to run over the path. But the man who sees through the *principium individuationis,* and recognizes the true nature of things-in-themselves, and thus the whole, is no longer susceptible of such consolation; he sees himself in all places simultaneously, and withdraws. His will turns about; it no longer affirms its own inner nature, mirrored in the phenomenon, but denies it. The phenomenon by which this becomes manifest is the transition from virtue to *asceticism.* In other words, it is no longer enough for him to love others like himself, and to do as much for them as for himself, but there arises in him a strong aversion to the inner nature whose expression is his own phenomenon, to the will-to-live, the kernel and essence of that world recognized as full of misery. He therefore renounces precisely this inner nature, which appears in him and is expressed already by his body, and his action gives the lie to his phenomenon, and appears in open contradiction thereto. Essentially nothing but phenomenon of the will, he ceases to will anything, guards against attaching his will to anything, tries to establish firmly in himself the greatest indifference to all things. His body, healthy and strong, expresses the sexual impulse through the genitals, but he denies the will, and gives the lie to the body; he desires no sexual satisfaction on any condition. Voluntary and complete chastity is the first step in asceticism or the denial of the will-to-live. It thereby denies the affirmation of the will that goes beyond the individual life, and thus announces that the will, whose phenomenon is the body, ceases with the life of this body. Nature, always true and naive, asserts that, if this maxim became universal, the human race would die out; and after what was said in the second book about the connection of all phenomena of will, I think I can assume that, with the highest phenomenon of will, the weaker reflection of it, namely, the animal world, would also be abolished, just as the half-shades vanish with the full light of day. With the complete abolition of knowledge the rest of the world would of itself also vanish into nothing, for there can be no object without a subject. Here I would like to refer to a passage in the *Veda* where it says: "As in this world hungry children press round their mother, so do all beings await the holy oblation." (*Asiatic Researches,* vol. 8; Colebrooke, *On the Vedas, Epitome of the Sama Veda; idem, Miscellaneous Essays,* vol. 1, p. 88.)[18] Sacrifice signifies resignation generally, and the rest of nature has to expect its salvation from man who is at the same time priest and sacrifice. In fact, it is worth mentioning as extremely remarkable that this thought has also been expressed by the admirable and immeasurably profound Angelus Silesius in the little poem entitled "Man brings all to God"; it runs:

> "Man! all love you; great is the throng around you:
> All flock to you that they may attain to God."

But an even greater mystic, Meister Eckhart, whose wonderful writings have at last (1857) become accessible to us through the edition of Franz Pfeiffer, says (p. 459) wholly in the sense here discussed: "I confirm this with Christ, for he says: 'I, if I be lifted up from the earth, will draw all things [men] unto me' (John 12:32). So shall the good man draw all things up to God, to the source whence they first came. The masters certify to us that all creatures are made for the sake of man. This is proved in all creatures by the fact that one creature makes use of another; the ox makes use of the grass, the fish of the water, the bird of the air, the animals of the forest. Thus all creatures come to the profit of the good man. A good man bears to God one creature in the other." He means that because, in and with himself, man also saves the animals, he makes use of them in this life. It seems to me indeed that that difficult passage in the Bible, Rom. 8:21-24, is to be interpreted in this sense.

Even in Buddhism there is no lack of expressions of this matter; for example, when the Buddha, while still a Bodhisattva, has his horse saddled for the last time, for the flight from his father's house into the wilderness, he says to the horse in verse: "Long have you existed in life and in death, but now you shall cease to carry and to draw. Bear me away from here just this once, O Kantakana, and when I have attained the Law (have become Buddha), I shall not forget you." (*Foe Koue Ki,* trans. by Abel Rémusat, p. 233.)

18. The passage is taken from the *Chandogya Upanishad,* 5:24, 5, and in literal translation is: Just as hungry children here sit round their mother, so do all beings sit round the agnihotram (the fire-sacrifice offered by the knower of Brahman).—Tr.

Asceticism shows itself further in voluntary and intentional poverty, which arises not only *per accidens,* since property is given away to alleviate the sufferings of others, but which is here an end in itself; it is to serve as a constant mortification of the will, so that satisfaction of desires, the sweets of life, may not again stir the will, of which self-knowledge has conceived a horror. He who has reached this point still always feels, as living body, as concrete phenomenon of will, the natural tendency to every kind of willing; but he deliberately suppresses it, since he compels himself to refrain from doing all that he would like to do, and on the other hand to do all that he would not like to do, even if this has no further purpose than that of serving to mortify the will. As he himself denies the will that appears in his own person, he will not resist when another does the same thing, in other words, inflicts wrong on him. Therefore, every suffering that comes to him from outside through chance or the wickedness of others is welcome to him; every injury, every ignominy, every outrage. He gladly accepts them as the opportunity for giving himself the certainty that he no longer affirms the will, but gladly sides with every enemy of the will's phenomenon that is his own person. He therefore endures such ignominy and suffering with inexhaustible patience and gentleness, returns good for all evil without ostentation, and allows the fire of anger to rise again within him as little as he does the fire of desires. Just as he mortifies the will itself, so does he mortify its visibility, its objectivity, the body. He nourishes it sparingly, lest its vigorous flourishing and thriving should animate afresh and excite more strongly the will, of which it is the mere expression and mirror. Thus he resorts to fasting, and even to self-castigation and self-torture, in order that, by constant privation and suffering, he may more and more break down and kill the will that he recognizes and abhors as the source of his own suffering existence and of the world's. Finally, if death comes, which breaks up the phenomenon of this will, the essence of such will having long since expired through free denial of itself except for the feeble residue which appears as the vitality of this body, then it is most welcome, and is cheerfully accepted as a longed-for deliverance. It is not merely the phenomenon, as in the case of others, that comes to an end with death, but the inner being itself that is abolished; this had a feeble existence merely in the phenomenon.[19] This last slender bond is now severed; for him who ends thus, the world has at the same time ended.

And what I have described here with feeble tongue, and only in general terms, is not some philosophical fable, invented by myself and only of today. No, it was the enviable life of so many saints and great souls among the Christians, and even more among the Hindus and Buddhists, and also among the believers of other religions. Different as were the dogmas that were impressed on their faculty of reason, the inner, direct, and intuitive knowledge from which alone all virtue and holiness can come is nevertheless expressed in precisely the same way in the conduct of life. For here also is seen the great distinction between intuitive and abstract knowledge, a distinction of such importance and of general application in the whole of our discussion, and one which hitherto has received too little notice. Between the two is a wide gulf; and, in regard to knowledge of the inner nature of the world, this gulf can be crossed only by philosophy. Intuitively, or *in concreto*, every man is really conscious of all philosophical truths; but to bring them into his abstract knowledge, into reflection, is the business of the philosopher, who neither ought to nor can do more than this.

Thus it may be that the inner nature of holiness, of self-renunciation, of mortification of one's own will, of asceticism, is here for the first time expressed in abstract terms and free from everything mythical, as *denial of the will-to-live*, which appears after the complete knowledge of its own inner being has become for it the quieter of all willing. On the other hand, it has been known directly and expressed in deed by all those saints and ascetics who, in spite of the same inner knowledge, used very different language according to the dogmas that their faculty of reason had accepted, and in consequence of which an Indian, a Christian, or a Lamaist saint must each give a very different account of his own conduct; but this is of no importance at all as regards the fact. A

19. This idea is expressed by a fine simile in the ancient Sanskrit philosophical work *Sankhya Karika:* "Yet the soul remains for a time clothed with the body, just as the potter's wheel continues to spin after the pot has been finished, in consequence of the impulse previously given to it. Only when the inspired soul separates itself from the body and nature ceases for it, does its complete salvation take place." Colebrooke, "On the Philosophy of the Hindus": *Miscellaneous Essays,* vol. 1, p. 259. Also in the *Sankhya Carica* by Horace Wilson, section 67, p. 184.

saint may be full of the most absurd superstition, or, on the other hand, may be a philosopher; it is all the same. His conduct alone is evidence that he is a saint; for, in a moral regard, it springs not from abstract knowledge, but from intuitively apprehended, immediate knowledge of the world and of its inner nature, and is expressed by him through some dogma only for the satisfaction of his faculty of reason. It is therefore just as little necessary for the saint to be a philosopher as for the philosopher to be a saint; just as it is not necessary for a perfectly beautiful person to be a great sculptor, or for a great sculptor to be himself a beautiful person. In general, it is a strange demand on a moralist that he should commend no other virtue than that which he himself possesses. To repeat abstractly, universally, and distinctly in concepts the whole inner nature of the world, and thus to deposit it as a reflected image in permanent concepts always ready for the faculty of reason, this and nothing else is philosophy. I recall the passage from Bacon quoted in the first book.

But my description, given above, of the denial of the will-to-live, or of the conduct of a beautiful soul, of a resigned and voluntarily expiating saint, is only abstract and general, and therefore cold. As the knowledge from which results the denial of the will is intuitive and not abstract, it finds its complete expression not in abstract concepts, but only in the deed and in conduct. Therefore, in order to understand more fully what we express philosophically as denial of the will-to-live, we have to learn to know examples from experience and reality. Naturally we shall not come across them in daily experience: *nam omnia praeclara tam difficilia quam rara sunt,*[20] as Spinoza admirably says. Therefore, unless we are made eyewitnesses by a specially favorable fate, we shall have to content ourselves with the biographies of such persons. Indian literature, as we see from the little that is so far known to us through translations, is very rich in descriptions of the lives of saints, penitents, Samanas, Sannyasis, and so on. Even the well-known *Mythologie des Indous* of Madame de Polier, although by no means praiseworthy in every respect, contains many excellent examples of this kind (especially in vol. 2, chapter 13). Among Christians there is also no lack of

---

20. For all that is excellent and eminent is as difficult as it is rare. [*Ethics, 5,* prop. 42 schol.]—Tr.

examples affording us the illustrations that we have in mind. Let us see the biographies, often badly written, of those persons sometimes called saintly souls, sometimes pietists, quietists, pious enthusiasts, and so on. Collections of such biographies have been made at various times, such as Tersteegen's *Leben heiliger Seelen,* Reiz's *Geschichte der Wiedergeborenen* in our own day, a collection by Kanne that, with much that is bad, yet contains some good, especially the *Leben der Beata Sturmin.* To this category very properly belongs the life of St. Francis of Assisi, that true personification of asceticism and prototype of all mendicant friars. His life, described by his younger contemporary St. Bonaventure, also famous as a scholastic, has recently been republished: *Vita S. Francisci a S. Bonaventura concinnata* (Soest, 1847), shortly after the appearance in France of an accurate and detailed biography that utilizes all the sources: *Histoire de S. François d'Assise,* by Chavin de Mallan (1845). As an oriental parallel to these monastic writings, we have the book of Spence Hardy: *Eastern Monachism, an Account of the Order of Mendicants Founded by Gotama Budha* (1850), which is very well worth reading. It shows us the same thing under a different cloak. We also see how immaterial it is whether it proceeds from a theistic or from an atheistic religion. But as a special and extremely full example and actual illustration of the conceptions I advance, I can particularly recommend the *Autobiography* of Madame de Guyon. To become acquainted with that great and beautiful soul, whose remembrance always fills me with reverence, and to do justice to the excellence of her disposition while making allowances for the superstition of her faculty of reason, must be gratifying to every person of the better sort, just as with common thinkers, in other words the majority, that book will always stand in bad repute. For everyone, always and everywhere, can appreciate only that which is to some extent analogous to him, and for which he has at any rate a feeble gift; this holds good of the ethical as well as of the intellectual. To a certain extent we might regard even the well-known French biography of Spinoza as a case in point, if we use as the key to it that excellent introduction to his very inadequate essay, *De Emendatione Intellectus.* At the same time, I can recommend this passage as the most effective means known to me of stilling the storm of the passions. Finally, even the great Goethe, Greek as he was, did not regard it as beneath his dignity to show us this most beautiful side of humanity in the elucidating mirror of the poetic art, since he presented to us in an idealized form the life of Fräulein Klettenberg in the *Confessions of a Beautiful Soul,* and later, in his own biography, gave us also a historical account of it. Besides this, he twice narrated the life of St. Philip Neri. The history of the world will, and indeed must, always keep silence about the persons whose conduct is the best and only adequate illustration of this important point of our investigation. For the material of world-history is quite different therefrom, and indeed opposed to it; thus it is not the denial and giving up of the will-to-live, but its affirmation and manifestation in innumerable individuals in which its dissension with itself at the highest point of its objectification appears with perfect distinctness, and brings before our eyes, now the superior strength of the individual through his shrewdness, now the might of the many through their mass, now the ascendancy of chance personified as fate, always the vanity and futility of the whole striving and effort. But we do not follow here the thread of phenomena in time, but, as philosophers, try to investigate the ethical significance of actions, and take this as the only criterion of what is significant and important for us. No fear of the always permanent majority of vulgarity and shallowness will prevent us from acknowledging that the greatest, the most important, and the most significant phenomenon that the world can show is not the conqueror of the world, but the overcomer of the world, and so really nothing but the quiet and unobserved conduct in the life of such a man. On this man has dawned the knowledge in consequence of which he gives up and denies that will-to-live that fills everything, and strives and strains in all. The freedom of this will first appears here in him alone, and by it his actions now become the very opposite of the ordinary. For the philosopher, therefore, in this respect those accounts of the lives of saintly, self-denying persons, badly written as they generally are, and mixed up with superstition and nonsense, are through the importance of the material incomparably more instructive and important than even Plutarch and Livy.

Further, a more detailed and complete knowledge of what we express in abstraction and generality through our method of presentation as denial of the will-to-live, will be very greatly facilitated by a consideration of the ethical precepts given in this sense and by people who were full of this spirit. These will at the same time show how old our view is, however new its purely philosophical expression may be. In the first place, Christianity is nearest at hand, the ethics of which is entirely in the spirit we have mentioned, and leads not only to the highest degrees of charity and human kindness, but also to renunciation. The germ of this last side is certainly distinctly present in the writings of the Apostles, yet only later is it fully developed and explicitly expressed. We find commanded by the Apostles love for our neighbor as for ourselves, returning of hatred with love and good actions, patience, meekness, endurance of all possible affronts and injuries without resistance, moderation in eating and drinking for suppressing desire, resistance to the sexual impulse, even complete if possible for us. Here we see the first stages of asceticism or of real denial of the will; this last expression denotes what is called in the Gospels denying the self and taking of the cross upon oneself. (Matt. 16:24, 25; Mark 8:34, 35; Luke 9:23, 24; 14:26, 27, 33.) This tendency was soon developed more and more, and was the origin of penitents, anchorites, and monasticism, an origin that in itself was pure and holy, but, for this very reason, quite unsuitable to the great majority of people. Therefore what developed out of it could be only hypocrisy and infamy, for *abusus optimi pessimus*.[21] In more developed Christianity, we see that seed of asceticism unfold into full flower in the writings of the Christian saints and mystics. Besides the purest love, these preach also complete resignation, voluntary and absolute poverty, true composure, complete indifference to all worldly things, death to one's own will and regeneration in God, entire forgetting of one's own person and absorption in the contemplation of God. A complete description of this is to be found in Fénelon's *Explication des maximes des Saints sur la vie intérieure*. But the spirit of this development of Christianity is certainly nowhere so perfectly and powerfully expressed as in the writings of the German mystics, e.g., those of Meister Eckhart, and the justly famous book *Theologia Germanica*. In the introduction to this last that Luther wrote, he says of it that, with the exception of the Bible and St. Augustine, he had learned more from it of what God, Christ, and man are than from any other book. Yet only in the year 1851 did we acquire

---

21. The worst is the abuse of the best.—TR.

its genuine and unadulterated text in the Stuttgart edition of Pfeiffer. The precepts and doctrines given in it are the most perfect explanation, springing from deep inward conviction, of what I have described as the denial of the will-to-live. One has therefore to make a closer study of it before dogmatizing about it with Jewish-Protestant assurance. Tauler's *Nachfolgung des armen Leben Christi,* together with his *Medulla Animae,* are written in the same admirable spirit, although not quite equal in value to that work. In my opinion, the teachings of these genuine Christian mystics are related to those of the New Testament as alcohol is to wine; in other words, what becomes visible to us in the New Testament as if through a veil and mist, stands before us in the works of the mystics without cloak or disguise, in full clearness and distinctness. Finally, we might also regard the New Testament as the first initiation, the mystics as the second, *small and great mysteries.*[22]

But we find what we have called denial of the will-to-live still further developed, more variously expressed, and more vividly presented in the ancient works in the Sanskrit language than could be the case in the Christian Church and the Western world. That this important ethical view of life could attain here to a more far-reaching development and a more decided expression, is perhaps to be ascribed mainly to the fact that it was not restricted by an element quite foreign to it, as the Jewish doctrine of faith is in Christianity. The sublime founder of Christianity had necessarily to adapt and accommodate himself, partly consciously, partly, it may be, unconsciously, to this doctrine; and so Christianity is composed of two very heterogeneous elements. Of these I should like to call the purely ethical element preferably, indeed exclusively, the Christian, and to distinguish it from the Jewish dogmatism with which it is found. If, as has often been feared, and especially at the present time, that excellent and salutary religion should completely decline, then I would look for the reason for this simply in the fact that it does not consist of one simple element, but of two originally heterogeneous elements, brought into combination only by means of world events. In such a case, dissolution would necessarily result through the breakup of these elements, which arises from their

22. The former celebrated by the Athenians in March, the latter in October.—TR.

different relationship and reaction to the advanced spirit of the times. Yet after this dissolution, the purely ethical part would still be bound always to remain intact, because it is indestructible. However imperfect our knowledge of Hindu literature still is, as we now find it most variously and powerfully expressed in the ethics of the Hindus, in the *Vedas, Puranas,* poetical works, myths, legends of their saints, in aphorisms, maxims, and rules of conduct,[23] we see that it ordains love of one's neighbor with complete denial of all self-love; love in general, not limited to the human race, but embracing all that lives; charitableness even to the giving away of one's hard-won daily earnings; boundless patience toward all offenders; return of all evil, however bad it may be, with goodness and love; voluntary and cheerful endurance of every insult and ignominy; abstinence from all animal food; perfect chastity and renunciation of all sensual pleasure for him who aspires to real holiness; the throwing away of all property; the forsaking of every dwelling place and of all kinsfolk; deep unbroken solitude spent in silent contemplation with voluntary penance and terrible slow self-torture for the complete mortification of the will, ultimately going as far as voluntary death by starvation, or facing crocodiles, or jumping over the consecrated precipice in the Himalaya, or being buried alive, or flinging oneself under the wheels of the huge car that drives round with the images of the gods amid the singing, shouting, and dancing of bayaderes. These precepts, whose origin reaches back more than four thousand years, are still lived up to by individuals even to the utmost extreme,[24] degenerate as that race is in many respects. That which has remained in practice for so long in a nation embracing so many millions, while it imposes the

23. See, for example, *Oupnek'hat,* studio Anquetil du Perron, vol. 2, Nos. 138, 144, 145, 146; *Mythologie des Indous,* by Madame de Polier, vol. 2, chaps. 13, 14, 15, 16, 17; *Asiatisches Magazin,* by Klaproth, in the first volume; *Ueber die Fo-Religion, also Bhaguat-Geeta oder Gespräche zwischen Kreeshna und Arjoon;* in the second volume, '*Moha-Mudgava;* then *Institutes of Hindu Law, or the Ordinances of Manu,* from the Sanskrit by Sir William Jones (German by Hüttner, 1797); especially the sixth and twelfth chapters. Finally, many passages in the *Asiatic Researches.* (In the last forty years Indian literature has grown so much in Europe, that if I now wished to complete this note to the first edition, it would fill several pages.)

24. At the procession of Jagganath in June 1840, eleven Hindus threw themselves under the car, and were instantly killed. (Letter from an East Indian landowner in the *Times* of December 30, 1840.)

heaviest sacrifices, cannot be an arbitrarily invented freak, but must have its foundation in the very nature of mankind. But besides this, we cannot sufficiently wonder at the harmony we find, when we read the life of a Christian penitent or saint and that of an Indian. In spite of such fundamentally different dogmas, customs, and circumstances, the endeavor and the inner life of both are absolutely the same; and it is also the same with the precepts for both. For example, Tauler speaks of the complete poverty that one should seek, and that consists in giving away and divesting oneself entirely of everything from which one might draw some comfort or worldly pleasure, clearly because all this always affords new nourishment to the will, whose complete mortification is intended. As the Indian counterpart of this, we see in the precepts of Fo that the Sannyasi, who is supposed to be without dwelling and entirely without property, is finally enjoined not to lie down too often under the same tree, lest he acquire a preference or inclination for it. The Christian mystics and the teachers of the Vedanta philosophy agree also in regarding all outward works and religious practices as superfluous for the man who has attained perfection. So much agreement, in spite of such different ages and races, is a practical proof that here is expressed not an eccentricity and craziness of the mind, as optimistic shallowness and dullness like to assert, but an essential side of human nature that appears rarely only because of its superior quality.

I have now mentioned the sources from which we can obtain a direct knowledge, drawn from life, of the phenomena in which the denial of the will-to-live exhibits itself. To a certain extent, this is the most important point of our whole discussion; yet I have explained it only quite generally, for it is better to refer to those who speak from direct experience, than to increase the size of this book unnecessarily by repeating more feebly what they say.

I wish to add only a little more to the general description of their state. We saw above that the wicked man, by the vehemence of his willing, suffers constant, consuming, inner torment, and finally that, when all the objects of willing are exhausted, he quenches the fiery thirst of his willfulness by the sight of others' pain. On the other hand, the man in whom the denial of the will-to-live has dawned, however poor, cheerless, and full of privation his state may be when looked at from outside, is full of inner cheerfulness and true heavenly peace. It is not the restless and turbulent pressure of life, the jubilant delight that has keen suffering as its preceding or succeeding condition, such as constitute the conduct of the man attached to life, but it is an unshakable peace, a deep calm and inward serenity, a state that we cannot behold without the greatest longing, when it is brought before our eyes or imagination, since we at once recognize it as that which alone is right, infinitely outweighing everything else, at which our better spirit cries to us the great *sapere aude*.[25] We then feel that every fulfillment of our wishes won from the world is only like the alms that keep the beggar alive today so that he may starve again tomorrow. Resignation, on the other hand, is like the inherited estate; it frees its owner from all care and anxiety forever.

It will be remembered from the third book that aesthetic pleasure in the beautiful consists, to a large extent, in the fact that, when we enter the state of pure contemplation, we are raised for the moment above all willing, above all desires and cares; we are, so to speak, rid of ourselves. We are no longer the individual that knows in the interest of its constant willing, the correlative of the particular thing to which objects become motives, but the eternal subject of knowing purified of the will, the correlative of the idea. And we know that these moments, when, delivered from the fierce pressure of the will, we emerge, as it were, from the heavy atmosphere of the earth, are the most blissful that we experience. From this we can infer how blessed must be the life of a man whose will is silenced not for a few moments, as in the enjoyment of the beautiful, but forever, indeed completely extinguished, except for the last glimmering spark that maintains the body and is extinguished with it. Such a man who, after many bitter struggles with his own nature, has at last completely conquered, is then left only as pure knowing being, as the undimmed mirror of the world. Nothing can distress or alarm him anymore; nothing can any longer move him; for he has cut all the thousand threads of willing that hold us bound to the world, and that as craving, fear, envy, and anger drag us here and there in constant pain. He now looks back calmly and with a smile on the phantasmagoria of this world that was once able to move and agonize even his mind, but now

25. Bring yourself to be reasonable!—Tr.

stands before him as indifferently as chessmen at the end of a game, or as fancy dress cast off in the morning, the form and figure of which taunted and disquieted us on the carnival night. Life and its forms merely float before him as a fleeting phenomenon, as a light morning dream to one half-awake, through which reality already shines, and which can no longer deceive; and, like this morning dream, they too finally vanish without any violent transition. From these considerations we can learn to understand what Madame Guyon means when, toward the end of her *Autobiography,* she often expresses herself thus: "Everything is indifferent to me; I *cannot* will anything more; often I do not know whether I exist or not." In order to express how, after the dying away of the will, the death of the body (which is indeed only the phenomenon of the will, and thus with the abolition of the will loses all meaning) can no longer have anything bitter, but is very welcome, I may be permitted to record here that holy penitent's own words, although they are not very elegantly turned: *"Midi de la gloire; jour où il n'y a plus de nuit; vie qui ne craint plus la mort, dans la mort même: parceque la mort a vaincu la mort, et que celui qui a souffert la première mort, ne goûtera plus la seconde mort."* (*Vie de Madame de Guion* [Cologne, 1720], vol. 2, p. 13.)[26]

However, we must not imagine that, after the denial of the will-to-live has once appeared through knowledge that has become a quieter of the will, such denial no longer wavers or falters, and that we can rest on it as on an inherited property. On the contrary, it must always be achieved afresh by constant struggle. For as the body is the will itself only in the form of objectivity, or as phenomenon in the world as representation, that whole will-to-live exists potentially so long as the body lives, and is always striving to reach actuality and to burn afresh with all its intensity. We therefore find in the lives of saintly persons that peace and bliss we have described, only as the blossom resulting from the constant overcoming of the will; and we see the constant struggle with the will-to-live as the soil from which it shoots up; for on earth no one can have lasting peace. We therefore see the histories of the inner life of saints full of spiritual conflicts, temptations, and desertion from

26. The noonday of glory; a day no longer followed by night; a life that no longer fears death, even in death itself, because death has overcome death, and because whoever has suffered the first death will no longer feel the second.—Tr.

grace, in other words, from that kind of knowledge that, by rendering all motives ineffectual, as a universal quieter silences all willing, gives the deepest peace, and opens the gate to freedom. Therefore we see also those who have once attained to denial of the will, strive with all their might to keep to this path by self-imposed renunciations of every kind, by a penitent and hard way of life, and by looking for what is disagreeable to them; all this in order to suppress the will that is constantly springing up afresh. Finally, therefore, because they already know the value of salvation, their anxious care for the retention of the hard-won blessing, their scruples of conscience in the case of every innocent enjoyment or with every little excitement of their vanity; this is also the last thing to die, the most indestructible, the most active, and the most foolish of all man's inclinations. By the expression *asceticism,* which I have already used so often, I understand in the narrower sense this *deliberate* breaking of the will by refusing the agreeable and looking for the disagreeable, the voluntarily chosen way of life of penance and self-chastisement, for the constant mortification of the will.

Now, if we see this practiced by persons who have already attained to denial of the will, in order that they may keep to it, then suffering in general, as it is inflicted by fate, is also a second way[27*] of attaining to that denial. Indeed, we may assume that most men can reach it only in this way, and that it is the suffering personally felt, not the suffering merely known, which most frequently produces complete resignation, often only at the approach of death. For only in the case of a few is mere knowledge sufficient to bring about the denial of the will, the knowledge namely that sees through the *principium individuationis,* first producing perfect goodness of disposition and universal love of mankind, and finally enabling them to recognize as their own all the sufferings of the world. Even in the case of the individual who approaches this point, the tolerable condition of his own person, the flattery of the moment, the allurement of hope, and the satisfaction of the will offering itself again and again, i.e., the satisfaction of desire, are almost invariably a constant obstacle to the denial of the will, and

27*. Cf. Stobaeus, *Florilegium,* vol. 2, p. 374. [In this chapter, footnotes indicated by an asterisk represent additions made by Schopenhauer in his interleaved copy of the third edition of 1859. He died in 1860, and so there are very few of these. Tr.]

a constant temptation to a renewed affirmation of it. For this reason, all those allurements have in this respect been personified as the devil. Therefore in most cases the will must be broken by the greatest personal suffering before its self-denial appears. We then see the man suddenly retire into himself, after he is brought to the verge of despair through all the stages of increasing affliction with the most violent resistance. We see him know himself and the world, change his whole nature, rise above himself and above all suffering, as if purified and sanctified by it, in inviolable peace, bliss, and sublimity, willingly renounce everything he formerly desired with the greatest vehemence, and gladly welcome death. It is the gleam of silver that suddenly appears from the purifying flame of suffering, the gleam of the denial of the will-to-live, of salvation. Occasionally we see even those who were very wicked purified to this degree by the deepest grief and sorrow; they have become different, and are completely converted. Therefore, their previous misdeeds no longer trouble their consciences, yet they gladly pay for such misdeeds with death, and willingly see the end of the phenomenon of that will that is now foreign to and abhorred by them. The great Goethe has given us a distinct and visible description of this denial of the will, brought about by great misfortune and by the despair of all deliverance, in his immortal masterpiece *Faust,* in the story of the sufferings of Gretchen. I know of no other description in poetry. It is a perfect specimen of the second path, which leads to the denial of the will not, like the first, through the mere knowledge of the suffering of a whole world that one acquires voluntarily, but through the excessive pain felt in one's own person. It is true that very many tragedies bring their violently willing heroes ultimately to this point of complete resignation, and then the will-to-live and its phenomenon usually end at the same time. But no description known to me brings to us the essential point of that conversion so distinctly and so free from everything extraneous as the one mentioned in *Faust*.

In real life we see those unfortunate persons who have to drink to the dregs the greatest measure of suffering, face a shameful, violent, and often painful death on the scaffold with complete mental vigour, after they are deprived of all hope; and very often we see them converted in this way. We should not, of course, assume that there is so great a difference between their character and that of most men as their fate seems to suggest; we have to ascribe the latter for the most part to circumstances; yet they are guilty and, to a considerable degree, bad. But we see many of them converted in the way mentioned, after the appearance of complete hopelessness. They now show actual goodness and purity of disposition, true abhorrence of committing any deed in the least degree wicked or uncharitable. They forgive their enemies, even those through whom they innocently suffered; and not merely in words and from a kind of hypocritical fear of the judges of the nether world, but in reality and with inward earnestness, and with no wish for revenge. Indeed, their suffering and dying in the end become agreeable to them, for the denial of the will-to-live has made its appearance. They often decline the deliverance offered them, and die willingly, peacefully, and blissfully. The last secret of life has revealed itself to them in the excess of pain, the secret, namely, that evil and wickedness, suffering and hatred, the tormented and the tormentor, different as they may appear to knowledge that follows the principle of sufficient reason, are in themselves one, phenomenon of the one will-to-live that objectifies its conflict with itself by means of the *principium individuationis*. They have learned to know both sides in full measure, the wickedness and the evil; and since they ultimately see the identity of the two, they reject them both at the same time; they deny the will-to-live. As we have said, it is a matter of complete indifference by what myths and dogmas they account to their faculty of reason for this intuitive and immediate knowledge, and for their conversion.

Matthias Claudius was undoubtedly a witness to a change of mind of this sort, when he wrote the remarkable essay that appears in the *Wandsbecker Bote* (pt. 1, p. 115) under the title *Bekehrungsgeschichte des* ... (History of the conversion of ...) which has the following ending: "Man's way of thinking can pass over from a point of the periphery to the opposite point, and back again to the previous point, if circumstances trace out for him the curved path to it. And these changes are not really anything great and interesting in man. But that *remarkable, catholic, transcendental change,* where the whole circle is irreparably torn up and all the laws of psychology become vain and empty, where the coat of skins is taken off, or at any rate turned inside out, and man's eyes are opened, is such that everyone who is conscious to some extent of the breath in his nostrils, forsakes father and mother, if he can hear and experience something certain about it."

The approach of death and hopelessness, however, are not absolutely necessary for such a purification through suffering. Even without them, the knowledge of the contradiction of the will-to-live with itself can, through great misfortune and suffering, violently force itself on us, and the vanity of all endeavor can be perceived. Hence men who have led a very adventurous life under the pressure of passions, men such as kings, heroes, or adventurers, have often been seen suddenly to change, resort to resignation and penance, and become hermits and monks. To this class belong all genuine accounts of conversion, for instance that of Raymond Lull, who had long wooed a beautiful woman, was at last admitted to her chamber, and was looking forward to the fulfillment of all his desires, when, opening her dress, she showed him her bosom terribly eaten away with cancer. From that moment, as if he had looked into hell, he was converted; leaving the court of the king of Majorca, he went into the wilderness to do penance.[28] This story of conversion is very similar to that of the Abbé de Rancé that I have briefly related in chapter 48 of volume 2. If we consider how, in both cases, the transition from the pleasure to the horror of life was the occasion, this gives us an explanation of the remarkable fact that it is the French nation, the most cheerful, merry, gay, sensual, and frivolous in Europe, in which by far the strictest of all monastic orders, namely, the Trappist, arose, was reestablished by Rancé after its decline, and maintains itself even to the present day in all its purity and fearful strictness, in spite of revolutions, changes in the Church, and the encroachments of infidelity.

However, a knowledge of the above-mentioned kind of the nature of this existence may depart again simultaneously with its occasion, and the will-to-live, and with it the previous character, may reappear. Thus we see that the passionate Benvenuto Cellini was converted in such a way, once in prison and again during a serious illness, but relapsed into his old state after the suffering had disappeared. In general, the denial of the will by no means results from suffering with the necessity of effect from cause; on the contrary, the will remains free. For here is just the one and

28. Brucker, *Hist. Philos.,* Tom. 4, pars 1, p. 10.

only point where its freedom enters directly into the phenomenon; hence the astonishment so strongly expressed by Asmus about the "transcendental change." For every case of suffering, a will can be conceived that surpasses it in intensity, and is unconquered by it. Therefore, Plato speaks in the *Phaedo* [116 E] of persons who, up to the moment of their execution, feast, carouse, drink, indulge in sexual pleasures, affirming life right up to the death. Shakespeare in Cardinal Beaufort[29] presents to us the fearful end of a wicked ruffian who dies full of despair, since no suffering or death can break his will that is vehement to the extreme point of wickedness.

The more intense the will, the more glaring the phenomenon of its conflict, and hence the greater the suffering. A world that was the phenomenon of an incomparably more intense will-to-live than the present one is, would exhibit so much the greater suffering; thus it would be a *hell*.

Since all suffering is a mortification and a call to resignation, it has potentially a sanctifying force. By this is explained the fact that great misfortune and deep sorrow in themselves inspire one with a certain awe. But the sufferer becomes wholly an object of reverence to us only when, surveying the course of his life as a chain of sorrows, or mourning a great and incurable pain, he does not really look at the concatenation of circumstances that plunged just his life into mourning; he does not stop at that particular great misfortune that befell him. For up till then, his knowledge still follows the principle of sufficient reason, and clings to the particular phenomenon; he still continues to will life, only not on the conditions that have happened to him. He is really worthy of reverence only when his glance has been raised from the particular to the universal, and when he regards his own suffering merely as an example of the whole and for him; for in an ethical respect he becomes inspired with genius, one case holds good for a thousand, so that the whole of life, conceived as essential suffering, then brings him to resignation. For this reason it is worthy of reverence when in Goethe's *Torquato Tasso* the princess speaks of how her own life and that of her relations have always been sad and cheerless, and here her regard is wholly toward the universal.

We always picture a very noble character to ourselves as having

29. *Henry VI, Part II,* act 3, scene 3.

a certain trace of silent sadness that is anything but constant pee-vishness over daily annoyances (that would be an ignoble trait, and might lead us to fear a bad disposition). It is a consciousness that has resulted from knowledge of the vanity of all possessions and of the suffering of all life, not merely of one's own. Such knowledge, however, may first of all be awakened by suffering personally experienced, especially by a single great suffering, just as a single wish incapable of fulfillment brought Petrarch to that resigned sadness concerning the whole of life that appeals to us so pathetically in his works; for the Daphne he pursued had to vanish from his hands, in order to leave behind for him the immortal laurel instead of herself. If the will is to a certain extent broken by such a great and irrevocable denial of fate, then practically nothing more is desired, and the character shows itself as mild, sad, noble, and resigned. Finally, when grief no longer has any definite object, but is extended over the whole of life, it is then to a certain extent a self-communion, a withdrawal, a gradual disappearance of the will, the visibility of which, namely, the body, is imperceptibly but inwardly undermined by it, so that the person feels a certain loosening of his bonds, a mild foretaste of the death that proclaims itself to be the dissolution of the body and of the will at the same time. A secret joy therefore accompanies this grief; and I believe it is this that the most melancholy of all nations has called "the joy of grief." Here, however, lies the danger of *sentimentality,* both in life itself and in its description in poetry; namely, when a person is always mourning and wailing without standing up courageously and rising to resignation. In this way heaven and earth are both lost, and only a watery sentimentality is retained. Only when suffering assumes the form of pure knowledge, and then this knowledge, as a *quieter of the will,* produces true resignation, is it the path to salvation, and thus worthy of reverence. But in this respect, we feel on seeing any very unfortunate person a certain esteem akin to that which virtue and nobility of character force from us; at the same time, our own fortunate condition seems like a reproach. We cannot help but regard every suffering, both those felt by ourselves and those felt by others, as at least a possible advance toward virtue and holiness, and pleasures and worldly satisfactions, on the other hand, as a departure therefrom. This goes so far that every man who under-goes great bodily or mental suffering, indeed everyone who performs a physical labor demanding the greatest exertion in the sweat of his brow and with evident exhaustion, yet does all this with patience and without grumbling, appears, when we consider him with close attention, somewhat like a sick man who applies a painful cure. Willingly, and even with satisfaction, he endures the pain caused by the cure, since he knows that the more he suffers, the more is the substance of the disease destroyed; and thus the present pain is the measure of his cure.

It follows from all that has been said, that the denial of the will-to-live, which is the same as what is called complete resignation or holiness, always proceeds from that quieter of the will; and this is the knowledge of its inner conflict and its essential vanity, expressing themselves in the suffering of all that lives. The difference, that we have described as two paths, is whether that knowledge is called forth by suffering that is merely and simply *known* and freely appropriated by our seeing through the *principium individuationis,* or by suffering immediately felt by ourselves. True salvation, deliverance from life and suffering, cannot even be imagined without complete denial of the will. Till then, everyone is nothing but this will itself, whose phenomenon is an evanescent existence, an always vain and constantly frustrated striving, and the world full of suffering as we have described it. All belong to this irrevocably and in like manner. For we found previously that life is always certain to the will-to-live, and its sole actual form is the present from which they never escape, since birth and death rule in the phenomenon. The Indian myth expresses this by saying that "they are born again." The great ethical difference of characters means that the bad man is infinitely remote from attaining that knowledge, whose result is the denial of the will, and is therefore in truth *actually* abandoned to all the miseries that appear in life as *possible.* For even the present fortunate state of his person is only a phenomenon brought about by the *principium individuationis,* and the illusion of Maya, the happy dream of a beggar. The sufferings that in the vehemence and passion of his pressing will he inflicts on others are the measure of the sufferings, the experience of which in his own person cannot break his will and lead to final denial. On the other hand, all true and pure affection, and even all free justice, result from seeing through the *principium individuationis;* when this penetration occurs in all its force, it produces perfect sanctification and salvation, the phenomenon of which are the state of resignation previously described, the unshakable peace accompanying this, and the highest joy and delight in death.[30]

Suicide, the arbitrary doing away with the individual phenomenon, differs most widely from the denial of the will-to-live, which is the only act of its freedom to appear in the phenomenon, and hence, as Asmus calls it, the transcendental change. The denial of the will has now been adequately discussed within the limits of our method of consideration. Far from being denial of the will, suicide is a phenomenon of the will's strong affirmation. For denial has its essential nature in the fact that the pleasures of life, not its sorrows, are shunned. The suicide wills life, and is dissatisfied merely with the conditions on which it has come to him. Therefore he gives up by no means the will-to-live, but merely life, since he destroys the individual phenomenon. He wills life, wills the unchecked existence and affirmation of the body; but the combination of circumstances does not allow of these, and the result for him is great suffering. The will-to-live finds itself so hampered in this particular phenomenon, that it cannot develop and display its efforts. It therefore decides in accordance with its own inner nature, which lies outside the forms of the principle of sufficient reason, and to which every individual phenomenon is therefore indifferent, in that it remains itself untouched by all arising and passing away, and is the inner core of the life of all things. For that same firm, inner assurance, which enables all of us to live without the constant dread of death, the assurance that the will can never lack its phenomenon, supports the deed even in the case of suicide. Thus the will-to-live appears just as much in this suicide (Shiva) as in the ease and comfort of self-preservation (Vishnu), and the sensual pleasure of procreation (Brahma). This is the inner meaning of the *unity of the Trimurti* which every human being entirely is, although in time it raises now one, now another of its three heads. As the individual thing is related to the Idea, so is suicide to the denial of the will. The suicide denies merely the individual, not the species. We have already found that, since life is always certain to the will-to-live, and suffering is essential to life, suicide, or the arbitrary destruction of an

30. Cf. chap. 48 of volume 2.

individual phenomenon, is a quite futile and foolish act, for the thing-in-itself remains unaffected by it, just as the rainbow remains unmoved, however rapidly the drops may change that sustain it for the moment. But in addition to this, it is also the masterpiece of Maya as the most blatant expression of the contradiction of the will-to-live with itself. Just as we have recognized this contradiction in the lowest phenomena of the will in the constant struggle of all the manifestations of natural forces and of all organic individuals for matter, time, and space, and as we saw that conflict stand out more and more with terrible distinctness on the ascending grades of the will's objectification; so at last at the highest stage, the Idea of man, it reaches that degree where not only the individuals exhibiting the same Idea exterminate one another, but even the one individual declares war on itself. The vehemence with which it wills life and revolts against what hinders it, namely suffering, brings it to the point of destroying itself, so that the individual will by an act of will eliminates the body that is merely the will's own becoming visible, rather than that suffering should break the will. Just because the suicide cannot cease willing, he ceases to live; and the will affirms itself here even through the cessation of its own phenomenon, because it can no longer affirm itself otherwise. But as it was just the suffering it thus shunned which, as mortification of the will, could have led it to the denial of itself and to salvation, so in this respect the suicide is like a sick man who, after the beginning of a painful operation that could completely cure him, will not allow it to be completed, but prefers to retain his illness. Suffering approaches and, as such, offers the possibility of a denial of the will; but he rejects it by destroying the will's phenomenon, the body, so that the will may remain unbroken. This is the reason why almost all ethical systems, philosophical as well as religious, condemn suicide, though they themselves cannot state anything but strange and sophistical arguments for so doing. But if ever a man was kept from suicide by purely moral incentive, the innermost meaning of this self-conquest (whatever the concepts in which his faculty of reason may have clothed it) was as follows: "I do not want to avoid suffering, because it can help to put an end to the will-to-live, whose phenomenon is so full of misery, by so strengthening the knowledge of the real nature of the world now already dawning on me, that such knowledge may become the final quieter of the will, and release me for ever."

It is well known that, from time to time, cases repeatedly occur where suicide extends to the children; the father kills the children of whom he is very fond, and then himself. If we bear in mind that conscience, religion, and all traditional ideas teach him to recognize murder as the gravest crime, but yet in the hour of his own death he commits this, and indeed without his having any possible egoistical motive for it, then the deed can be explained only in the following way. The will of the individual again recognizes itself immediately in the children, although it is involved in the delusion of regarding the phenomenon as the being-in-itself. At the same time, he is deeply moved by the knowledge of the misery of all life; he imagines that with the phenomenon he abolishes the inner nature itself, and therefore wants to deliver from existence and its misery both himself and his children in whom he directly sees himself living again. It would be an error wholly analogous to this to suppose that one can reach the same end as is attained by voluntary chastity by frustrating the aims of nature in fecundation, or even by men, in consideration of the inevitable suffering of life, countenancing the death of the new-born child, instead of rather doing everything to ensure life to every being that is pressing into it. For if the will-to-live exists, it cannot, as that which alone is metaphysical or the thing-in-itself, be broken by any force, but that force can destroy only its phenomenon in such a place and at such a time. The will itself cannot be abolished by anything except *knowledge*. Therefore the only path to salvation is that the will should appear freely and without hindrance, in order that it can *recognize or know* its own inner nature in this phenomenon. Only in consequence of this knowledge can the will abolish itself, and thus end the suffering that is inseparable from its phenomenon. This, however, is not possible through physical force, such as the destruction of the seed or germ, the killing of the new-born child, or suicide. Nature leads the will to the light, just because only in the light can it find its salvation. Therefore the purposes of nature are to be promoted in every way, as soon as the will-to-live, that is her inner being, has determined itself.

There appears to be special kind of suicide, quite different from the ordinary, which has perhaps not yet been adequately verified.

This is voluntarily chosen death by starvation at the highest degree of asceticism. Its manifestation, however, has always been accompanied, and thus rendered vague and obscure, by much religious fanaticism and even superstition. Yet it seems that the complete denial of the will can reach that degree where even the necessary will to maintain the vegetative life of the body, by the assimilation of nourishment, ceases to exist. This kind of suicide is so far from being the result of the will-to-live, that such a completely resigned ascetic ceases to live merely because he has completely ceased to will. No other death than that by starvation is here conceivable (unless it resulted from a special superstition), since the intention to cut short the agony would actually be a degree of affirmation of the will. The dogmas that satisfy the faculty of reason of such a penitent delude him with the idea that a being of a higher nature has ordered for him the fasting to which his inner tendency urges him. Old instances of this can be found in the *Breslauer Sammlung von Natur- und Medicin-Geschichten,* September 1719, p. 363 *seq.;* in Bayle's *Nouvelles de la république des lettres,* February 1685, p. 189 *seq.;* in Zimmermann, *Ueber die Einsamkeit,* vol. 1, p. 182; in the *Histoire de l'Académie des Sciences* of 1764, an account by Houttuyn; the same account is repeated in the *Sammlung für praktische Aerzte,* vol. 1, p. 69. Later reports are to be found in Hufeland's *Journal für praktische Heilkunde,* vol. 10, p. 181, and vol. 48, p. 95; also in Nasse's *Zeitschrift für psychische Aerzte,* 1819, part 3, p. 460; in the *Edinburgh Medical and Surgical Journal,* 1809, vol. 5, p. 319. In the year 1833, all the papers reported that the English historian, Dr. Lingard, had died of voluntary starvation at Dover in January; according to later accounts it was not Lingard himself but a kinsman of his who died. But in these accounts the individuals are for the most part described as mad, and it is no longer possible to ascertain how far this may have been the case. But I will here give a more recent account of this kind, if only to ensure the preservation of one of the rare instances of the striking and extraordinary phenomenon of human nature just mentioned, which, at any rate, apparently belongs to where I should like to assign it, and could hardly be explained in any other way. This recent account is to be found in the *Nürnberger Korrespondent* of July 29, 1813, in the following words:

"It is reported from Bern that in a dense forest near Thurnen a small hut was discovered in which was lying the decomposed corpse of a man who had been dead for about a month. His clothes gave little information about his social position. Two very fine shirts lay beside him. The most important thing was a Bible, interleaved with blank pages, which had been partly written on by the deceased. In it he announced the day of his departure from home (but it did not mention where his home was). He then said that he was driven into the wilderness by the spirit of God to pray and fast. On his journey to that spot, he had already fasted for seven days, and had then eaten again. After settling down here, he began to fast again, and indeed fasted for as many days. Every day was now indicated by a stroke, of which there were five, after which the pilgrim had presumably died. There was also found a letter to a clergyman about a sermon that the deceased had heard him preach; but the address was missing." Between this voluntary death springing from the extreme of asceticism and that resulting from despair there may be many different intermediate stages and combinations, which are indeed hard to explain; but human nature has depths, obscurities, and intricacies, whose elucidation and unfolding are of the very greatest difficulty.

We might perhaps regard the whole of our discussion (now concluded) of what I call the denial of the will as inconsistent with the previous explanation of necessity, that appertains just as much to motivation as to every other form of the principle of sufficient reason. As a result of that necessity, motives, like all causes, are only occasional causes on which the character unfolds its nature, and reveals it with the necessity of a natural law. For this reason we positively denied freedom as *liberum arbitrium indifferentiae*. Yet far from suppressing this here, I call it to mind. In truth, real freedom, in other words, independence of the principle of sufficient reason, belongs to the will as thing-in-itself, not to its phenomenon, whose essential form is everywhere this principle of sufficient reason, the element of necessity. But the only case where that freedom can become immediately visible in the phenomenon is the one where it makes an end of what appears, and because the mere phenomenon, insofar as it is a link in the chain of causes, namely the living body, still continues to exist in time that contains only phenomena, the will, manifesting itself through this phenomenon, is then in contradiction with it, since it denies what the phenomenon expresses. In such a case the genitals, for example, as the visibility of the sexual impulse, are there and in health; but yet in the innermost consciousness no sexual satisfaction is desired. The whole body is the visible expression of the will-to-live, yet the motives corresponding to this will no longer act; indeed the dissolution of the body, the end of the individual, and thus the greatest suppression of the natural will, is welcome and desired. Now the contradiction between our assertions, on the one hand, of the necessity of the will's determinations through motives according to the character, and our assertions, on the other, of the possibility of the whole suppression of the will, whereby motives become powerless, is only the repetition in the reflection of philosophy of this *real* contradiction that arises from the direct encroachment of the freedom of the will-in-itself, knowing no necessity, on the necessity of its phenomenon. But the key to the reconciliation of these contradictions lies in the fact that the state in which the character is withdrawn from the power of motives does not proceed directly from the will, but from a changed form of knowledge. Thus, so long as the knowledge is only that which is involved in the *principium individuationis,* and which positively follows the principle of sufficient reason, the power of the motives is irresistible. But when the *principium individuationis* is seen through, when the ideas, and indeed the inner nature of the thing-in-itself, are immediately recognized as the same will in all, and the result of this knowledge is a universal quieter of willing, then the individual motives become ineffective, because the kind of knowledge that corresponds to them is obscured and pushed into the background by knowledge of quite a different kind. Therefore the character can never partially change, but must, with the consistency of a law of nature, realize in the particular individual the will whose phenomenon it is in general and as a whole. But this whole, the character itself, can be entirely eliminated by the above-mentioned change of knowledge. It is this elimination or suppression at which Asmus marvels, as said above, and which he describes as the "catholic, transcendental change." It is also that which in the Christian Church is very appropriately called *new birth* or *regeneration,* and the knowledge from which it springs, the *effect of divine grace.* Therefore, it is not a question of a change, but of an entire suppression of the character; and so it happens that, however different the characters that arrived at that suppression were before it, they nevertheless show after it a great similarity in their mode of conduct, although each *speaks* very differently according to his concepts and dogmas.

Therefore, in this sense, the old philosophical argument about the freedom of the will, constantly contested and constantly maintained, is not without ground, and the Church dogma of the effect of grace and the new birth is also not without meaning and significance. But now we unexpectedly see both coincide into one, and can understand in what sense the admirable Malebranche could say: *"La liberté est un mystère"*;[31] and he was right. For just what the Christian mystics call the *effect of grace* and the *new birth*, is for us the only direct expression of the *freedom of the will*. It appears only when the will, after arriving at the knowledge of its own inner nature, obtains from this a *quieter*, and is thus removed from the effect of *motives* that lie in the province of a different kind of knowledge, whose objects are only phenomena. The possibility of the freedom that thus manifests itself is man's greatest prerogative, which is for ever wanting in the animal, because the condition for it is the deliberation of the faculty of reason, enabling him to survey the whole of life independently of the impression of the present moment. The animal is without any possibility of freedom, as indeed it is without the possibility of a real, and hence deliberate, elective decision after a previous complete conflict of motives, which for this purpose would have to be abstract representations. Therefore the hungry wolf buries its teeth in the flesh of the deer with the same necessity with which the stone falls to the ground, without the possibility of the knowledge that it is the mauled as well as the mauler. *Necessity is the kingdom of nature; freedom is the kingdom of grace.*

Now since, as we have seen, that *self-suppression of the will* comes from knowledge, but all knowledge and insight as such are independent of free choice, that denial of willing, that entrance into freedom, is not to be forcibly arrived at by intention or design, but comes from the innermost relation of knowing and willing in man; hence it comes suddenly, as if flying in from without. Therefore, the Church calls it the *effect of grace;* but just as she still represents it as depending on the acceptance of grace, so too the effect of the

---

31. Freedom is a mystery.—Tr.

quieter is ultimately an act of the freedom of the will. In consequence of such an effect of grace, man's whole inner nature is
fundamentally changed and reversed, so that he no longer wills
anything of all that he previously willed so intensely; thus a new
man, so to speak, actually takes the place of the old. For this
reason, the Church calls this consequence of the effects of grace
new birth or *regeneration.* For what she calls the *natural man,* to
whom she denies all capacity for good, is that very will-to-live that
must be denied if salvation is to be attained from an existence
like ours. Behind our existence lies something else that becomes
accessible to us only by our shaking off the world.

Considering not the individuals according to the principle of
sufficient reason, but the idea of man in its unity, the Christian
teaching symbolizes *nature,* the *affirmation of the will-to-live, in
Adam.* His sin bequeathed to us, in other words, our unity with
him in the idea, which manifests itself in time through the bond of
generation, causes us all to partake of suffering and eternal death.
On the other hand, the Christian teaching symbolizes *grace,* the
denial of the will, salvation, in the God become man. As he is free
from all sinfulness, in other words, from all willing of life, he cannot, like us, have resulted from the most decided affirmation of the
will; nor can he, like us, have a body that is through and through
only concrete will, phenomenon of the will, but, born of a pure
virgin, he has only a phantom body. This last is what was taught
by the Docetae, certain Fathers of the Church, who in this respect
are very consistent. It was taught especially by Apelles, against
whom and his followers Tertullian revolted. But even Augustine
comments on the passage, Rom. 8:3, "God sending his Son in the
likeness of sinful flesh," and says: *"Non enim caro peccati erat,
quae non de carnali delectatione nata erat: sed tamen inerat ei
similitudo carnis peccati, quia mortalis caro erat"* (*Liber 83 Quaes-
tionum, qu.* 66).[32] He also teaches in his work entitled *Opus Imper-
fectum,* 1:47, that original sin is sin and punishment at the same
time. It is already to be found in newborn children, but shows itself
only when they grow up. Nevertheless the origin of this sin is to
be inferred from the will of the sinner. This sinner was Adam, but

---

32. For it was not a sinful flesh, as it was not born of carnal desire; but yet
the form of sinful flesh was in it, because it was a mortal flesh.—TR.

we all existed in him; Adam became miserable, and in him we have all become miserable. The doctrine of original sin (affirmation of the will) and of salvation (denial of the will) is really the great truth that constitutes the kernel of Christianity, while the rest is in the main only clothing and covering, or something accessory. Accordingly, we should interpret Jesus Christ always in the universal, as the symbol or personification of the denial of the will-to-live, but not in the individual, whether according to his mythical history in the Gospels, or according to the probably true history lying at the root thereof. For neither the one nor the other will easily satisfy us entirely. It is merely the vehicle of that first interpretation for the people, who always demand something founded on fact. That Christianity has recently forgotten its true significance, and has degenerated into shallow optimism, does not concern us here.

It is further an original and evangelical doctrine of Christianity, which Augustine, with the consent of the heads of the Church, defended against the platitudes of the Pelagians; and to purify this of errors and reestablish it was the principal aim of Luther's efforts, as is expressly declared in his book *De Servo Arbitrio;* namely, the doctrine that the *will is not free,* but is originally subject to a propensity for evil. Therefore the works of the will are always sinful and imperfect, and can never satisfy justice; finally, these works can never save us, but faith alone can do this. Yet this faith itself does not originate from resolution and free will, but through the *effect of grace* without our participation, like something coming to us from outside. Not only the dogmas previously mentioned, but also this last genuinely evangelical dogma is among those that an ignorant and dull opinion at the present day rejects as absurd or conceals, since, in spite of Augustine and Luther, this opinion adheres to the Pelagian plain common sense, which is just what present-day rationalism is. It treats as antiquated precisely those profound dogmas that are peculiar and essential to Christianity in the narrowest sense. On the other hand, it clings to, and regards as the principal thing, only the dogma originating in and retained from Judaism, and connected with Christianity only in a historical way.[33] We, however, recognize in the above-mentioned doctrine the

---

33. How much this is the case is seen from the fact that all the contradictions and inconceivable mysteries contained in the Christian dogmatics and consistently systematized by Augustine, which have led precisely to the opposite Pelagian insipid-

truth that is in complete agreement with our own investigations. Thus we see that genuine virtue and saintliness of disposition have their first origin not in deliberate free choice (works), but in knowledge (faith), precisely as we developed it also from our principal idea. If it were works, springing from motives and deliberate intention, that led to the blissful state, then, however we may turn it, virtue would always be only a prudent, methodical, farseeing egoism. But the faith to which the Christian Church promises salvation is this: that as through the fall of the first man we all partake of sin, and are subject to death and perdition, we are also all saved through grace and by the divine mediator taking upon himself our awful guilt, and this indeed entirely without any merit of our own (of the person). For what can result from the intentional (motive-determined) action of the person, namely, works, can never justify us, by its very nature, just because it is *intentional* action brought

---

ity, vanish, as soon as we abstract from the fundamental Jewish dogma, and recognize that man is not the work of another, but of his own will. Then all is at once clear and correct; then there is no need of a freedom in the *operari*, for it lies in the *esse;* and here also lies the sin as original sin. The effect of grace, however, is our own. With the present-day rationalistic view, on the other hand, many doctrines of the Augustinian dogmatics, established in the New Testament, appear absolutely untenable and even revolting, for example, predestination. Accordingly, what is really Christian is then rejected, and a return is made to crude Judaism. But the miscalculation or primary defect of Christian dogmatics lies where it is never sought, namely, in what is withdrawn from all investigation as settled and certain. Take this away, and the whole of dogmatics is rational; for that dogma ruins theology, as it does all the other sciences. Thus, if we study the Augustinian theology in the books *De Civitate Dei* (especially in the fourteenth book), we experience something analogous to the case when we try to make a body stand, whose center of gravity falls outside it; however we may turn and place it, it always topples over again. So also here, in spite of all the efforts and sophisms of Augustine, the guilt of the world and its misery always fall back on God, who made everything and everything that is in everything, and who also knew how things would turn out. I have already shown in my essay *On the Freedom of the Will* (chap. 4, pp. 66-68 of the first edition) that Augustine himself was aware of the difficulty, and was puzzled by it. In the same way, the contradiction between the goodness of God and the misery of the world, as also that between the freedom of the will and the foreknowledge of God, is the inexhaustible theme of a controversy, lasting nearly a hundred years, between the Cartesians, Malebranche, Leibniz, Bayle, Clarke, Arnauld, and many others. The only dogma fixed for the disputants is the existence of God together with his attributes, and they all incessantly turn in a circle, since they try to bring these things into harmony, in other words, to solve an arithmetical sum that never comes right, but the remainder of which appears now in one place, now in another, after it has been concealed elsewhere. But it does not occur to anyone that the source of the dilemma is to be looked for in the fundamental assumption, although it palpably obtrudes itself. Bayle alone shows that he notices this.

about by motives, and hence *opus operatum*. Thus in this faith it is implied first of all that our state is originally and essentially an incurable one, and that we need *deliverance* from it; then that we ourselves belong essentially to evil, and are so firmly bound to it that our works according to law and precept, i.e., according to motives, can never satisfy justice or save us, but salvation is to be gained only through faith, in other words, through a changed way of knowledge. This faith can come only through grace, and hence as from without. This means that salvation is something quite foreign to our person, and points to a denial and surrender of this very person being necessary for salvation. Works, the observance of the law as such, can never justify, because they are always an action from motives. Luther requires (in his book *De Libertate Christiana*) that, after faith has made its appearance, good works shall result from it entirely of themselves, as its symptoms, its fruits; certainly not as something that in itself pretends to merit, justification, or reward, but occurs quite arbitrarily and gratuitously. We also represented, as resulting from an ever-clearer discernment of the *principium individuationis,* first of all merely free justice, then affection extending to the complete surrender of egoism, and finally resignation or denial of the will.

Here I have introduced these dogmas of Christian theology, in themselves foreign to philosophy, merely in order to show that the ethics that results from the whole of our discussion, and is in complete agreement and connection with all its parts, although possibly new and unprecedented according to the expression, is by no means so in essence. On the contrary, this system of ethics fully agrees with the Christian dogmas proper, and, according to its essentials, was contained and present even in these very dogmas. It is also just as much in agreement with the doctrines and ethical precepts of the sacred books of India, which again are presented in quite different forms. At the same time, the calling to mind of the dogmas of the Christian Church served to explain and elucidate the apparent contradiction between the *necessity* of all the manifestations of the character with the presentation of motives (kingdom of nature) on the one hand, and the *freedom* of the will-in-itself to deny itself and to abolish the character, on the other, together with all the necessity of the motives that is based on this character (kingdom of grace).

In now bringing to a conclusion the main points of ethics, and with these the whole development of that one idea the imparting of which was my object, I do not wish by any means to conceal an objection concerning this last part of the discussion. On the contrary, I want to show that this objection lies in the nature of the case, and that it is quite impossible to remedy it. This objection is that, after our observations have finally brought us to the point where we have before our eyes in perfect saintliness the denial and surrender of all willing, and thus a deliverance from a world whose whole existence presented itself to us as suffering, this now appears to us as a transition into empty *nothingness*.

On this I must first of all observe that the concept of *nothing* is essentially relative, and always refers to a definite something that it negates. This quality has been attributed (especially by Kant) merely to the *nihil privativum* indicated by − in contrast to +. This negative sign (−) from the opposite point of view might become +, and, in opposition to this *nihil privativum*, the *nihil negativum* has been set up, which would in every respect be nothing. For this purpose, the logical contradiction that does away with itself has been used as an example. But considered more closely, an absolute nothing, a really proper *nihil negativum*, is not even conceivable, but everything of this kind, considered from a higher standpoint or subsumed under a wider concept, is always only a *nihil privativum*. Every nothing is thought of as such only in relation to something else; it presupposes this relation, and thus that other thing also. Even a logical contradiction is only a relative nothing; it is no thought of our faculty of reason; yet it is not on that account an absolute nothing. For it is a word combination; it is an example of the unthinkable that is necessarily required in logic to demonstrate the laws of thought. Therefore, if for this purpose we look for such an example, we shall stick to the nonsense as the positive we are just looking for, and skip the sense as the negative. Thus every *nihil negativum* or absolute nothing, if subordinated to a higher concept, will appear as a mere *nihil privativum* or relative nothing, which can always change signs with what it negates, so that that would then be thought of as negation, but it itself as affirmation. This also agrees with the result of the difficult dialectical investigation on the conception of nothing that is given by Plato in the *Sophist* [258 D] (pp. 277-287, *Bip.*): *It is the nature of* being different, *of which we have demonstrated that it exists and is dispersed piecemeal over all being in* mutual relationship, *and since we opposed to being every single particle of this nature, we have ventured to assert that precisely this is in truth* nonbeing.

What is universally assumed as positive, what we call *being*, the negation of which is expressed by the concept *nothing* in its most general significance, is exactly the world as representation, which I have shown to be the objectivity, the mirror, of the will. We ourselves are also this will and this world, and to it belongs the representation in general as one aspect of it. The form of this representation is space and time; and so, for this point of view, everything that exists must be in some place and at some time. Then the concept, the material of philosophy, and finally the word, the sign of the concept, also belong to the representation. Denial, abolition, turning of the will are also abolition and disappearance of the world, of its mirror. If we no longer perceive the will in this mirror, we ask in vain in what direction it has turned, and then, because it no longer has any *where* and any *when*, we complain that it is lost in nothingness.

If a contrary point of view were possible for us, it would cause the signs to be changed, and would show what exists for us as nothing, and this nothing as that which exists. But so long as we ourselves are the will-to-live, this last, namely, the nothing as that which exists, can be known and expressed by us only negatively, since the old saying of Empedocles, that like can be known only by like, deprives us here of all knowledge, just as, conversely, on it ultimately rests the possibility of all our actual knowledge, in other words, the world as representation, or the objectivity of the will; for the world is the self-knowledge of the will.

If, however, it should be absolutely insisted on that somehow a positive knowledge is to be acquired of what philosophy can express only negatively as denial of the will, nothing would be left but to refer to that state that is experienced by all who have attained to complete denial of the will, and that is denoted by the names ecstasy, rapture, illumination, union with God, and so on. But such a state cannot really be called knowledge, since it no longer has the form of subject and object; moreover, it is accessible only to one's own experience that cannot be further communicated.

We, however, who consistently occupy the standpoint of philosophy, must be satisfied here with negative knowledge, content to have reached the final landmark of the positive. If, therefore, we have recognized the inner nature of the world as will, and have seen in all its phenomena only the objectivity of the will; and if we have followed these from the unconscious impulse of obscure natural forces up to the most conscious action of man, we shall by no means evade the consequence that, with the free denial, the surrender, of the will, all those phenomena also are now abolished. That constant pressure and effort, without aim and without rest, at all grades of objectivity in which and through which the world exists; the multifarious forms succeeding one another in gradation; the whole phenomenon of the will; finally, the universal forms of this phenomenon, time and space, and also the last fundamental form of these, subject and object; all these are abolished with the will. No will: no representation, no world.

Before us there is certainly left only nothing; but that which struggles against this flowing away into nothing, namely, our nature, is indeed just the will-to-live that we ourselves are, just as it is our world. That we abhor nothingness so much is simply another way of saying that we will life so much, and that we are nothing but this will and know nothing but it alone. But we now turn our glance from our own needy and perplexed nature to those who have overcome the world, in whom the will, having reached complete self-knowledge, has found itself again in everything, and then freely denied itself, and who then merely wait to see the last trace of the will vanish with the body that is animated by that trace. Then, instead of the restless pressure and effort; instead of the constant transition from desire to apprehension and from joy to sorrow; instead of the never-satisfied and never-dying hope that constitutes the life dream of the man who wills, we see that peace that is higher than all reason, that oceanlike calmness of the spirit, that deep tranquillity, that unshakable confidence and serenity, whose mere reflection in the countenance, as depicted by Raphael and Correggio, is a complete and certain gospel. Only knowledge remains; the will has vanished. We then look with deep and painful yearning at that state, beside which the miserable and desperate nature of our own appears in the clearest light by the contrast. Yet this consideration is the only one that can permanently console us, when, on the one hand, we have recognized incurable suffering and endless misery as essential to the phenomenon of the will, to the world, and on the other see the world melt away with the abolished will, and retain before us only empty nothingness. In this way, therefore, by contemplating the life and conduct of saints, to meet with whom is of course rarely granted to us in our own experience, but who are brought to our notice by their recorded history, and, vouched for with the stamp of truth by art, we have to banish the dark impression of that nothingness, which as the final goal hovers behind all virtue and holiness, and which we fear as children fear darkness. We must not even evade it, as the Indians do, by myths and meaningless words, such as reabsorption in *Brahman,* or the *Nirvana* of the Buddhists. On the contrary, we freely acknowledge that what remains after the complete abolition of the will is, for all who are still full of the will, assuredly nothing. But also conversely, to those in whom the will has turned and denied itself, this very real world of ours with all its suns and galaxies, is—nothing.[34*]

Translated by E. F. J. Payne

Nothing but the Death Wish by one living on Death Wealth (inheritance)

[34*]. This is also the Prajna-Paramita of the Buddhists, the "beyond all knowledge," in other words, the point where subject and object no longer exist. See I. J. Schmidt, *Ueber das Mahajana und Pradschna-Paramita.*

the caste system — the will to leave a will.
who invented

PART 3

13

The Foundation of Ethics

16

Statement and Proof of the Only
Genuine Moral Incentive

After the foregoing, absolutely necessary preliminary remarks, I now come to the demonstration of the true incentive underlying all actions of genuine moral worth. As such, it will prove by its seriousness and unquestionable reality to be very far removed from all hairsplitting, subtle sophistries, airy assertions, and a priori soap bubbles, which things all previous systems have tried to make the source of moral conduct and the basis of ethics. I will not *advance* this moral incentive, to be accepted or not as the case may be, but will actually *prove* that it is the only one possible. But as such a proof requires the joining of many ideas, I mention first a few premises that are the hypotheses of the argument and may well be regarded as *axioms,* with the exception of the last two, which refer to the discussions previously given.

(1) No action can take place without a sufficient motive, any more than a stone can move without a sufficient push or pull.

(2) In precisely the same way, an action cannot fail to take place when there is present a motive that is sufficient for the character of the doer, unless a stronger countermotive renders inevitable its nonperformance.

(3) What moves the will is simply weal and woe in general and is taken in the widest sense of the term; just as, conversely, weal

and woe signify "in agreement with or contrary to a will." Hence every motive must have a reference to weal and woe.

(4) Consequently, every action refers to, and has as its ultimate object, a being susceptible to weal and woe.

(5) This being is either the doer himself or another, who then takes a *passive* part in the action, since it is done to his detriment or his advantage and benefit.

(6) Every action that has as its ultimate object the weal and woe of the doer himself is *egoistic*.

(7) All that is said here about actions applies equally to the nonperformance of such actions for which motive and countermotive exist.

(8) As a result of the discussion given in the previous section, *egoism* and the *moral worth* of an action absolutely exclude each other. If an action has as its motive an egoistic aim, it cannot have any moral worth. If it is to have moral worth, its motive cannot be egoistic aim, direct or indirect, near or remote.

(9) In consequence of the elimination, carried out in section 5, of the so-called duties to ourselves, the moral significance of an action can lie only in its reference to others. Only in respect to these can it have moral worth or worthlessness, and accordingly be an action of justice or philanthropy, as well as the reverse of them.

From these premises the following is evident: the *weal and woe* that (according to premise 3) must, as its ultimate object, underlie everything done or left undone, are those either of the doer himself, or of someone else who plays a passive part in the action. *In the first case* the action is necessarily *egoistic*, since an interested motive underlies it. This is not merely the case with actions we obviously undertake for our own profit and advantage, which are the most usual, but is precisely the same whenever we expect from an action some remote result *for ourselves*, either in this world or the next. It is no different when we have in view our honor, our reputation in the eyes of others, the esteem of anyone, the sympathy of onlookers, and so on. It is no less true when we intend through this action to uphold a maxim from whose general observance we expect *eventualiter* an advantage *to ourselves*, as, for instance, the maxim of justice, of universal support and assistance, and so on. The action is also egoistic when we consider it advisable to obey some absolute command that comes from an admittedly unknown but obviously superior authority; for nothing can induce us to obey except *fear* of the evil consequences of *disobedience,* although they may be conceived only generally and indefinitely. Again, it is egoism that prompts us when we endeavor to assert, by something done or left undone, our own high opinion of ourselves (clearly or vaguely conceived), and of our worth and dignity, an opinion that we should otherwise have to give up and thereby see our pride humbled. Finally, it is also egoism when, in accordance with Wolff's principles, we try by an action to work out our own perfection. In short, we can put what we like as the ultimate motive of an action, the result will always be that, in some roundabout way, the real incentive is ultimately *the doer's own weal and woe.* The action is, therefore, *egoistic,* and consequently *without moral worth.* There is only one single case in which this does not take place, namely, when the ultimate motive for doing or omitting to do a thing is precisely and exclusively centered in the *weal and woe of someone else,* who plays a passive part; thus the man who plays the active part in doing or omitting to do something has in view simply and solely the weal and woe *of another;* he has absolutely no other object than that the other man will be left unharmed, or will even receive help, assistance, and relief. It is *this aim alone* that gives what is done or left undone the stamp of *moral worth.* This, then, depends exclusively on the fact that something is done or left undone merely for the benefit and advantage *of another.* Whenever this is *not* the case, the *weal and woe* that incite to or deter from *every* action can be only those *of the doer himself;* but then the action or its nonperformance is always *egoistic* and consequently *without moral worth.*

But now if my action is to be done simply and solely *for the sake of another,* then *his weal and woe* must be *directly my motive,* just as *my* weal and woe are so in the case of all other actions. This narrows the expression of our problem, which can be stated as follows: how is it possible for *another's* weal and woe to move my will immediately, that is to say, in exactly the same way in which it is usually moved only by my own weal and woe? Thus, how is it possible for *another's* weal and woe to become directly my motive, and this sometimes to such a degree that I more or less subordinate to them my own weal and woe, normally the sole source of my motives? Obviously only through that other man's becoming *the ultimate object* of my will in the same way as I myself otherwise am and hence through my directly desiring *his* weal and not *his* woe just as immediately as I ordinarily do only *my own.* But this necessarily presupposes that, in the case of his *woe* as such, I suffer directly with him. I feel *his* woe just as I ordinarily feel only my own; and, likewise, I directly desire his weal in the same way I otherwise desire only my own. But this requires that I am in some way *identified with him,* in other words, that this entire *difference* between me and everyone else, which is the very basis of my egoism, is eliminated, to a certain extent at least. Now since I do not exist *inside the other man's skin,* then only by means of the *knowledge* I have of him, that is, of the representation of him in my head, can I identify myself with him to such an extent that my deed declares that difference abolished. However, the process here analyzed is not one that is imagined or invented; on the contrary, it is perfectly real and indeed by no means infrequent. It is the everyday phenomenon of *compassion,* of the immediate *participation,* independent of all ulterior considerations, primarily in the *suffering* of another, and thus in the prevention or elimination of it; for all satisfaction and all well-being and happiness consist in this. It is simply and solely this compassion that is the real basis of all *voluntary* justice and *genuine* loving-kindness. Only insofar as an action has sprung from compassion does it have moral value; and every action resulting from any other motives has none. As soon as this compassion is aroused, the weal and woe of another are nearest to my heart in exactly the same way, although not always in the same degree, as otherwise only my own are. Hence the difference between him and me is now no longer absolute.

This event is certainly astonishing, indeed, mysterious. In fact it is the great mystery of ethics; it is the primary and original phenomenon of ethics, the boundary mark beyond which only metaphysical speculation can venture to step. In that event we see abolished the partition that, by the light of nature (as the old theologians call the faculty of reason), absolutely separates one being from another; the nonego has to a certain extent become the ego. For the present, however, we will leave untouched the metaphysical explanation of the phenomenon, and will first see whether all actions of voluntary justice and genuine philanthropy really proceed from this event. Our problem will then be solved, since we shall have demonstrated the ultimate foundation of morality to be in human nature itself. That foundation itself cannot again be a problem of *ethics,* but rather, like everything that exists *as such,* of *metaphysics.* But the metaphysical explanation of the primary ethical phenomenon lies outside the question set by the Royal Society, which is directed to the basis of ethics, and at all events, such explanation can be added only as a supplement to be given and taken at our discretion. Now before I turn to the derivation of the cardinal virtues from the fundamental incentive just given, I have still to add two essential observations.

(1) For the purpose of easier comprehension, I have simplified the above derivation of compassion, as the sole source of actions of moral worth, by intentionally leaving out of account the incentive of *malice.* Like compassion, this too is without self-interest, and makes its ultimate aim the *pain* of another. But by including it, we can now state the above proof more completely and rigorously: There are generally only *three fundamental incentives* of human actions, and all possible motives operate solely through their stimulation:

(a) Egoism: this desires one's own weal (is boundless).

(b) Malice: this desires another's woe (goes to the limits of extreme cruelty).

(c) Compassion: this desires another's weal (goes to the length of nobleness and magnanimity).

Every human action must be attributable to one of these incentives, although two can also act in combination. Now as we have assumed that actions of moral worth are given facts, they too must result from one of these fundamental incentives. But by virtue of the eighth premise, they cannot spring from the *first* still less from the *second:* for all actions that arise from the second are morally bad, while the first incentive produces actions that, from a moral point of view, are in part neither good nor bad. They must, therefore, come from the *third* incentive; and this will receive its confirmation a posteriori in what follows.

(2) Direct sympathy with another is restricted to his *suffering.* It is not roused, at any rate not directly, by his *well-being* on the contrary, in and by itself this leaves us unmoved. J.-J. Rousseau also says the same thing in *Émile* (book 4): *Première maxime: Il*

*n'est pas dans le coeur humain de se mettre à la place des gens,
qui sont plus heureux que nous, mais seulement de ceux, qui sont
plus à plaindre,* etc.[1]

The reason for this is that pain, suffering that includes all want,
privation, need, in fact every wish or desire, is *that which is positive
and directly felt and experienced.* On the other hand, the nature
of satisfaction, enjoyment, and happiness consists solely in the re-
moval of a privation, the stilling of a pain; and so these have a
negative effect. Therefore, need and desire are the condition of
every pleasure or enjoyment. Plato recognized this, and excepted
only pleasant odors and intellectual pleasures (*Republic* 9, pages
264f. Bip.). Voltaire also says: *Il n'est de vrais plaisirs, qu'avec de
vrais besoins.*[2] Thus pain is something *positive* that automatically
makes itself known; satisfaction and pleasures are something *negative,* the mere elimination of the former. To this is due, first of all,
the fact that only another's suffering, want, danger, and helplessness awaken our sympathy directly and as such. The fortunate
and contented man *as such* leaves us indifferent really because his
state is negative, namely, an absence of pain, want, and distress. It
is true that we can take pleasure in the good fortune, well-being,
and enjoyment of others; but then this is secondary, brought about
by the fact that their suffering and privation had previously dis-
tressed us. Or else we share the joys and pleasures of a man not
as such, but insofar as he is our child, father, friend, relation,
servant, subject, and so on. Our immediate sympathy is not stirred
by the good fortune or pleasure of another *purely as such,* as it is
by the suffering, privation, and misfortune of another *purely as
such.* If, even *for ourselves,* our activity is stirred only by our sufferings, which also include all wants, needs, desires, and indeed boredom, whereas a state of contentedness and prosperity leaves us
inactive and in idle unconcern, how could it not be just the same
in regard to others? For indeed our sympathy rests on an identifica-
tion with them. Even the sight of success and enjoyment *purely as
such* can very easily excite envy, to which everyone is prone, and

1. First maxim: it is not peculiar to the human heart to put itself in the position
of those who are more fortunate than we, but only of those who are more pitiable.—Tr.

2. There are no true pleasures without true needs. (*Summary of Ecclesiastes
[Précis de l'Écclésiaste],* 5:30.)—Tr.

which has found a place among the antimoral forces previously mentioned.

In consequence of the above discussion on compassion as a state of being immediately motivated by the sufferings of another, I must censure the error of Cassina, which has since been so often repeated (*Analytical Essay on Compassion [Saggio analitico sulla compassione]*, 1788; German translation by Pockels, 1790). His view is that compassion arises from an instantaneous deception of the imagination, since we put ourselves in the position of the sufferer, and have the idea that we are suffering *his* pains in *our* person. This is by no means the case; on the contrary, at every moment we remain clearly conscious that *he* is the sufferer, not *we;* and it is precisely in *his* person, not in ours, that we feel the suffering, to our grief and sorrow. We suffer *with* him and hence *in* him; we feel his pain as *his*, and do/not imagine that it is ours. In fact, the happier our state, and hence the more the consciousness of it is contrasted with other man's fate, the more susceptible we are to compassion. But the explanation of the possibility of this highly important phenomenon is not so easy; nor can it be reached on the purely psychological path, as was attempted by Cassina. It can be arrived at only metaphysically, and in the last section I shall attempt to give such an explanation.

But I now turn to the derivation of actions of genuine moral worth from the source already indicated. In the previous section I laid down the rule as the universal maxim of such actions and consequently as the supreme principle of ethics: *Neminem laede; imo omnes, quantum potes, juva.*[3] As this maxim contains *two* clauses, the actions that correspond to it automatically fall into two classes.

17

The Virtue of Justice

If we consider more closely the occurrence of compassion, which previously was shown to be the primary ethical phenomenon, it is at once evident that there are two clearly separate degrees wherein another's suffering can directly become my motive, in other words,

3. Injure no one; on the contrary, help everyone as much as you can.—TR.

can determine me to do or omit to do something. In the first degree, by counteracting egoistic and malicious motives, compassion prevents me from causing suffering to another and hence from becoming myself the cause of another's pain, and thus from bringing about something that does not yet exist. In the second place, there is the higher degree where compassion works positively and incites me to active help. The separation between so-called duties of law and duties of virtue, more correctly between justice and philanthropy, which was effected by Kant in so forced and unnatural a manner,[4] results here entirely of itself and thereby testifies to the correctness of the principle. It is the natural, unmistakable, and sharp boundary between the negative and positive, between doing no injury and helping. The terms used before, namely, duties of law and duties of virtue, the latter also called duties of love—imperfect duties—are in the first place at fault because they coordinate the *genus* with the *species;* for justice is also a virtue. Then underlying these terms is the much too wide extension of the concept *duty,* which I shall later reduce to its true limits. I shall therefore put in the place of the above two duties two virtues, those of justice and philanthropy. I call them cardinal virtues, since from them all the others follow practically, and may be derived theoretically. Both have their roots in natural compassion. But this itself is an undeniable fact of human consciousness, is essential to it, and does not depend on presuppositions, concepts, religions, dogmas, myths, training, and education. On the contrary, it is original and immediate, it resides in human nature itself, and for this very reason, it endures in all circumstances and appears in all countries and at all times. Therefore, everywhere appeal is confidently made to it as something necessarily existing in everyone, and nowhere is it among the "strange gods." Furthermore, anyone appearing to be wanting in compassion is called inhuman, and so "humanity" is often used as its synonym.

Thus the first degree of the effectiveness of this genuine and natural moral incentive is called *negative.* Originally, we are all inclined to injustice and violence, because our needs, desires, anger, and hatred immediately enter consciousness and thus have the *jus primi occupantis.*[5] On the other hand, the sufferings of others that

4. In *Foundations,* Academy 424.—Tr.
5. The right of first occupancy.—Tr.

are caused by our injustice and violence, enter consciousness merely on the secondary path of the *representation* and only through experience, thus *indirectly*. And so Seneca says, *Ad neminem ante bona mens venit, quam mala* (*Epistles* 50:7).[6] Therefore the first degree of the effect of compassion is that it opposes and impedes those sufferings that I intend to cause to others by my inherent antimoral forces. It calls out to me "Stop!"; it stands before the other man like a bulwark, protecting him from the injury that my egoism or malice would otherwise urge me to do. Thus there arises from this first degree of compassion the maxim, *Neminem laede*,[7] i.e., the fundamental principle of *justice*. Only here does this virtue have its origin—genuine, purely moral, and free from all admixture—and nowhere else, since then it would have to rest on egoism. If my disposition is susceptible to compassion up to that degree, it will restrain me, wherever and whenever I feel inclined to use another's sufferings as a means to the attainment of my ends; it is immaterial whether that suffering is instantaneous or comes later, whether it is direct or indirect, or effected through intermediate links. Consequently, I shall just as little seize another man's property as I shall his person; I shall cause him just as little mental suffering as bodily; I shall, therefore, refrain not only from every physical injury, but also from the infliction of mental suffering through mortification, alarm, annoyance, or slander. The same compassion will prevent me from seeking to satisfy my desires at the expense of women's happiness or from seducing another man's wife, or even from ruining youths morally and physically by tempting them to commit pederasty. However, it is by no means necessary for compassion actually to be stirred in each individual case, for it would often come too late. On the contrary, the maxim, *Neminem laede,* arises in noble dispositions from the knowledge, gained once for all, of the suffering that every unjust action necessarily brings to others and that is intensified by the feeling of enduring wrong, that is, of someone else's superior strength. Rational reflection raises noble dispositions to the firm resolution, grasped once and for all, of respecting the rights of everyone, of never allowing themselves to encroach on them, of keeping themselves

6. To no one do good feelings come before the bad.—Tʀ.
7. Injure no one.—Tʀ.

free from the self-reproach of being the cause of another's suffering. Accordingly, noble dispositions will not shift to the shoulders of others, by force or cunning, the burdens and sorrows of life that circumstances bring everyone; but, on the contrary, will bear their allotted share in order not to double that of another. For although *principles* and abstract knowledge generally are by no means the original source or first foundation of morality, they are nevertheless indispensable to a moral course of life: they are the receptacle or reservoir that stores the habit of mind that has sprung from the fount of all morality, a habit of mind that does not flow at every moment, but when the occasion for its application arises, flows along the proper channel. There is thus an analogy between what is moral and what is physiological, for example, the gallbladder is necessary as the reservoir for the product of the liver, and many similar cases. Without *principles* firmly held, we should inevitably be at the mercy of antimoral tendencies when, through external impressions, these tendencies were stirred to emotions. *Self-control* is the steadfast adherence to and observance of principles, in spite of the motives that act against them. Here too is to be found the reason why women are as a rule inferior to men in the virtue of justice, and thus of uprightness and conscientiousness. Owing to the weakness of their reasoning faculty, they are far less capable than men of understanding and sticking to universal *principles*, and of taking them as a guide. Hence injustice and deceitfulness are the most frequent vices of women, and lies are their proper element. On the other hand, they surpass men in the virtue of *philanthropy* or *loving-kindness*, for the origin of this is in most cases *intuitive* and therefore appeals directly to compassion, to which women are decidedly more easily susceptible. But for women, only what is intuitive, present, and immediately real truly exists; what is knowable only by means of concepts, what is remote, absent, past, or future, cannot really be grasped by them. Here too we have compensation; justice is more a masculine virtue, loving-kindness more a feminine. The very thought of seeing women administer justice raises a laugh; but the sisters of mercy surpass even the brothers of charity. Now as the *animal* totally lacks abstract or rational knowledge, it is quite incapable of resolutions, to say nothing of principles; it is consequently incapable of *self-control* and is helplessly abandoned to impression and emotion. This is precisely why the animal has no conscious *morality*, although the species show great differences of goodness and badness of character, and in the highest genera, even great individuality. As a result of what has been said, compassion operates in the individual actions of the just man only indirectly, by means of principles, and not so much *actu* as *potentiâ;* much in the same way as in statics the greater *velocity,* which is produced by the greater length of one scalebeam and by virtue of which the smaller mass keeps the greater in equilibrium, operates in a state of rest only *potentiâ,* and yet wholly as though it did so *actu.* Compassion, however, always remains ready to come forward *actu.* Therefore, when, in individual cases, the established maxim of justice shows signs of breaking down, no motive (egoistic motives excluded of course) is more effective for supporting it and putting new life into just resolutions than that drawn from the fountainhead itself, namely, compassion. This holds good not merely where it is a question of personal injury, but also where damage to property is concerned, for example, when anyone feels inclined to keep something of value he has found. If in such cases we exclude all motives prompted by worldly wisdom and religion, nothing will bring us back to the path of justice so readily as the mental picture of the trouble, grief, and lamentation of the loser. This truth is felt; for it often happens that the public appeal for the return of lost money has the assurance added that the loser is poor, a domestic servant, and so on.

It is hoped that these observations will clarify that, however little this appears to be the case at first sight, justice as a genuine voluntary virtue certainly has it origin in compassion. If, however, anyone should suppose this soil too poor and meager for that great and really cardinal virtue to be capable of taking root, he should bear in mind the above remarks, and remember how small is the amount of genuine, voluntary, unselfish, and plain justice to be found among men. He should note how justice always occurs only as a surprising exception, and its counterfeit, the justice that rests on mere prudence and is everywhere advertised, is related to it in quality and quantity as copper is to gold. I would like to call counterfeit justice *copper* and the genuine *gold.* For it is the latter that, according to Hesiod, leaves the earth in the iron age in order to dwell with the celestial gods. The root we have indicated is vigorous enough for this rare and always only delicate plant.

Accordingly, *injustice or wrong* always consists in *injuring* another. The concept of *wrong* is, therefore, *positive*, and antecedent to that of *right*. The concept of right is *negative*, and denotes merely those actions that can be done without injury to others, that is, without *wrong* being done. It is easy to see that to such actions also belong all those whose sole object is to ward off an attempted wrong. For no participation in the interests of another, no sympathy for him, can require me to let myself be injured by him, that is to say, to suffer wrong. That the concept of *right* is *negative* in contrast to that of *wrong*, which is *positive*, is also seen in the first interpretation of this idea, given at the beginning of his work, by Hugo Grotius, the father of philosophical jurisprudence: *Jus hic nihil aliud, quam quod justum est significat, idque negante magis sensu, quam ajente, ut jus sit, quod injustum non est* (*De jure belli et pacis,* book 1, chap. 1, section 3).[8] Contrary to appearance, the negative nature of justice is established even in the trite definition, "Give to each his own." If a man has his own, there is no need to give it to him; and so the meaning is, "Take from no one what is his own." Since the demand of justice is merely negative, it can be enforced; for the *Neminem laede*[9] can be practiced simultaneously by all. Here the compulsory institution is *the State,* whose sole purpose is to protect individuals from one another and the whole from external foes. A few German philosophasters of this mercenary age would like to distort the State into an institution for spreading morality and edifying instruction; but here lurks in the background the Jesuitical purpose of doing away with personal freedom and individual development, in order to make men into mere wheels of a Chinese machine of state and religion. This is the path that once led to inquisitions, autos-da-fé, and religious wars. Frederick the Great declared that he would never tread it, when he said: "In my country everyone shall be able to work out his own salvation in his own way." On the other hand, we still see everywhere (with the exception of North America, which is more ap-

---

8. Justice here denotes nothing but what is just, and indeed more in the negative sense than in the positive, insofar as justice is that which is not unjust. *The Law of War and Peace.*—Tr.

9. Injure no one.—Tr.

parent than real) the State undertake even the provision for the metaphysical needs of its members. Governments appear to have chosen as their principle the aphorism of Quintus Curtius: *Nulla res efficacius multitudinem regit, quam superstitio: alioquin impotens, saeva, mutabilis; ubi vana religione capta est, melius vatibus, quam ducibus suis paret.*[10]

The concepts *wrong* and *right* are synonymous with doing harm and not doing harm, and to the latter belongs also the warding off of injury. They are obviously independent of, and antecedent to, all positive legislation. Hence there is a purely ethical or natural right and a pure doctrine of right, in other words, one that is independent of all positive statute. It is true that the principles of this doctrine have an empirical origin insofar as they arise from the concept of *doing injury*. In themselves, however, they rest on the pure understanding that a priori furnishes ready to hand the principle *Causa causae est causa effectus,*[11] which here says that the other man, not I, is the cause of whatever I must do to ward off the injury he intends to do to me; and so I can resist all encroachments on his part without doing him any wrong. It is, so to speak, a law of moral repercussion. Therefore the union of the empirical concept of wrongdoing with that rule that is supplied by the pure understanding gives rise to the fundamental concepts of wrong and right, which everyone grasps a priori and applies at once at the instance of experience. The empiric who denies this, because only experience is of any value to him, may simply be referred to savages, who all distinguish quite correctly, and often indeed with nice precision, between right and wrong. This is very obvious in their bartering and other transactions with the crews of European ships, and in their visits to them. They are bold and full of confidence when right is on their side; on the other hand, they are anxious and uneasy when it is not. In disputes they approve of a just settlement; on the other hand, an unjust method drives them to war. *Jurisprudence,* or the *doctrine of right,* is a branch of morals that determines those actions we are not allowed to commit unless we intend to injure others, that is, to do wrong; thus moral-

10. Nothing rules the masses so effectively as superstition. As a rule they are unbridled, cruel, fickle, and irresolute, so that as soon as they are caught by some delusion of religion, they prefer to obey their priests rather than their leaders.—TR.

11. The cause of a cause is also the cause of its effect.—TR.

ity has in view here the *active* part. Legislation, however, takes this chapter of morality in order to use it with regard to the *passive* side, and hence conversely, and to consider as such the same actions that no one need endure, since no wrong should befall him. Now against these actions the state constructs the bulwark of the laws, as positive right. Its intention is that no one shall *suffer* wrong, whereas the intention of moral jurisprudence is that no one shall *do* wrong.[12]

With every unjust action the wrong is *qualitatively* the same, namely, injury to another, whether it be to his person, freedom, property, or honor. But *quantitatively* it can be very different. Such difference in the *amount of wrong* does not yet seem to have been properly investigated by moralists, although it is everywhere recognized in real life, since the amount of censure passed corresponds to that of wrong done. It is the same regarding the *justice* of actions. To explain this: whoever steals a loaf when dying of starvation commits a wrong; but how small his injustice is when compared with that of a rich man who in any way defrauds a poor man of his last possession! The rich man who pays his day laborer acts justly; but how small this justice is compared with that of a poor man who voluntarily returns to the rich man the purse of gold he has found! However, the measure of this very significant difference in the *quantity* of justice and injustice (the quality always being equal) is not direct and absolute, like that on a graduated scale, but indirect and relative, like that of sines and tangents. I therefore lay down the following formula: the amount of injustice in my conduct is equal to that of the evil I thereby inflict on another divided by the amount of advantage I thereby obtain: and the amount of justice in my action equals that of advantage that the injury to another would bring me divided by the amount of harm that he would thereby suffer. But there is in addition a *double injustice* that is specifically different from every simple one, however great. This is seen through the amount of indignation of the impartial witness, which always proves proportional to the amount of injustice, and reaches its highest degree only in the case of the double injustice. This is loathed and detested as something revolt-

12. The doctrine of right will be found in detail in the *World as Will and Representation*, vol. 1, section 62.

ing and outrageous, as a monstrous crime, at which the gods, so to speak, cover their faces. This *double injustice* occurs when anyone has expressly undertaken the obligation to protect someone else in a definite respect; consequently, the nonfulfillment of the obligation would in itself be an injury to the other person, and thus a wrong; but in addition, he now attacks and injures the other man at the very spot where he should protect him. Such is the case, for example, when the appointed watchman or attendant becomes a murderer, the trusted custodian becomes a thief, the guardian defrauds his ward of her property, the lawyer prevaricates, the judge allows himself to be bribed, and the man asked for advice deliberately gives some dangerous and pernicious counsel. All these things are thought of under the concept of *treachery*, and are detested by the whole world. Dante accordingly places traitors at the very bottom of hell, where Satan himself dwells (*Inferno*, 11:61–66).

Now as the concept of *obligation* has here come under discussion, this is the place to determine that of *duty*, which is so frequently applied in ethics as well as in real life, and yet is given too great an extension. We have found that wrong always consists in injury to another, whether to his person, freedom, property, or honor. From this it seems to follow that every wrong must be a postive attack, a deed. But there are actions whose mere *omission* is a wrong; and they are called *duties*. This is the true philosophical definition of the concept of *duty*, which, however, is deprived of every characteristic and thereby lost when, as in all previous morality, every mode of praiseworthy conduct is called *duty*; and thus it is forgotten that what is *duty* must also be *indebtedness*. *Duty, le devoir, die Pflicht, is therefore an action by the mere omission of which an injury is done to another, that is, a wrong is committed.* Obviously this can be the case only if the man who neglects to do such an action has undertaken to carry it out, in other words, has *bound* or *pledged* himself. All duties accordingly depend on an obligation entered into. As a rule, this is an express and mutual agreement, as, for example, between prince and people, government and civil servants, master and servant, counsel and client, physician and patient, and generally between everyone who has undertaken to carry out any kind of task, and his employer in the broadest sense of the word. Therefore every duty confers a right, since no one can undertake an obligation without a motive, which here means without some advantage to himself. Only *one* obligation is known to me that is undertaken *not* by means of an agreement, but immediately through a mere act, since the person with whom it is concerned was not yet in existence when it was undertaken; I refer to the obligation of parents to their children. Whoever brings a child into the world has a *duty* to support it until it is capable of supporting itself; and should this time *never* come, as in the case of one who is born blind, a cripple, cretin, and so on, then the duty also never comes to an end. For by the mere nonprovision of assistance, and hence through an omission, he would injure his child—would, in fact, bring about its ruin. The moral duty of children to their parents is not so immediate and positive. It rests on the fact that, because every duty confers a right, parents must also have a right as regards their children, which is the basis of children's duty of obedience to their parents; but later this duty also ceases, along with the right from which it originated. In its place will appear gratitude for what the parents did over and above their strict duty. However unpleasant and even revolting a vice ingratitude may be, gratitude cannot really be called a *duty,* since its omission causes no harm to another and hence is not a *wrong.* Moreover, the benefactor would inevitably be under the impression that he was tacitly striking a bargain. At all events, reparation for harm done could be regarded as an obligation arising directly out of an action. As the elimination of the consequences of an unjust action, however, this reparation is a mere attempt to efface it, something purely negative resting on the fact that the action itself ought not to have taken place. Further, it should be noted here that equity [*Billigkeit*] is the enemy of justice and often comes into violent collision with it; and so we should not concede too much to it. The German is a friend of equity, the Englishman sticks to justice.

The law of motivation is just as strict as that of physical causality; and so it involves just as irresistible an obligation and want of freedom. Accordingly, there are two ways of doing wrong, those of *violence* and of *cunning*. Just as through violence I can kill another, or rob him, or force him to obey me, so too by means of cunning I can do all these things, since I confront his intellect with false motives, in consequence of which he must do what he otherwise would not. This is effected by means of the *lie*, whose objectionable nature rests on this alone, and therefore sticks to it only insofar as it is an instrument of cunning, that is, of compulsion by means of motivation. But as a rule, this is what it is. For in the first place, my lies themselves cannot occur without a motive; but with the rarest of exceptions this will be unjust, namely, the intention to guide, in accordance with my will, others over whom I have no power, that is, to compel them by means of motivation. This intention also underlies even the merely bombastic lie, since whoever uses it tries by its means to put himself higher in the sight of others than is his due. The binding force of the *promise* and *contract* rests on the fact that, if they are not fulfilled, they are the most grave and serious lie; its intention is to exercise moral compulsion over others, and here it is the more evident since the motive of the lie, namely, the desired performance by the opposite party, is expressly declared. The contemptible aspect of the fraud arises from the fact that, by dissimulation and hypocrisy, it disarms its man before attacking him. *Treachery* is the height of fraud, and, because it belongs to the category of the *double injustice,* is regarded with deep loathing. But just as I can repel force by force without doing wrong and thus with right, so can I repel force by cunning if I lack the power, or if it appears more convenient to me. Therefore, in cases where I have a right to use force, I also have a right *to tell lies;* for example, I can resort to lies against robbers and ruffians of every sort, whom I accordingly entice into a trap through cunning. Thus a promise extorted by force is not binding. Indeed the *right to tell lies* goes even further; it occurs in the case of every wholly unauthorized question concerning my personal or business affairs, which is therefore prompted by curiosity. For I should be exposed to danger not only by answering it, but also by merely putting it off and incurring suspicion by saying, "I won't tell you." Here the lie is the legitimate means of defense against unauthorized inquisitiveness, whose motive is hardly ever benevolent. For I have the right to oppose the implied bad will of others, and accordingly to anticipate with physical resistance, at the risk of the aggressor, the presumed physical violence. Thus, as a preventative measure, I can protect my garden wall with sharp spikes, turn savage dogs loose in my yard at night, and even, according to circumstances, set mantraps and spring guns, for the evil consequences of which the intruder has only himself to thank. In the same way, I also have the right to keep secret by every means that which, if known, would lay me open to the attack of others. Moreover, I have good cause for doing this, because even here I must assume that the bad will of others is quite possible, and must take in advance the necessary precautions. Hence Ariosto says:

> Quantunque il simular sia le più volte
> Ripreso, e dia di mala mente indici,
> Si trova pure in molte cose e molte
> Avere fatti evidenti benefici,
> E danni e biasmi e morti avere tolte:
> Che non conversiam' sempre con gli amici,
> In questa assai più oscura che serena
> Vita mortal, tutta d'invidia piena.[13]
>
> (*Orlando furioso*, Canto 4:1)

Therefore, without doing wrong, I can cunningly oppose in advance even the merely presumed harm through cunning; and so I need not give an account to anyone who unwarrantedly pries into my private affairs, or, by answering, "I wish to keep this a secret," show him the place where there is a secret that is dangerous to me and possibly advantageous to him, but which in any case puts me in his power:

> Scire volunt secreta domus, atque inde timeri.[14]

On the contrary, I am entitled to put him off with a lie at his risk, in the event of its leading him into an error detrimental to himself. For here the lie is the only means of averting inquisitive and suspicious curiosity, and is therefore a case of self-defense. Here the correct maxim is, "Ask me no questions and I'll tell you no lies." Thus the English consider the reproach of telling lies the gravest insult, and for that reason actually tell fewer lies than do other nations. Accordingly, they regard as a piece of impertinence and

13. However much dissimulation is often censured and is evidence of a bad intention, yet in very many things it has obviously done good by preventing harm, disgrace, and death. For not always with friends do we speak in this mortal life, which is much more gloomy than cheerful, and is bursting with envy.—Tr.

14. They wish to know secrets in order thus to become feared. Juvenal. *Satires* 3:113.—Tr.

The truth is theft. People have to earn the right to be told the truth. They are not asking questions, they are ordering you to answer. "None of your business" is a false escape. It is implies confirmation of the accusation.

ill breeding all unauthorized questions concerning other people's affairs; this is denoted by the expression "to ask questions." Every sensible and prudent man also goes to work in accordance with the above principle, even if he is of the strictest integrity and honesty. For example, if he is returning from a remote place where he has raised money, and an unknown traveler joins him and first asks him the usual *whence* and *whither* and gradually comes to the question what may have taken him to that place, he will give the traveler a false answer to obviate the risk of robbery. If a man is found in the house of another whose daughter he is wooing, and is asked the reason for his unexpected presence, he will, unless he is a fool, unhesitatingly give a fasle answer. And so very many cases occur in which every reasonable man, without any scruple of conscience, tells a lie. It is this view alone that removes the glaring contradiction between morality as taught and morality as daily practiced even by the best and most upright of men. However, the above-stated limitation to the case of self-defense must be strictly observed, for otherwise this doctrine would be open to terrible abuse; for in itself the lie is a very dangerous instrument. But just as, in spite of general peace, the law allows everyone to carry arms and to use them in case of self-defense, so does morality also allow the use of the lie for the same purpose, but *only* for this. With the exception of this case of self-defense against violence or cunning, every lie is an instrument for wrongdoing; and so justice demands truthfulness and veracity toward everyone. But there is much to be said against the wholly unconditional, and by the nature of the thing, universal condemnation of lies; for there are cases where telling lies is even a *duty,* especially for doctors; there are also *magnanimous* lies, for example, that of the Marquis Posa in *Don Carlos,* that in the *Gerusalemme liberata,* 2:22, and generally all cases where one man wishes to take on his shoulders the guilt of another; finally, there is Jesus Christ, who on one occasion intentionally told an untruth (John 7:8). Accordingly, Campanella frankly states in his *Poesie filosofiche,* Madr. 9: *Bello è il mentir, se a fare gran ben' si trova.*[15] On the other hand, the current theory of the white lie is a wretched patch on the garment of a miserable morality. The derivations of the unlawful nature of lies that, at

15. It is fine to tell lies when they result in much good.—TR.

the instigation of Kant, are given in many textbooks, namely, the derivations from man's *faculty of speech*,[16] are so insipid, childish, and absurd that one might be tempted, if only to ridicule them, to embrace the devil and say with Talleyrand: *L'homme a reçu la parole pour pouvoir cacher sa pensée*.[17] The unconditional and boundless abhorrence of lies that Kant evinces on every occasion is due either to affectation or prejudice. In the chapter of his *Doctrine of Virtue* that deals with lies,[18] he inveighs against them with every defamatory epithet, but does not quote a single adequate reason for their condemnation, which, after all, would have been more effective. Declamation is easier than demonstration and moralizing easier than being sincere. Kant would have done better to launch his special indignation against the *malicious joy at the misfortune of others;* this, not lying, is the really devilish vice. For it is the very opposite of compassion and is nothing but impotent cruelty. Unable itself to bring about the sufferings it so gladly beholds in others, such cruelty thanks chance for having done so instead. According to the principle of knightly honor, the reproach of being a liar is regarded as extremely grave and really to be washed out with the accuser's blood. This is not because the lie is *wrong,* for then the accusation of wrongdoing through violence would inevitably be just as gravely offensive, and we know that this is not the case. On the contrary, it is because, according to the principle of knightly honor, right is really based on might. Now whoever has recourse to lies in order to do wrong, shows that he lacks the strength or necessary courage to apply it. Every lie is evidence of fear; it is this that passes on him the fatal sentence.

18

The Virtue of Loving-Kindness

Justice is, therefore, the first and fundamentally essential cardinal virtue. Even the philosophers of antiquity regarded it as such,

16. Kant, *Metaphysical Principles of the Doctrine of Virtue,* section 9 (Academy 429).—Tr.

17. Man has received speech to be able to conceal his thoughts. (Talleyrand to the Spanish Ambassador Izquierdo. From Barère, *Memoirs* [Paris, 1842], 4:447).—Tr.

18. See n. 16 above.—Tr.

though they coordinated it with three others that were unsuitably chosen. On the other hand, they did not set up philanthropy, loving-kindness, *caritas,* as a virtue; even Plato, who rises to the greatest heights in morality, gets only as far as voluntary, disinterested justice. It is true that philanthropy has existed at all times, in practice and in fact; but it was first theoretically mentioned, formulated as a virtue—indeed as the greatest of all virtues—and extended even to enemies, by Christianity. This is Christianity's greatest merit, although only in respect to Europe; for in Asia a thousand years earlier the boundless love of one's neighbor had been the subject of theory and precept as well as of practice, in the Veda and Dharma-Sastra, Itihasa and Purana, as well as the teaching of the Buddha Sakya-Muni, never weary of preaching it. And to be strictly accurate, we must mention that traces of a recommendation to loving-kindness are to be found even among the ancients, for example, in Cicero, *De finibus* 5:23, even in Pythagoras, according to Iamblichus, *De vita Pythagorae* 33. It is now incumbent on me to give the philosophical derivation of this virtue, from my principle.

In the second degree, another's suffering in itself and as such directly becomes my motive by means of *compassion,* which was previously shown to be a fact, although of mysterious origin. This second degree is clearly distinguished from the first by the *positive character* of the actions resulting from it, since compassion now not only restrains me from injuring another, but even impels me to help him. Now according as, on the one hand, that direct participation is keenly and deeply felt, and, on the other, the distress of someone else is great and urgent, I shall be induced by that purely moral motive to make a greater or smaller sacrifice for another's needs or distress. Such sacrifice may consist in an expenditure of my bodily and mental powers on his behalf, in the loss of property, health, freedom, and even life itself. Thus in that direct participation, resting on and requiring no arguments, is to be found the only true origin of loving-kindness, *caritas,* in other words, that virtue whose maxim is *Omnes, quantum potes, juva.*[19] From it flows all that is prescribed by ethics under the name of duties of virtue, duties of love, imperfect duties. This wholly direct and even

19. Help everyone as much as you can.—Tr.

instinctive participation in another's sufferings—compassion—is the sole source of such actions when they are said to *have moral worth*, that is, to be free from all egoistic motives and, for that very reason, to awaken in us that inward contentment called the good, satisfied, approving conscience. Such actions also stir within the spectator that characteristic assent, esteem, admiration, and even a humiliating glance at himself; this is an undeniable fact. If, on the other hand, a charitable action has any other motive, it cannot be anything but egoistic, if it is not actually malicious. For in keeping with the previously mentioned fundamental springs of all actions, namely, egoism, malice, and compassion, the *motives* that are capable generally of moving men and women can be grouped into three general and principal classes: (1) one's own weal, (2) another's woe, (3) another's weal. Now if the motive of a charitable action is not from the *third* class, it must naturally belong to the *first* or *second*. The second actually is sometimes the case, for example, when I do good to one man in order to annoy another whom I do not benefit, or to make the other man's sufferings more acute, or even to put to shame a third who does not benefit the first, or finally, by my action to humiliate the man whom I benefit. The *first* class, however, is much more often the case, namely, as soon as I have *my own weal*, however remote and indirect, in view when doing a good deed, and thus whenever I am urged by considerations of reward in this world or the next, or by the attainment of high esteem and the reputation for nobleheartedness, or by the reflection that the person I help today may one day be able to help me in return, or otherwise to serve and benefit me; or finally, also when I am urged by the thought that the maxim of magnanimity or charitableness must be upheld because it may one day benefit me. In short, this is the case whenever my aim is anything but the purely *objective* one of wanting to know that the other person is helped, is rescued from his need and distress, or is freed from his suffering, and absolutely nothing else but this! Only with the purely objective aim have I really shown that lovingkindness, *caritas*, the preaching of which is the great and distinguishing merit of Christianity. The very precepts, added by the Gospel to its commandment of love, such as *Sinistra tua manus haud cognoscat, quae dextra facit*[20] and the like, are based on a

20. Let not thy left hand know what thy right hand doeth. (Matthew 6:3.)—Tr.

feeling of what I have deduced here, namely, that another's distress alone, and no other consideration, must be my motive if my action is to have moral worth. And in the same place (Matthew 6:2) it is said quite rightly that those who give with ostentation have their reward. But even here the Vedas give us, so to speak, the higher inspiration; for they repeatedly assure us that whoever desires any reward for his works is still wandering on the path of darkness, and is not yet ripe for deliverance. If anyone were to ask me what he gets from giving alms, my answer in all conscience would be: "This, that the lot of that poor man is made so much the lighter; otherwise, absolutely nothing. Now if this is of no use and of no importance to you, then your wish was really not to give alms, but to make a purchase; and in that case you are defrauded of your money. If, however, it is a matter of importance to you that that man who is oppressed by want suffers less, then you have attained your object from the fact that he suffers less, and you see exactly how far your gift is rewarded."

But now how is it possible for a suffering that is not *mine* and does not touch *me* to become just as directly a motive as only my own normally does, and to move me to action? As I have said, only by the fact that although it is given to me merely as something external, merely by means of external intuitive perception or knowledge, I nevertheless *feel it with him, feel it as my own*, and yet not *within me*, but *in another person*; and thus there occurs what is expressed by Calderón:

> que entre el ver
> Padecer y el padecer
> Ninguna distancia habia.
> (That there is no difference between suffering and
> seeing suffering.)
>
> ("No siempre el peor es cierto")

But this presupposes that to a certain extent I have identified myself with the other man, and in consequence the barrier between the ego and nonego is for the moment abolished; only then do the other man's affairs, his need, distress, and suffering, directly become my own. I no longer look at him as if he were something given to me by empirical intuitive perception, as something strange and foreign, as a matter of indifference, as something entirely different from me. On the contrary, I share the suffering *in him*, in spite of the fact that his skin does not enclose my nerves. Only in this way can *his* woe, *his* distress, become a motive *for me;* otherwise it can be absolutely only my own. I repeat that this *occurrence is mysterious,* for it is something our faculty of reason can give no direct account of, and its grounds cannot be discovered on the path of experience. And yet it happens every day; everyone has often experienced it within himself; even to the most hard-hearted and selfish it is not unknown. Every day it comes before our eyes, in single acts on a small scale, wherever, on the spur of the moment, and without much reflection, one man helps another, hastens to the assistance of one whom he has seen for the first time, and in fact sometimes exposes even his own life to the most obvious danger for the sake of that man, without thinking of anything except that he sees the other's great distress and danger. It appears on a large scale when, after long deliberation and difficult debates, the magnanimous British nation gave twenty million pounds to purchase the freedom of the negro slaves in its colonies; this it did with the joy and approbation of the whole world. Whoever feels inclined to deny that the motive of this fine action on a grand scale is traceable to compassion, in order to ascribe it instead to Christianity, should bear in mind that in the whole of the New Testament not one word is said against slavery; at that time the thing was so universal. Further, he should remember that as late as 1860 in North America, during the debates on slavery, a man quoted in support of his argument that Abraham and Jacob kept slaves.

Now what in each particular case will be the practical results of that mysterious inner occurrence may be analyzed by ethics in chapters and paragraphs on duties of virtue, duties of love, imperfect duties, or any other way. The root, the basis of all this is the one here indicated, from which springs the principle *Omnes, quantum potes, juva;* and from this everything else can be very easily derived, just as from the first half of my principle, from the *Neminem laede,*[21] all duties of justice can be derived. Indeed, ethics is the easiest of all the branche. of knowledge, as is only to be expected, for everyone is obliged to construct it for himself, and to derive the rule, for each case as it occurs, from the supreme principle that is rooted in his heart; for few have the leisure and

21. Injure no one.

patience to learn a ready-made system of ethics. All the virtues flow from justice and loving-kindness; these are therefore the cardinal virtues, and with their derivation, the cornerstone of ethics is laid. Justice is the entire ethical content of the Old Testament, and loving-kindness that of the New. This is the new commandment (John 13:34) in which according to Paul (Romans 13:8–10), all the Christian virtues are contained.

19

Confirmations of the Expounded Basis of Morals

The truth I have now expressed, that compassion, as the sole non-egoistic motive, is also the only genuinely moral one, is strangely, indeed almost incomprehensibly paradoxical. I will therefore attempt to bring it home to the reader's convictions by showing that it is confirmed by experience and by the statements of universal humane feeling.

(1) For this purpose I will first take as an example an imaginary case, which can be regarded in this investigation as an *experimentum crucis*.[22] But not to make the matter too easy, I am not taking a case of philanthropy, but a violation of right, and indeed the gravest. Let us suppose that two young men, Caius and Titus, are both passionately in love each with a different girl, and that, on account of external circumstances, each is thwarted absolutely by a specially favored rival. They have both decided to put their rivals out of the way, and are perfectly secure from all detection, even from all suspicion. When, however, each comes to make more detailed arrangements for the murder, he desists after an inward struggle. They are now to give us a sincere and clear account of the reasons for abandoning their decision. Now, that given by Caius is to be left entirely to the reader's choice. He may have been prevented through religious reasons, such as the will of God, the retribution to come, the Day of Judgment, and so on. Or he may say: "I consider that the maxim for my proceeding in this case would not have been calculated to give a universally valid rule for all possible rational beings, since I should have treated my rival only

22. A crucial test. Tʀ.

as a means and not at the same time as an end."[23] Or he may say with Fichte: "Every human life is a means to the realization of the moral law; hence I cannot, without being indifferent to that realization, destroy one who is destined to contribute to it" (*Moral Philosophy*, p. 373). (Incidentally, he could get over this scruple by hoping, when once in possession of his beloved, to produce soon a new instrument of the moral law.) Or he may say in accordance with Wollaston: "I considered that this action would be the expression of a false proposition." Or like Hutcheson he may say: "The moral sense whose feelings, like those of any other, are incapable of further explanation, prevailed on me not to do it." Or like Adam Smith: "I foresaw that my action would not excite any sympathy at all for me in those who witnessed it." Or in the words of Christian Wolff: "I recognized that I should thus work against my own perfection and not help that of another." Or he may use the words of Spinoza: *Homini nihil utilius homine: ergo hominem interimere nolui.*[24] In short, he may say what he likes. But Titus, whose account I reserve for myself, may say: "When it came to making the arrangements, and so for the moment I had to concern myself not with my passion but with that rival, I clearly saw for the first time what would really happen to him. But I was then seized with compassion and pity; I felt sorry for him; I had not the heart to do it, and could not." Now I ask any honest and unbiased reader: Which of the two is the better man? To which of them would he prefer to entrust his own destiny? Which of them has been restrained by the purer motive? Accordingly, where does the foundation of morality lie?

(2) Nothing shocks our moral feelings so deeply as cruelty does. We can forgive every other crime, but not cruelty. The reason for this is that it is the very opposite of compassion. When we obtain information of a very cruel deed, as, for example, the case, recently reported in the papers, of a mother who murdered her five-year-old son by pouring boiling oil down his throat and her younger child by burying it alive; or the case, just reported from Algiers, where, after a casual dispute and fight between a Spaniard and an Algerine, the latter, as the stronger, tore away the whole of the

23. Kant. *Foundations of the Metaphysics of Morals*, Academy 429.—Tr.
24. To man nothing is more useful than man; I was therefore unwilling to kill the man. (*Ethics*, 4, prop. 18, schol.)—Tr.

lower jawbone of the former, and carried it off as a trophy, leaving the other man still alive; when we hear of such things, we are seized with horror and exclaim: "How is it possible to do such a thing?" What is the meaning of this question? Is it: How is it possible to have so little fear for the punishments of the future life? Hardly. Or: How is it possible to act according to a maxim that is so absolutely unfitted to become a general law for all rational beings? Certainly not. Or: How is it possible so utterly to neglect one's own perfection and that of another? Again, certainly not. The sense of that question is certainly only this: How is it possible to be so utterly bereft of compassion? Thus it is the greatest lack of compassion that stamps a deed with the deepest moral depravity and atrocity. Consequently, compassion is the real moral incentive.

(3) In general, the foundation of morals or the incentive to morality as laid down by me is the only one that can boast of a real, and extensive, effectiveness. For surely no one will venture to assert this of all the other moral principles laid down by philosophers; these consist of abstract, sometimes even hairsplitting propositions with no foundation except an artificial combination of concepts, so that their application to actual conduct would often even have its ludicrous side. A good deed performed merely out of regard for Kant's moral principle would at bottom be the work of a philosophical pedantry; or it would lead to self-deception, since the reasoning faculty of the doer would interpret a deed that had other and possibly nobler motives as the product of the categorical imperative and of the concept of duty that rests on nothing. However, it is rarely possible to establish a definite effectiveness, not only of *philosophical* moral principles that are adapted to mere theory, but even of *religious* moral principles that are laid down entirely for practical purposes. We first see this in that, despite the great variety of religions in the world, the degree of morality, or rather immorality, shows absolutely no corresponding variety, but is essentially pretty much the same everywhere. And we must not confuse rudeness and refinement with morality and immorality. The religion of the Greeks had an exceedingly small moral tendency, restricted almost entirely to the oath; no dogma was taught, and no system of morals was publicly preached. But taking everything into consideration, we do not see that the Greeks were for that reason morally inferior to men of the Christian era. The morality of Christianity

is of a much higher nature than that of all the other religions ever appearing in Europe. But whoever felt inclined to believe that European morality had therefore improved to the same level, and now surpassed at any rate other current systems of morality, might soon be convinced that among Mohammedans, Guebres, Hindus, and Buddhists there was at least as much honesty, fidelity, tolerance, gentleness, benevolence, nobleness, and self-denial as there is among Christian nations. Indeed, the long list of inhuman cruelties that have been the concomitants of Christianity would rather cause the scale to turn against this religion. Such a list includes the numerous religious wars, the inexcusable Crusades, the extermination of a large part of the aborigines of America, the peopling of that continent with black slaves,[25] dragged from Africa illegally and without a shadow of right, torn from their families, their native land, their quarter of the globe, and condemned to penal servitude for life; the indefatigable persecution of heretics, the outrageous courts of the Inquisition, the Massacre of St. Bartholomew, the execution by the duke of Alba of eighteen thousand in the Netherlands, and so on and so on. Speaking generally, however, if the excellent morality that is preached by Christianity and more or less by every religion is compared with the performance of its followers, and if we picture to ourselves how far we should get with it if the secular arm did not prevent crimes—in fact, what we should have to face if all laws were abolished even only for a day—then we are bound to confess that the effect of all religions on morality is really very small. Naturally, weakness of faith is to blame for this. Theoretically, and as long as it remains a question of pious meditation, everyone's faith appears to him to be firm. But the deed is the hard touchstone of all our convictions: when it comes to the point, and faith is now to be tested by great renunciations and heavy sacrifices, faith's feebleness is then revealed. If a man is seriously meditating a crime, he has already broken the bounds of genuine and pure morality. Thereafter, the first thing that stops him is always the thought of justice and the police. If he banishes this by hoping to escape detection, then the second barrier that opposes him is a regard for his honor. If he now surmounts

25. According to Buxton, *The African Slave-trade* (1839), even now their number is *annually* increased by approximately 150,000 fresh Africans. In the capture and transport of these, over 200,000 others perish miserably.

this rampart, then after those two strong resistances have been overcome, the odds are very great against any religious dogma's having sufficient power to keep him back from the deed. For whoever is not deterred by near and certain dangers will hardly be kept in check by those that are remote and rest merely on faith. Moreover, to every good action that results solely from religious convictions, it may still be objected that it was not disinterested but done out of regard for reward and punishment, and consequently had no purely moral worth. We find this view vigorously expressed in a letter by the famous grand duke, Karl August of Weimar. "Baron Weyhers was himself of the opinion that whoever is good through religion and not by natural inclination must be a bad fellow. *In vino veritas.*" (*Letters to J. H. Merck,* no. 229.) On the other hand, let us now consider the moral incentive that is put forward by me. Who ventures to deny for a moment that it displays a decided and truly wonderful effectiveness at all times, among all nations, in all the situations of life, even in a state of anarchy and amid the horrors of revolutions and wars, in small things and in great, every day and every hour? Who will say that it does not daily prevent much wrong, that it does not call into existence many a good deed without any hope of reward, and often quite unexpectedly? Will anyone deny that where it and it alone has been effective, we all with deep feeling and esteem unreservedly attribute genuine moral worth to the deed?

(4) Boundless compassion for all living beings is the firmest and surest guarantee of pure moral conduct, and needs no casuistry. Whoever is inspired with it will assuredly injure no one, will wrong no one, will encroach on no one's rights; on the contrary, he will be lenient and patient with everyone, will forgive everyone, will help everyone as much as he can, and all his actions will bear the stamp of justice, philanthropy, and loving-kindness. On the other hand, if we attempt to say, "This man is virtuous but knows no compassion," or, "He is an unjust and malicious man yet he is very compassionate," the contradiction is obvious. Tastes differ, but I know of no finer prayer than the one that ends old Indian dramas (just as in former times English plays ended with a prayer for the King). It runs: "May all living beings remain free from pain."

(5) Even from isolated characteristics it may be inferred that the

true moral incentive is compassion. For example, it is just as wrong to defraud a rich man of a hundred talers by legal tricks involving no danger, as it is to defraud a poor man of the same sum. The reproaches of conscience, however, and the censure of impartial witnesses will prove to be very much louder and more emphatic in the case of the poor man. And so Aristotle also says, *It is more shameful to injure one who is unfortunate than one who is fortunate.* (*Problems* 29:2) On the other hand, the reproaches will be fainter in the case of anyone who is rich; and will be fainter still when it is a public exchequer that has been defrauded, for this cannot be an object of compassion. We see that material for self-reproach and the reproach of others is furnished not directly by violation of the law, but primarily by the suffering thereby brought on another. The mere violation of right as such, for example, the defrauding of the public exchequer, will naturally be disapproved by our conscience and by others, but only insofar as the maxim of respecting every right, which makes the truly honorable man, is thereby broken, and thus indirectly and to a lesser degree. If, however, the fraud is on a state treasury that is *entrusted with private funds,* the case is then quite different, since here we have the previously established concept of *the double injustice* with its specific characteristics. It is due to this analysis that the gravest reproach ever brought on grasping extortioners and legal rogues is that of having seized the property of widows and orphans, just because they more than any others, by their utter helplessness, should have excited compassion. Therefore, an entire want of compassion is that which convicts a person of wickedness.

(6) Compassion is the basis of loving-kindness even more obviously than of justice. A man will not obtain demonstrations of genuine philanthropy from others as long as he is well-off in every respect. The lucky man can, of course, frequently experience the goodwill of relations and friends; but the expressions of that pure, disinterested, objective participation in the lot and condition of another, which are the effect of loving-kindness, are reserved for him who in any way suffers. For the lucky man *as such* we feel no sympathy; on the contrary, *as such* he remains a stranger to our hearts: *Habeat sibi sua.*[26] Indeed, if he has many advantages over others he may easily excite envy, which, if he should once fall

26. May he retain for himself what is his own.—Tr.

from the heights of fortune, threatens to turn into malicious joy. However, this menace often remains unfulfilled and rarely comes to the Sophoclean *his enemies laugh triumphantly*.[27] For as soon as the lucky man falls, there occurs a great transformation in the hearts of others, which for our consideration is instructive. In the first place, we now see what sort of interest was taken in him by the friends of his fortune: *Diffugiunt cadis cum faece siccatis amici*.[28] On the other hand, what he dreaded more than misfortune itself and could not bear to think of, namely, the exultation of those envious of his good fortune, the mocking laughter of malicious joy, rarely comes to pass. Envy is reconciled and has disappeared with its own cause; compassion takes its place and gives birth to loving-kindness. Those who were envious of and hostile to the man of fortune have often become, after his downfall, his considerate, consoling, and helpful friends. Who has not experienced something of the sort in himself, at any rate to a lesser extent? Has not the man struck by some misfortune seen with surprise how those who previously showed him the greatest coldness and even ill will now came to him with sincere and genuine sympathy? For misfortune is the condition of compassion, and this is the source of philanthropy. Closely associated with this view is the observation that nothing so quickly appeases our anger, even when it is righteous, as this statement about the object of our anger: "He is unfortunate." For rain is to fire what compassion is to anger. Therefore whoever would fain have nothing to regret should note the following advice. When he is inflamed with anger and is thinking of doing someone else a grave injury, let him vividly picture it in his mind as though he had already done it. He would then see the victim struggle with mental and physical pain, or with misery and distress, and would be forced to say to himself: "This is my work!" If anything can assuage his wrath, it is this. For compassion is the true antidote against anger, and by practicing this artifice on ourselves, we anticipate, while there is still time,

> la pitié, dont la voix,
> Alors qu'on est vengé, fait entendre ses lois.[29]
> (Voltaire, *Sémiramis*, 5:6)

27. Sophocles, *Electra* 1153.—Tr.
28. As soon as the jugs are emptied, friends flee. (Horace, *Odes* 1:35, 26.)—Tr.
29. Compassion, whose voice makes her laws heard when we take revenge.—Tr.

Nothing removes our spiteful attitude toward others so easily as adopting a point of view in which they appeal to our compassion. Parents are, as a rule, most fond of the delicate child, due to the fact that it constantly excites their compassion.

(7) The moral incentive advanced by me as the genuine, is further confirmed by the fact that *the animals* are also taken under its protection. In other European systems of morality they are badly provided for, which is most inexcusable. They are said to have no rights, and there is the erroneous idea that our behavior to them is without moral significance, or, as it is said in the language of that morality, there are no duties to animals. All this is revoltingly crude, a barbarism of the West, the source of which is to be found in Judaism. In philosophy it rests, despite all evidence to the contrary, on the assumed total difference between man and animal. We all know that such difference was expressed most definitely and strikingly by Descartes as a necessary consequence of his errors. Thus when the philosophy of Descartes, Leibniz, and Wolff built up rational psychology out of abstract concepts and constructed an immortal *anima rationalis,* the natural claims of the animal world obviously stood up against this exclusive privilege, this patent of immortality of the human species, and nature, as always on such occasions, entered her silent protest. With an uneasy intellectual conscience, the philosophers then had to try to support rational psychology by means of the empirical. They were therefore concerned to open up a vast chasm, an immeasurable gulf between man and animal in order to represent them as fundamentally different, in spite of all evidence to the contrary. Such efforts were ridiculed even by Boileau: Holy cow

> Les animaux ont-ils des universités?
> Voit-on fleurir chez eux des quatre facultés?[30]

In the end animals would be quite incapable of distinguishing themselves from the external world and would have no consciousness of themselves, no ego! To answer such absurd statements, we can point simply to the boundless egoism inherent in every animal,

30.　Have the animals their universities?
　　Do we see the four faculties flourish with them?
(*Satires,* 8:165)—Tr.

even the smallest and lowest, which shows clearly enough how very conscious they are of their ego in face of the world or the nonego. If any Cartesian were to find himself clawed by a tiger, he would become aware in the clearest possible manner of the sharp distinction such a beast draws between its ego and the nonego. In keeping with such sophisms of philosophers, we find a popular peculiarity in many languages, especially German, of giving animals special words of their own for eating, drinking, pregnancy, parturition, dying, and their bodies, so that we need not use the same words that describe those acts among human beings: and thus we conceal under a diversity of words the perfect and complete identity of the thing. Since the ancient languages did not recognize any such duplication, but rather frankly and openly denoted the same thing by the same word, that miserable artifice is undoubtedly the work of European priests and parsons. In their profanity these men think they cannot go far enough in disavowing and reviling the eternal essence that lives in all animals, and thus have laid the foundation of that harshness and cruelty to animals that is customary in Europe, but that no native of the Asiatic uplands can look at without righteous horror. In the English language we do not meet with this contemptible trick, doubtless because the Saxons, when they conquered England, were not yet Christians. On the other hand, we do find an analogy to it in the strange fact that in English all animals are of the neuter gender and so are represented by the pronoun *it*, just as if they were inanimate things. The effect of this artifice is quite revolting, especially in the case of primates, such as dogs, monkeys, and the like; it is unmistakably a priestly trick for the purpose of reducing animals to the level of things. The ancient Egyptians, whose whole life was dedicated to religious purposes, put the mummies of the ibis, crocodile, and so on, in the same vault with those of human beings. In Europe, however, it is an abomination and a crime for a faithful dog to be buried beside the resting place of his master, though at times, from a faithfulness and attachment not to be found among the human race, he there awaited his own death. Nothing leads more definitely to a recognition of the identity of the essential nature in animal and human phenomena than a study of zoology and anatomy. What, then, are we to say when in these days (1839) a bigoted and canting zootomist[31] has the audacity to emphasize an absolute and radical difference between man and animal, and goes so far as to attack and disparage honest zoologists who keep aloof from all priestly guile, toadyism, and hypocrisy, and pursue their course under the guidance of nature and truth?

One must be really quite blind or totally chloroformed not to recognize that the essential and principal thing in the animal and man is the same, and that what distinguishes the one from the other is not to be found in the primary and original principle, in the archaeus, in the inner nature, in the kernel of the two phenomena, such kernel being in both alike the *will* of the individual; but only in the secondary, in the intellect, in the degree of the cognitive faculty. In man this degree is incomparably higher through the addition of the faculty of *abstract* knowledge, called *reason*. Yet this superiority is traceable only to a greater cerebral development, and hence to the somatic difference of a single part, the brain, and in particular, its quantity. On the other hand, the similarity between animal and man is incomparably greater, both psychically and somatically. And so we must remind the Western, Judaized despiser of animals and idolater of the faculty of reason that, just as he was suckled by *his* mother, so too was the dog by *his*. Even Kant fell into this mistake of his contemporaries and countrymen; this I have already censured. The morality of Christianity has no consideration for animals, a defect that is better admitted than perpetuated. This is the more surprising since, in other respects, that morality shows the closest agreement with that of Brahmanism and Buddhism, being merely less strongly expressed, and not carried through to its very end. Therefore we can scarcely doubt that, like the idea of a god become man (avatar), the Christian morality originates from India and may have come to Judaea by way of Egypt, so that Christianity would be a reflected splendor of the primordial light of India from the ruins of Egypt; but unfortunately it fell on Jewish soil. The circumstance of John the Baptist coming before us quite like an Indian sannyasi, yet clad in the skin of an animal, could be viewed as an odd *symbol* of the defect in Christian morality just censured, in spite of its otherwise close agreement

31. Rudolph Wagner (1805–1864), physiologist and anthropologist, professor at Erlangen and Göttingen.—Tr.

with the Indian. We know, of course, that to every Hindu such a thing would be an abomination. Even the Royal Society of Calcutta received their copy of the Vedas only on their promising not to have it bound in leather, in the European style; it is therefore to be seen bound in silk in their library. Again, the Gospel story of Peter's draft of fishes, which the Savior blesses by a miracle to such an extent that the boats are overloaded with fish to the point of sinking (Luke 5:1–10), affords a similar characteristic contrast to the story of Pythagoras. Initiated as he was in the wisdom of the Egyptians, he bought up the draft from the fishermen while the net was still under water, in order to give all the captured fish their freedom (Apuleius, *De magia,* p. 36 Bip.). Since compassion for animals is so intimately associated with goodness of character, it may be confidently asserted that whoever is cruel to animals cannot be a good man. This compassion also appears to have sprung from the same source as the virtue that is shown to human beings has. Thus, for example, persons of delicate feelings, on realizing that in a bad mood, in anger, or under the influence of wine, they unnecessarily or excessively, or beyond propriety, ill-treated their dog, horse, or monkey—these people will feel the same remorse, the same dissatisfaction with themselves as is felt when they recall a wrong done to human beings, where it is called the voice of reproving conscience. I recall having read of an Englishman who, while hunting in India, had shot a monkey; he could not forget the look that the dying animal gave him, and since then had never again fired at monkeys. Similarly, William Harris, a true Nimrod, in 1836 and 1837 traveled far into the interior of Africa merely to enjoy the pleasure of hunting. In his book, published in Bombay in 1838, he describes how he shot his first elephant, a female. The next morning he went to look for the dead animal; all the other elephants had fled from the neighborhood except a young one, who had spent the night with his dead mother. Forgetting all fear, he came toward the sportsmen with the clearest and liveliest evidence of inconsolable grief, and put his tiny trunk round them in order to appeal to them for help. Harris says he was then filled with real remorse for what he had done, and felt as if he had committed a murder. We see this English nation of fine feelings distinguished above all others by a conspicuous sympathy for animals, which appears at every opportunity, and has been strong enough to induce the English, in spite of the "cold superstition" that otherwise degrades them, to repair by legislation the gap their religion has left in morality. For this is the very reason why in Europe and America societies for the protection of animals are needed, and they are effective only with the help of justice and the police. In Asia the religions afford sufficient protection to animals, and thus no one ever thinks of such societies. Meanwhile, in Europe a sense of the rights of animals is gradually awakening, in proportion to the slow dying and disappearing of the strange notions that the animal world came into existence simply for the benefit and pleasure of man. Such notions result in animals being treated exactly like things, for they are the source of their rough and quite ruthless treatment in Europe. In the second volume of the *Parerga,* section 177, I have shown that they are of Old Testament origin. To the glory of the English, then, let it be said that they are the first nation whose laws have quite seriously protected even the animals from cruel treatment. The ruffian must actually make amends for having committed an outrage on animals, even when they belong to him. Not content with this, the English have voluntarily formed in London a society for the protection of animals, known as the Society for the Prevention of Cruelty to Animals. By private means and at considerable expense, it does a great deal to counteract the tortures that are inflicted. Its emissaries are secretly on the watch to appear later and denounce the torturers of dumb, sensitive creatures, and everywhere their presence is feared.[32]

32. How seriously the matter is taken is shown by the following quite recent example that I quote from the *Birmingham Journal* of December 1839: "Arrest of a company of eighty-four promoters of dogfights. When it became known that a dogfight was to take place yesterday on the square in Fox Street, Birmingham, the Society of Animals' Friends took precautionary measures to secure the help of the police. A strong detachment of police went to the spot, and as soon as they got there, they arrested the whole company who were present. The accomplices were now handcuffed in pairs, and then the whole party was made fast by a long rope running down the middle. They were thus taken off to the police station where the mayor and magistrate were in session. The two ringleaders were each fined one pound and eight shillings and sixpence costs, and in default were sentenced to fourteen days' hard labor. The rest were released." The coxcombs whose habit is never to miss such noble sport must have looked very embarrassed in the procession. But we find in the *Times* of April 6, 1855, on p. 6, an even more striking example from recent times, and indeed the paper itself settling the matter. Thus it reports the case, brought before the courts, of the daughter of a very wealthy Scottish baronet. She had used with the greatest cruelty a cudgel and knife on her horse,

* * *

At steep bridges in London the society keeps a pair of horses that are attached gratis to every heavily loaded wagon. Is this not a fine thing? Does it not command our approbation precisely as does a good deed done to human beings? In 1837 the Philanthropic Society of London on its part offered a prize of thirty pounds for the best statement of the moral reasons against torturing animals. Such, however, had to be taken mainly from Christianity, and this naturally made the problem more difficult. In 1839 the prize was awarded to Mr. Macnamara. For similar purposes there is in Philadelphia an Animals' Friends' Society. T. Forster, an Englishman, dedicated to its president his book entitled *Philozoia, Moral Reflections on the Actual Condition of Animals and the Means of Improving the Same* (Brussels, 1839). The book is original and well written. As an Englishman, the author naturally attempts to make the Bible the basis of his exhortations to the humane treatment of animals, but he is always on slippery ground, so that in the end he resorts to the argument that Jesus Christ was born in a stable among oxen and asses. This was understood to mean symbolically that we had to regard animals as our brothers and treat them accordingly. All that I have mentioned here is evidence that the moral chord in question is at last beginning to vibrate even in the West. For the rest, sympathy for animals should not carry us to the length of having to abstain from animal food, like the Brahmans; for in nature the capacity for suffering keeps pace with intelligence, and thus man would suffer more by going without animal food, especially in the North, than the animal does through a quick

---

and for this she had been fined five pounds. But for such a girl this was nothing, and therefore would have amounted to no punishment at all, had not the *Times* intervened with a severe and proper reprimand by giving twice in large letters the girl's Christian name and surname and adding: "We cannot help saying that a few months' imprisonment with some whippings, administered in private, but by the most muscular woman in Hampshire, would have been a much more fitting punishment for Miss N. N. A miserable creature of this kind has forfeited all the consideration and privileges attaching to her sex. We can no longer regard her as a woman." I dedicate these newspaper reports especially to the societies against cruelty to animals that are now being formed in Germany, so that they will see how the problem must be tackled, if they are to obtain any result. However, I fully acknowledge the praiseworthy efforts of Herr Hofrath Perner in Munich, who has devoted himself entirely to this branch of doing good and has aroused interest all over Germany.

and always unforeseen death—which should, however, be made even easier by means of chloroform. Without animal food the human race could not even exist in the North. By the same token, man may also have the animal to work for him; cruelty occurs only when it is subjected to undue strain.

(8) If we entirely disregard for once all possible metaphysical examination of the ultimate ground of that compassion, from which alone nonegoistical actions can result; and if we consider it from the empirical point of view, merely as a natural arrangement, it will be clear to everyone that, for the greatest possible alleviation of the countless sufferings of every kind to which our life is exposed and from which no one entirely escapes, and at the same time as a counterbalance to the burning egoism that fills all beings and often develops into malice, nature could not have done anything more effective than plant that wonderful disposition in the human heart. By virtue of it, one man shares the sufferings of another, and we hear the voice that calls firmly and clearly to one, "Show forbearance!" and to another, "Give help!" according to the occasion. From the resultant mutual assistance one could certainly expect more for the welfare of all than from a strict command of duty couched in general and abstract terms and resulting from certain rational considerations and combinations of concepts. From such a command the expected result would be less, since universal propositions and abstract truths are quite unintelligible to the untutored, for whom only the concrete has any meaning. But with the exception of an extremely small part, the whole of mankind was always rough and uncultured and must remain so, since the large amount of physical work, inevitably necessary for the race as a whole, leaves no time for the cultivation of the mind. On the other hand, to awaken that compassion that is shown to be the *sole source of disinterested actions and hence the true basis of morality*, there is no need for abstract knowledge, but only for that of intuitive perception, for the mere apprehension of the concrete case to which compassion at once appeals without any further mediation of ideas.

(9) We shall find the following circumstance to be wholly in agreement with this last observation. The foundation I have given to ethics certainly leaves me without a predecessor among the school philosophers; in fact, with reference to their teachings, it is

paradoxical. For many of them, the Stoics, for instance (Seneca, *De clementia* 2:5), Spinoza (*Ethics*, 4, prop. 50), Kant (*Critique of Practical Reason*, p. 213, R. 257 [Academy 118]), positively reject and condemn compassion. On the other hand, my foundation is supported by the authority of J.J. Rousseau, who was undoubtedly the greatest moralist of modern times. He is the profound judge of the human heart, who drew his wisdom not from books but from life, and intended his doctrine not for the professorial chair but for humanity. He is the enemy of all prejudice, the pupil of nature; he alone was endowed by nature with the gift of being able to moralize without being tedious, for he hit upon the truth and touched the heart. Having been in my previous remarks as sparing as possible with quotations, I will now venture to quote in confirmation of my own view a few passages from Rousseau.

In the *Discourse on the Origin of Inequality [Discours sur l'origine de l'inégalité]*, p. 91 (Bip.), he says:

> There is another principle that Hobbes has not observed at all, which, having been given to man to soothe in certain circumstances the ferocity of his egoism and self-esteem, moderates the ardor he has for his own well-being by means of *an innate repugnance at seeing his fellow men suffer*. I do not think that I have any contradiction to fear in ascribing to man the *sole natural virtue* that the most strenuous and zealous detractor of human virtues has been forced to acknowledge. I speak of *pity and compassion*, etc. . . . . (p. 92): Mandeville has rightly recognized that, with all their morality, men would never have been anything but hideous monsters, had not nature given them *compassion* as a support for their faculty of reason. But he did not see that *from this one quality spring all the social virtues* that he wishes to deny men. In fact, what are generosity, clemency, and humanity if not *compassion* that is applied to the weak, the guilty, or even the entire human race? Properly understood, benevolence and even friendship are the result of a constant pity that is fixed on a particular object. For to desire that someone will not suffer at all is simply nothing but to desire that he may be happy. . . . The commiseration will be the more energetic, the more intimately *the spectator identifies himself with the sufferer*. (p. 91): It is therefore quite certain that compassion is a natural feeling that moderates in every individual his self-esteem, and contributes to the mutual preservation of the entire race. It is pity that in the state of nature takes the place of laws, customs,

and virtues, with the added advantage that no one will be tempted to disobey its gentle voice. It is pity that will dissuade every rough and brutal savage from depriving a weak child or an infirm old man of the sustenance acquired through much trouble, if he himself hopes to find his own elsewhere. It is pity that, instead of that sublime maxim of reasoned justice, 'Let us do unto others as we would be done by,' inspires all men with that other less perfect but perhaps more useful maxim of natural kindness, "Achieve your well-being with the least possible harm to others." In a word, *in this natural feeling, rather than in subtle arguments, does one have to look for the cause of the repugnance that everyone would experience in doing something wicked,* quite independently of the maxims of education.

Compare this with what he says in *Émile,* book 4, p. 115–20 (Bip.), where, among other things, it states:

> In fact, how can we let ourselves be moved to pity unless by transporting ourselves outside ourselves and *identifying ourselves with the suffering animal, by quitting, so to speak, our own being in order to assume his?* Here we suffer only to the extent that we think he suffers; *it is not in ourselves but in him that we suffer.* . . . *We must offer to a young man* objects on which the expansive force of his heart can act, which expand and extend it to other beings, and which cause him everywhere *to find himself again outside himself.* On the other hand, he must carefully avoid those objects that might restrain and repress his heart and stretch the mainspring of the *human I or ego,* etc. —Tr.

As I have said, no authorities from the schools support my case; yet I state that the *Chinese* accept five cardinal virtues (*Chang*) headed by compassion (*Sin*), the other four being justice, politeness, wisdom, and sincerity.[33] Similarly, we see also with the Hindus that on the commemorative tablets, erected to the memory of deceased princes, compassion for human beings and animals occupies first place among the virtues with which they were credited. In Athens, compassion had an altar in the marketplace: *The Athenians have in the marketplace an altar to compassion. They are the only Greeks who worship this god, because of all the gods he is the*

---

33. *Journal asiatique,* vol. 9:62, to be compared with *Meng-Tseu,* ed. Stan. Julien (1824), book 1, section 45, also with *Meng-Tseu* in the *Livres sacrés de l'orient* (Pauthier), p. 281.

most influential in human life and its vicissitudes.[34] Lucian also mentions this altar in the *Timon*, section 99. A saying of Phocion, preserved by Stobaeus, describes compassion as the most sacred thing in man: *We must not tear the altar from a temple, or compassion from the human heart.*[35] In the *Sapientia Indorum*, which is the Greek translation of the *Panchatantra*, it says (section 3, p. 220): *For it says that compassion is the first of all the virtues.*[36] We see that all ages and countries have clearly recognized the source of morality; Europe alone has not, and for this only the *foetor Judaicus* is to blame, for it pervades everything. To Europeans, the source positively must be a command of duty, a moral law, an imperative—in short, an order and decree that is obeyed. From this they will not depart, nor see that such things always have ony egoism as their basis. Of course, isolated individuals of superior insight have felt and become aware of the truth. Rousseau was such a man, as I have previously shown, and in a letter written in 1756, Lessing also says, "The most compassionate man is the best, the one most disposed to all the social virtues and to all forms of magnanimity."

20

On the Ethical Difference of Characters

The last question that needs to be answered, for the completeness of the foundation of ethics as expounded by me, is as follows. On what rests the great difference in the moral behavior of human beings? If compassion is the fundamental incentive of all genuine, i.e., disinterested, justice and loving-kindness, why is it that one man is influenced by it whereas another is not? Is it possible that ethics, in discovering the moral incentive, is also capable of setting it in motion? Can ethics transform the man who is hard-hearted into one who is compassionate, and thereby just and humane? Certainly not; the difference of characters is innate and ineradicable. The wicked man is born with his wickedness as much as the serpent is with its poisonous fangs and glands; and he is as little

34. Pausanias, 1:17:1.—Tr.
35. Stobaeus, *Florilegium* 1:31.—Tr.
36. The *Panchatantra* is a collection of fables of Indian origin, in five books, compiled in the fifth century.—Tr.

able to change his character as the serpent its fangs. *Velle non discitur*[37] was a saying of Nero's tutor. In the *Meno*, Plato investigates in detail whether or not virtue can be taught; he quotes a passage from Theognis:

> *Indeed, by instruction a bad man is never made good.*[38]

and arrives at the result:

> *Virtue does not come to us naturally, nor can it be taught; but whoever is endowed with it has it apportioned to him by divine ordinance and without intellect.*[39]

Here the difference seems to indicate one between physical and metaphysical. Socrates, the father of ethics, asserts, according to the statement of Aristotle:

> *It is not in our power to be either good or bad.*[40]

Aristotle also expresses himself in the same sense:

> *For, as it seems, the particular traits of character are already in some way by nature peculiar to all; for a tendency to justice, moderation, bravery, and the like is already peculiar to us from birth.*

Similarly, we find this conviction very definitely expressed in the fragments of the Pythagorean Archytas, which are in any case very old, though possibly not genuine, and have been preserved by Stobaeus in the *Florilegium* 1:77. They are also given by Orelli in his *Short and Concise Moral Works of the Greeks* [*Opuscula Graecorum sententiosa et moralia*] (vol. 2, p. 240). It says there in the Dorian dialect:

> *For those virtues, relying on reason and demonstration, must be called sciences. On the other hand, ethical virtue, which is the best, is understood to be a disposition of the soul's irrational*

37. Seneca, *Epistle* 81:14.—Tr.
38. *Meno* 96a.—Tr.
39. *Meno* 99e.—Tr.
40. *Magna moralia* 1:9.—Tr.

part *on the basis whereof we are regarded as possessing a definite ethical nature, for example, as being generous, just, and
temperate.*

If we survey all the virtues and vices, concisely summarized by
Aristotle in his book *On Virtues and Vices* [*De virtutibus et vitiis*],
we shall find that they are all conceivable only as inborn qualities,
in fact, that only as such can they be genuine. If, on the other
hand, in consequence of rational reflection they were assumed to
be voluntary or arbitrary, they would really end in fictions and be
spurious; and so their continued existence and confirmation under
the pressure of circumstances could not be counted on at all. It
is the same with regard to philanthropy or loving-kindness, not
mentioned by Aristotle or by any of the ancients. Although keeping
up his skeptical tone, Montaigne therefore says, in the same sense:
*Seroit-il vrai, que pour être bon tout-à-fait, il nous le faille être par
occulte, naturelle et universelle propriété, sans loi, sans raison, sans
exemple?* (book 2, chap. 11)[41] But Lichtenberg says quite plainly:
"All virtue arising from premeditation is not worth much. Feeling
or habit is the thing" (*Miscellaneous Writings* [*Vermischte Schriften*], "Moral Observations"). But even the original teaching of
Christianity agrees with this view, since it says in the Sermon on
the Mount itself (Luke 6:45):

> *A good man out of the good treasure of his heart bringeth forth
> that which is good; and an evil man out of the evil treasure of
> his heart bringeth forth that which is evil.*[42]

In the two previous verses (Luke 6:43–44), an allegorical explanation of the matter was given, of the fruit that always turns out in
accordance with its tree.

But it was Kant who first completely cleared up this important
point through his great doctrine that the *intelligible character* underlies the *empirical,* the latter as phenomenon appearing in time
and a plurality of actions. The intelligible character is the essential
constitution of the thing-in-itself of that phenomenon and is, there-

---

41. Would it be true that, to be thoroughly good, it would be necessary for
us to be so through an occult, natural, and universal quality, without law, reason,
or example? *(Essays.)*—TR.
42. King James version.—TR.

fore, independent of space and time, of plurality and change. Only in this way can we explain the rigid unalterability of characters that is so astonishing and familiar to anyone of experience. Ethical writers who promise to produce a system of ethics that will morally improve man and who speak of a progress in virtue are always triumphantly refuted by reality and experience, which have demonstrated that virtue is inborn and cannot result from sermons. As something original, character is unchangeable, and therefore impervious to all improvement by means of a rectification of knowledge. If this were not so, and again if, as that shallow ethics asserts, an improvement of the character could occur through morality and accordingly "a constant advance toward the good" were possible, then the older half of humanity would inevitably be considerably better, at any rate on the average, than the younger, unless all the many religious institutions and attempts at moralizing were to have failed in their purpose. But there is so little trace of such an improvement that, on the contrary, we hope for something good rather from the young than from the old, the latter having become worse through experience. It is true that in old age one man may seem better and another worse than he was in his youth. But this is due merely to the fact that in old age, as a result of riper and constantly corrected knowledge, the character stands out more clearly and distinctly; whereas in youth, ignorance, errors and chimeras at one moment presented false motives, and at another concealed the real ones. This follows from what was said in the previous essay on the *Freedom of the Will,* on pages seqq. under section 3.[43] Among convicted criminals there are very many more young people than old, for this reason, that where a tendency to such criminal actions exists in the character, it soon finds the opportunity to appear as a deed and attains its goal, namely, the galleys or gallows. On the other hand, the man who could not be induced to commit a crime by all the opportunities of a long life, is not likely, on the strength of motives, to plunge into crime at the eleventh hour. And so the real reason for the respect paid to old age seems to me to be that an old man has passed the test of a long life and has preserved his integrity; for this is the condition

---

43. *Essay on the Freedom of the Will,* trans. Konstantin Kolenda, "Library of Liberal Arts," no. 70 (New York: Liberal Arts Press, Inc., 1960), pp. 51ff.—Tr.

of such respect. According to this view, we have never been led astray in real life by those promises of the moralists; on the contrary, we have never again trusted the man who has once proved himself to be bad, and we have always viewed with confidence the magnanimity of him who had once shown proofs of it, even when everything else might have changed. *Operari sequitur esse*[44] is a pregnant proposition of scholasticism; everything in the world acts in accordance with its unchangeable nature; this constitutes its true being, its *essentia*. It is the same with man. As a man *is*, so will he, so must he, act, and the *liberum arbitrium indifferentiae*[45] is an invention from the childhood of philosophy that has long since been exploded, but that a few old women in doctor's hats still like to trail around.

Man's three fundamental ethical incentives, egoism, malice, and compassion, are present in everyone in different and incredibly unequal proportions. In accordance with them, motives will operate on man and actions will ensue. Over an egoistical character only egoistical motives will have any influence, and those appealing to compassion or malice will make no headway. Such a man will as little sacrifice his interests to vengeance on his enemy, as to assistance to his friend. Another man, very susceptible to malicious motives, will often not shrink from great harm to himself in order to injure others. For there are characters who, in causing suffering to others, find a pleasure that outweighs their own equally great suffering. *Dum alteri noceat sui negligens* (Seneca, *De ira* 1:1).[46] These characters plunge with passionate delight into the encounter in which they expect to receive as many wounds as they hope to inflict. In fact, experience has very often shown that they will deliberately murder the man who has done them an injury and will then, to escape punishment, at once commit suicide. On the other hand, *goodness of heart* consists in a deeply felt, universal compassion for every living thing, but primarily for man; for susceptibility to suffering keeps pace with enhancement of intelligence, and therefore man's innumerable mental and physical sufferings have a much stronger claim to compassion than have the sufferings of animals, which are only physical and themselves less acute. Accord-

44. What we do follows from what we are.—TR.
45. The free decision of the will, not influenced in any direction.—TR.
46. He pays no regard to himself, if only he can injure another.—TR.

ingly, goodness of character will first refrain from doing any injury to others, whatever it be, and will then urge us to help wherever the suffering of another presents itself. And even in this direction, one can go just as far as one can in the opposite direction, with malice; namely, there are characters of rare goodness who take more to heart the sufferings of others than their own, and who, therefore, make sacrifices for others whereby they themselves suffer more than did the man whom they helped. Where several or even very many are to be helped simultaneously, in this way, such characters will, if need be, completely sacrifice themselves; Arnold von Winkelried did so. In the fifth century, while the Vandals from Africa invaded Italy, it is related of Paulinus, bishop of Nola (Johannes von Müller's *Universal History* [*Weltgeschichte*], book 10, chap. 10): "In order to ransom prisoners, he had already disposed of the treasures of the Church, his own and his friends' property, when he saw a widow's great distress. Her only son was being carried off, and Paulinus offered himself for servitude in his place. For whoever was of the right age and had not fallen by the sword, was taken prisoner to Carthage."

In consequence of this incredibly great, inborn, and original difference, everyone will be powerfully stirred by *those* motives to which he is predominantly susceptible, just as one body reacts only to acids and another only to alkalies: the one, like the other, cannot be changed. The motives of loving-kindness that are for the good character such powerful incentives, can as such have no influence on a man who is susceptible only to egoistical motives. If, however, we wish to induce the egoist to perform actions of loving-kindness, we can do it only by deluding him with ideas that the alleviation of another's suffering contributes indirectly in some way *to his own advantage* (indeed, most doctrines of morals are really attempts of different kinds in this sense). In this way, however, his will is merely misled, not improved. For a real improvement, it would be necessary to transform the entire nature of his susceptibility to motives. Thus, for example, one man should no longer be indifferent to another's sufferings as such; a second should no longer feel pleasure in causing suffering to another; and for a third, no increase of his own well-being, not even the smallest, should far outweigh and render ineffective all motives of a different kind. This, however, is certainly much more impossible than changing lead into gold. For it would be necessary to turn the man's heart around in his body, so to speak, to transform the very essence of his being. On the contrary, all that we can do is clear the *head,* correct the *insight,* bring the man to a better comprehension of what objectively exists, of the true circumstances of life. Yet nothing further is gained from this than that the nature of his will reveals itself more consistently, distinctly, and definitely, and expresses itself more genuinely and sincerely. For, just as many a good action at bottom rests on false motives, on well-meant but deluded notions of an advantage to oneself to be thereby obtained in this world or the next, so does many a misdeed rest merely on false knowledge of the circumstances of human life. The American penitentiary system is based on this, in which the intention is not to improve the *heart* of the criminal, but merely to put his *head* on the right lines, so that he will come to see that work and honesty are a surer, indeed easier way to his own prosperity than are roguery and knavery.

Legality may be enforced through motives, but not *morality;* we can remodel *what we do,* but not really *what we will to do,* to which alone moral worth attaches. We cannot change the goal that the will aspires to, but only the path it follows there. Instruction can alter the choice of means, but not that of the ultimate general aims; every will determines these for itself in accordance with its original nature. We can point out to the egoist that by giving up small advantages, he will obtain the greater, and we can show a malicious person that by causing suffering to others, he will bring on himself greater afflictions. But we shall not dissuade anyone from egoism itself, from malice itself, any more than we can talk a cat out of her propensity for catching mice. Through an increase in insight, through instruction concerning the circumstances of life, and thus by enlightening the mind, even goodness of character can be brought to a more logical and complete expression of its true nature. This happens, for example, when the remoter consequences that our action has for others are pointed out to us, such as the sufferings that come to them indirectly and only in the course of time, and that arise from this or that action that we did not consider to be so bad. The same thing occurs when we hear of the harmful consequences of many a good-hearted action, for example, the excusing of a criminal, and especially when we learn of the precedence that the *neminem laede* has always over the *omnes juva*. In this respect, there certainly is a moral education, an ethical system that improves; but it does not go beyond this, and its limits can easily be seen. The head becomes clear; the heart remains unreformed. The fundamental element, the positive factor, in the moral as well as the intellectual and the physical, is *that which is inborn;* art can everywhere only help. Everyone is what he is "by the grace of God," so to speak, *jure divino.*

> You're after all—just what you are.
> Wear wigs of a million ringlets as you will,
> Put ell-thick soles beneath your feet, and still
> You will remain just what you are.[47]

But I have long been listening to the reader put the question: Where are guilt and merit to be found? For the answer to this I refer to section 10. What would otherwise have to be stated *here* found its place in that section because it was closely connected with Kant's doctrine of the coexistence of freedom with necessity. I therefore request the reader to study once more what was said there. In accordance with that statement, the *operari* (what we do) is absolutely necessary when the motives make their appearance; and therefore *freedom,* which proclaims itself alone through *responsibility,* can be found only in the *esse* (what we are). It is true that the reproaches of conscience primarily and ostensibly concern what we *have done,* but really and ultimately what we *are;* for our deeds alone afford us conclusive evidence of what we are, since they are related to our character as the symptoms to the disease. Thus guilt and merit must also lie in this *esse,* in what we *are.* What we either esteem and love or despise and hate in others is not something changeable and transient, but enduring and existing once for all; it is what they *are.* And if at any time we alter our opinion of them, we do not say that they have changed, but that we have been mistaken about them. In the same way, the object of our satisfaction and dissatisfaction with ourselves is *what we are,* what we irrevocably are and remain; this extends even to qualities of the intellect and, indeed, to those of physiognomy. Therefore

47. Goethe, *Faust,* trans. Charles Passage, part 1, "Study Room," lines 1806–9.—Tr.

how could guilt and merit lie anywhere else than in *what we are?*
Conscience is the acquaintance with ourselves that becomes ever
more complete; it is the *register of deeds* that becomes more and
more filled up. The theme of conscience is primarily our actions,
indeed, either those in which, because we were guided by egoism
or even malice, we gave no ear to compassion, who urged us at
least not to injure others and even to afford them help and support;
or those in which, with the renunciation of egoism and malice, we
followed compassion's call. Both cases indicate the extent of the
difference we make *between ourselves and others.* On such *difference* ultimately rest the degrees of morality or immorality, in other
words, of justice and philanthropy as also of their opposite. The
recollection of actions that are significant in this respect becomes
ever richer, and forms an ever more complete picture of our character, the true acquaintance with ourselves. But from this there arises
satisfaction or dissatisfaction with ourselves, with what we are,
according as we have been ruled by egoism, malice, or compassion,
that is to say, according as the difference we have made between
our own person and others has been greater or smaller. By the
same standard, we likewise judge others whose characters we get
to know just as empirically as we do our own, only less perfectly.
What showed itself as satisfaction or dissatisfaction (the latter can
become pangs of conscience) when we sat in judgment on ourselves, appears here as praise, approbation, and esteem, or censure,
vexation, and contempt. Many very frequently used expressions
are also evidence of the fact that the reproaches we cast on others
are directed only *in the first instance* to their deeds, but *really* to
their unchangeable character, and that virtue and vice are regarded
as inherent and enduring qualities. Thus, for example, we have:
Jetzt sehe ich, wie du bist! (Now I see what you are!) *In dir habe
ich mich geirrt* (I was mistaken in you). *Voilà donc, comme tu es!*
(There, that's the kind of person you are!) *So bin ich nicht!* (I am
not such a person!) *Ich bin nicht der Mann, der fähig wäre, Sie zu
hintergehn* (I am not the man who would be capable of deceiving
you). And many others. Also *les âmes bien nées* (persons of excellent disposition); again, in Spanish, *bien nacido* (wellborn); *gener-
osioris animi amicus* (a friend of nobler spirit), and so on.
  Conscience is conditioned by the faculty of reason merely because a clear and connected recollection is possible only by virtue

of it. It lies in the nature of the case that conscience speaks only *afterward;* and thus conscience is said to *pronounce judgment.* Conscience can speak *beforehand* only in a figurative, not in a literal sense, and thus indirectly, since reflection infers from the recollection of similar cases the future disapproval of a deed that is as yet only contemplated. The ethical fact of consciousness goes thus far; it is itself a metaphysical problem that does not directly form part of our question; however, I shall touch on it in the last section. Conscience is an acquaintance with our own unalterable character, which we make only through the medium of our deeds. This knowledge harmonizes perfectly with the fact that *susceptibility* to the motives of selfishness, malice, and compassion, which differs so widely in different men and on which the whole of man's moral worth depends, is not a thing that can be explained from something else or acquired through instruction, and therefore something originating in time, and changeable—in fact, dependent on chance. On the contrary, it is something that is inborn, unchangeable, and incapable of further explanation. The course of life itself with all its manifold activities accordingly is nothing but a clockface of that inner original mechanism; or it is the mirror in which alone the nature of everyone's own will, that is the very core of his being, can become clear to his intellect.

Whoever takes the trouble to think over carefully what has been said here and in section 10, will discover in my foundation of ethics a consistency and well-rounded completeness that are wanting in all other ethical systems. On the other hand, between my system and the facts of experience, he will discover an agreement that those others have to an even lesser degree. For only truth can be universally in harmony with itself and with nature; on the other hand, all false fundamental views are internally at variance with one another, and externally contrary to experience, which at every step enters its silent protest.

I am well aware, yet without any feelings of remorse or regret, that the truths expounded in this essay, especially here at the end, strike directly at many deeply rooted prejudices and errors, particularly at a certain nursery-school morality that is now in vogue. For in the first place, I am here addressing not children or ordinary people, but an enlightened academy whose purely theoretical question is directed to the ultimate fundamental truths of ethics, and who also expects a serious answer to an extremely serious question. In the second place, I am of the opinion that there cannot be either privileged, useful, or even harmless errors, but that every error does infinitely more harm than good. On the other hand, if it were the intention to make prevailing prejudices the standard of truth or the boundary mark beyond which the expounding of truth may not go, then it would be more honest to abolish philosophical faculties and academies entirely; for what does not exist should also not appear.

Translated by E. F. J. Payne

14

Aphorisms on the Wisdom of Life

Fundamental Division

Aristotle (*Nicomachean Ethics*, 8) has divided the good things of human life into three classes, those outside, those of the soul, and those of the body. Now retaining nothing of this except the number three, I say that what establishes the difference in the lot of mortals may be reduced to three fundamental qualifications. They are:

(1) What a man *is* and therefore personality in the widest sense. Accordingly, under this are included health, strength, beauty, temperament, moral character, intelligence and its cultivation.

(2) What a man *has* and therefore property and possessions in every sense.

(3) What a man *represents;* we know that by this expression is understood what he is in the eyes of others and thus how he *is represented* by them. Accordingly, it consists in their opinion of him and is divisible into honor, rank, and reputation.

The differences to be considered under the first heading are those established by nature herself between one man and another. From this it may be inferred that their influence on the happiness or unhappiness of mankind will be much more fundamental and radical than what is produced by the differences that are mentioned under the two following headings and result merely from human decisions and resolutions. Compared with *genuine personal advantages,* such as a great mind or a great heart, all the privileges of rank, birth, even royal birth, wealth, and so on, are as kings on the stage to kings in real life. Metrodorus, the first disciple of Epicurus, gave the title to a chapter: *The cause of happiness that lies within us is greater than the cause that comes from things.* (Cf. Clement of Alexandria, *Stromata*, lib. 2, c. 21, p. 362 of the Würzburg edition of the polemical works.) And it is certain that for man's well-being, indeed for his whole mode of existence, the main thing is obviously what exists or occurs within himself. For here is to be found immediately his inner satisfaction or dissatisfaction that is primarily the result of his feeling, his willing, and his thinking. On the other hand, everything situated outside him has on him only an indirect influence; and so the same external events and circumstances affect each of us quite differently; and indeed with the same environment each lives in a world of his own. For a man is directly concerned only with his own conceptions, feelings, and voluntary movements; things outside influence him only insofar as they give rise to these. The world in which each lives depends first on his interpretation thereof and therefore proves to be different to different men. Accordingly, it will result in being poor, shallow, and superficial, or rich, interesting, and full of meaning. For example, while many envy another man the interesting events that have happened to him in his life, they should rather envy his gift of interpretation that endowed those events with the significance they have when he describes them. For the same event that appears to be so interesting in the mind of a man of intelligence would be only a dull and vapid scene from the commonplace world when conceived in the shallow mind of an ordinary man. This is seen in the highest degree in many of Goethe's and Byron's poems that are obviously based on real events. Here it is open to the foolish reader to envy the poet the most delightful event, instead of envying him the mighty imagination that was capable of making something so great and beautiful from a fairly commonplace occurrence. In the same way, a man of melancholy disposition sees a scene from a tragedy, where one of sanguine temperament sees only an interesting conflict and someone phlegmatic sees something trifling and unimportant. All this is due to the fact that every reality, in other words, every moment of actual experience, consists of two halves, the subject and the object, although in just as necessary and close a connection as are oxygen and hydrogen in water. Therefore when the objective half is exactly the same, but the subjective is different, the present reality is quite different, just as it is in the reverse case; thus the finest and best objective half with a dull and inferior subjective half furnishes only an inferior reality, like a beautiful landscape in bad weather or in the reflected light of a bad camera obscura. In plainer language, everyone is confined to his consciousness as he is within his own skin and only in this does he really live; thus he cannot be helped very much from without. On the stage one man is a prince, another a councillor, a third a servant, a soldier, or a general, and so on. These differences, however, exist only on the outer surface; in the interior, as the kernel of such a phenomenon, the same thing is to be found in all of them, namely, a poor player with his wants and worries. In life it is also the same. Differences of rank and wealth give everyone his part to play, but there is certainly not an internal difference of happiness and satisfaction that corresponds to that role. On the contrary, here too there is in everyone the same poor wretch with his worries and wants. Materially these may be different in everyone, but in form and thus in their essential nature they are pretty much the same in all, although with differences of degree that do not by any means correspond to position and wealth, in other words, to the part a man plays. Thus since everything existing and happening for man directly exists always in his own *consciousness* and happens only for this, the nature thereof is obviously the first essential and in most cases this is more important than are the forms that present themselves therein. All the pomp and pleasure that are mirrored in the dull consciousness of a simpleton are very poor when compared with the consciousness of Cervantes writing *Don Quixote* in a miserable prison. The objective half of the present reality is in the hands of fate and is accordingly changeable; we ourselves are the subjective half that is, therefore, essentially unchangeable. Accordingly, the life of every man bears throughout the same character in spite of all change from without and is comparable to a series of variations on one theme. No one can get outside his own individuality. In all the circumstances in which the animal is placed, it remains confined to the narrow circle, irrevocably drawn for it by nature, so that, for instance, our endeavors to make a pet happy must always keep within narrow bounds precisely on account of those limits of its true nature and consciousness. It is the same with man; the measure of his possible happiness is determined beforehand by his individuality. In particular, the limits of his mental powers have fixed once for all his capacity for pleasures of a higher order. (Cf. *World as Will and Representation*, vol. 2, chap. 7.) If those powers are small, all the efforts from without, everything done for him by mankind or good fortune, will not enable him to rise above the ordinary half-animal human happiness and comfort. He is left to depend on the pleasures of the senses, on a cosy and cheerful family life, on low company and vulgar pastimes. Even education, on the whole, cannot do very much, if anything, to broaden his horizon. For the highest, most varied, and most permanent pleasures are those of the mind, however much we may deceive ourselves on this point when we are young; but these pleasures depend mainly on innate mental powers. Therefore it is clear from this how much our happiness depends on what we *are*, our individuality, whereas in most cases we take into account only our fate, only what we *have* or *represent*. Fate, however, can improve; moreover, if we are inwardly wealthy we shall not demand much from it. On the other hand, a fool remains a fool, a dull blockhead a dull blockhead, till the end of his life, even if he were surrounded by houris in paradise. Therefore Goethe says;

> Mob, menial, and master
> At all time admit,
> The supreme fortune of mortals
> Is their personality alone.
>
> *Westöstlicher Diwan*

Everything confirms that the subjective is incomparably more essential to our happiness and pleasures than is the objective, namely, from the fact that hunger is the best sauce, hoary old age regards the goddess of youth with indifference, up to the life of the genius and the saint. In particular, health so far outweighs all external blessings that a healthy beggar is indeed more fortunate than a monarch in poor health. A quiet and cheerful temperament, resulting from perfect health and a prosperous economy, an understanding that is clear, lively, penetrating, and sees things correctly, a moderate and gentle will and hence a good conscience—these are advantages that no rank or wealth can make good or replace. For what a man is by himself, what accompanies him into solitude, and what no one can give him or take from him is obviously more essential to him than everything he possesses, or even what he may be in the eyes of others. A man of intellect, when entirely alone, has excellent entertainment in his own thoughts and fancies, whereas the continuous diversity of parties, plays, excursions, and amusements cannot ward off from a dullard the tortures of boredom. A good, moderate, gentle character can be contented in needy circumstances, whereas one who is covetous, envious, and malicious is not so, in spite of all his wealth. Indeed for the man who constantly has the delight of an extraordinary and intellectually eminent individuality, most of the pleasures that are generally sought after are entirely superfluous; indeed they are only a bother and a burden. Therefore Horace says of himself:

> Gemmas, marmor, ebur, Tyrrhena sigilla, tabellas,
> Argentum, vestes Gaetulo murice tinctas,
> Sunt qui non habeant, est qui non curat habere;[1]

and when Socrates saw luxury articles displayed for sale, he said: "How many things there are I do not need!"

Accordingly, for our life's happiness, what we *are*, our personality, is absolutely primary and most essential, if only because it is operative at all times and in all circumstances. Moreover, unlike the blessings under the other two headings, it is not subject to fate and cannot be wrested from us. To this extent its value can be described as absolute in contrast to the merely relative value of the other two. Now it follows from this that it is much more difficult to get at a man from without than is generally supposed. Only the all-powerful agent, Time, here exercises its right; physical and mental advantages gradually succumb to it; moral character alone remains inaccessible to it. In this respect, it would naturally appear that the blessings which are enumerated under the second and third headings, of which time cannot directly deprive us, have an advantage over those of the first. A second advantage might be found in the fact, that, as such blessings lie in the objective, they are by their nature attainable and everyone has before him at least the

---

1. Ivory, marble, trinkets, Tyrrhenian statues, pictures, silver plate, clothes dyed with Gaetulian purple, many do without such things, and some do not bother about them. *Epistles*, 2:2:180.—Tr.

possibility of coming into possession of them, whereas the subjective is certainly not given into our power, but has entered *jure divino*[2] and is unalterably fixed for the whole of life, so that here Goethe's words inexorably apply:

> As on the day that lent you to the world
> The sun received the planets' greetings,
> At once and eternally you have thrived
> According to the law whereby you stepped forth.
> So must you be, from yourself you cannot flee,
> So have the Sibyls and the Prophets said;
> No time, no power breaks into little pieces
> The form here stamped and in life developed.

The only thing that in this respect lies within our power is for us to take the greatest possible advantage of the given personality and accordingly to follow only those tendencies that are in keeping with it and to strive for the kind of development that is exactly suitable to it, while avoiding every other, and consequently to choose the position, occupation, and way of life that are suited to it. . . .

What a Man Is

We have in general recognized that this contributes much more to a man's happiness than what he *has* or *represents*. It always depends on what a man is and accordingly has in himself; for his individuality always and everywhere accompanies him and everything experienced by him is tinged thereby. In everything and with everything he first of all enjoys only himself; this already applies to physical pleasures and how much truer is it of those of the mind! Therefore the English words "to enjoy oneself"[3] are a very apt expression; for example, we do not say "he enjoys Paris," but "he enjoys *himself* in Paris."[4] Now if the individuality is ill-conditioned, all pleasures are like choice wines in a mouth that is made bitter with gall. Accordingly, if we leave out of account cases

---

2. By divine right.—TR.
3. Schopenhauer's own words.—TR.
4. Schopenhauer's own words.—TR.

of grave misfortune, less depends, in the good things as well as in the bad, on what befalls and happens to us in life than on the way in which we feel it, and thus on the nature and degree of our susceptibility in every respect. What a man is and has in himself, that is to say, personality and its worth, is the sole immediate factor in his happiness and well-being. Everything else is mediate and indirect and so the effect thereof can be neutralized and frustrated; that of personality never. For this reason, the envy excited by personal qualities is the most implacable, as it is also the most carefully concealed. Further, the constitution of consciousness is what is permanent and enduring and individuality is at work constantly and incessantly more or less at every moment. Everything else, on the other hand, acts only at times, occasionally, temporarily, and in addition is subject to variation and change. Therefore Aristotle says: *For we can depend on nature, not on money.* (*Eudemian Ethics*, 7:2.) To this is due the fact that we can bear with more composure a misfortune that has befallen us entirely from without than one that we have brought upon ourselves, for fate can change, but our own nature never. Therefore subjective blessings, such as a noble character, a gifted mind, a happy temperament, cheerful spirits, and a well-conditioned thoroughly sound body, and so generally *mens sana in corpore sano*[5] (Juvenal, *Satires*, 10:356), are for our happiness primary and the most important. We should, therefore, be much more concerned to promote and preserve such qualities than to possess external wealth and external honor.

Now of all those qualities the one that most immediately makes us happy is cheerfulness of disposition; for this good quality is its own instantaneous reward. Whoever is merry and cheerful has always a good reason for so being, namely, the very fact that he is so. Nothing can so completely take the place of every other blessing as can this quality, whilst it itself cannot be replaced by anything. A man may be young, handsome, wealthy, and esteemed; if we wish to judge of his happiness, we ask whether he is cheerful. On the other hand, if he is cheerful, it matters not whether he is young or old, straight or humpbacked, rich or poor; he is happy. In my youth, I once opened an old book in which it said: "Whoever laughs a lot is happy, and whoever weeps a lot is unhappy," a very simple remark, but because of its plain truth I have been unable to

---

5. A healthy mind in a healthy body.—Tr.

forget it, however much it may be the superlative of a truism. For this reason, we should open wide the doors to cheerfulness whenever it makes its appearance, for it never comes inopportunely. Instead of doing this, we often hesitate to let it enter, for we first want to know whether we have every reason to be contented; or because we are afraid of being disturbed by cheerfulness when we are involved in serious deliberations and heavy cares. But what we improve through these is very uncertain, whereas cheerfulness is an immediate gain. It alone is, so to speak, the very coin of happiness and not, like everything else, merely a check on a bank; for only it makes us immediately happy in the present moment. And so it is the greatest blessing for beings whose reality takes the form of an indivisible present moment between an infinite past and an infinite future. Accordingly, we should make the acquisition and encouragement of this blessing our first endeavor. Now it is certain that nothing contributes less to cheerfulness than wealth and nothing contributes more than health. The lower classes or the workers, especially those in the country, have the more cheerful and contented faces; peevishness and ill humor are more at home among the wealthy upper classes. Consequently, we should endeavor above all to maintain a high degree of health, the very bloom of which appears as cheerfulness. The means to this end are, as we know, avoidance of all excesses and irregularities, of all violent and disagreeable emotions, and also of all mental strain that is too great and too prolonged, two hours' brisk exercise every day in the open air, many cold baths, and similar dietetic measures. Without proper daily exercise no one can remain healthy; all the vital processes demand exercise for their proper performance, exercise not only of the parts wherein they occur, but also of the whole. Therefore Aristotle rightly says: *life begins in movement*. Life consists in movement and has its very essence therein. Ceaseless and rapid motion occurs in every part of the organism; the heart in its complicated double systole and diastole beats strongly and untiringly; with its twenty-eight beats it drives the whole of the blood through all the arteries, veins, and capillaries; the lungs pump incessantly like a steam-engine; the intestines are always turning in *motus peristalticus*;[6] all the glands are constantly absorbing and secreting; even the brain has a double motion with every heartbeat and every

6. "Wormlike movement."—Tr.

breath. Now when there is an almost total lack of external movement, as is the case with numberless people who lead an entirely sedentary life, there arises a glaring and injurious disproportion between external inactivity and internal tumult. For the constant internal motion must be supported by something external. That want of proportion is analogous to the case where, in consequence of some emotion, something boils up within us that we are obliged to suppress. In order to thrive even trees require movement through wind. Here a rule applies which may be briefly expressed in Latin: *omnis motus, quo celerior, eo magis motus.*[7] How much our happiness depends on cheerfulness of disposition, and this on the state of our health, is seen when we compare the impression, made on us by external circumstances or events when we are hale and hearty, with that produced by them when ill health has made us depressed and anxious. It is not what things are objectively and actually, but what they are for us and in our way of looking at them, that makes us happy or unhappy. This is just what Epictetus says: *It is not things that disturb men, but opinions about things.* In general, however, nine-tenths of our happiness depend on health alone. With it everything becomes a source of pleasure, whereas without it nothing, whatever it may be, can be enjoyed, and even the other subjective blessings, such as mental qualities, disposition, and temperament, are depressed and dwarfed by ill health. Accordingly, it is not without reason that, when two people meet, they first ask about the state of each other's health and hope that it is good; for this really is for human happiness by far the most important thing. But from this it follows that the greatest of all follies is to sacrifice our health for whatever it may be, for gain, profit, promotion, learning, or fame, not to mention sensual and other fleeting pleasures; rather should we give first place to health.

Now however much health may contribute to the cheerfulness that is so essential to our happiness, this does not depend solely on health; for even with perfect health we may have a melancholy temperament and a predominantly gloomy frame of mind. The ultimate reason for this is undoubtedly to be found in the original and thus unalterable constitution of the organism and generally in the more or less normal relation of sensibility to irritability and

7. "The more rapid a movement is, the more it is movement."—Tr.

power of reproduction. An abnormal excess of sensibility will produce inequality of spirits, periodical excess of cheerfulness and prevailing melancholy. . . .

Beauty is partly akin to health. Although this subjective good quality does not really contribute directly to our happiness, but only indirectly by impressing others, it is nevertheless of great importance even to a man. Beauty is an open letter of recommendation that wins hearts for us in advance; and so Homer's words are here specially applicable: *Not to be despised are the divine gifts of the gods that they alone bestow and none can obtain at will.*[8]

The most general survey shows that pain and boredom are the two foes of human happiness. In addition, it may be remarked that, in proportion as we succeed in getting away from the one, we come nearer to the other, and vice versa. And so our life actually presents a violent or feeble oscillation between the two. This springs from the fact that the two stand to each other in a double antagonism, an outer or objective and an inner or subjective. Thus externally, want and privation produce pain; on the other hand, security and affluence give rise to boredom. Accordingly, we see the lower classes constantly struggling against privation and thus against pain; on the other hand, the wealthy upper classes are engaged in a constant and often really desperate struggle against boredom.[9] But the inner or subjective antagonism between pain and boredom is due to the fact that in the individual a susceptibility to the one is inversely proportional to a susceptibility to the other since it is determined by the measure of his mental ability. Thus feebleness of mind is generally associated with dullness of sensation and a lack of sensitiveness, qualities that render a man less susceptible to pains and afflictions of every kind and intensity. On the other hand, the result of this mental dullness is that *inner vacuity and emptiness* that is stamped on innumerable faces and also betrays itself in a constant and lively attention to all the events in the external world, even the most trivial. This vacuity is the real source of boredom and always craves for external excitement in order to set the mind and spirits in motion through something. Therefore in the choice

---

8. *Iliad*, 3:65.
9. The *nomadic life*, indicating the lowest stage of civilization, is again found at the highest in the *tourist life* that has become general. The first was produced by *want*, the second by *boredom*.

thereof it is not fastidious, as is testified by the miserable and wretched pastimes to which people have recourse and also by the nature of their sociability and conversation, and likewise by the many who gossip at the door or gape out of the window. The principal result of this inner vacuity is the craze for society, diversion, amusement, and luxury of every kind that lead many to extravagance and so to misery. Nothing protects us so surely from this wrong turning as *inner* wealth, the wealth of the mind, for the more eminent it becomes, the less room does it leave for boredom. The inexhaustible activity of ideas, their constantly renewed play with the manifold phenomena of the inner and outer worlds, the power and urge always to make different combinations with them, all these put the eminent mind, apart from moments of relaxation, quite beyond the reach of boredom. On the other hand, this enhanced intelligence is directly conditioned by a heightened sensibility and is rooted in a greater vehemence of will and hence of impulsiveness. From its union with these qualities, there now result a much greater intensity of all the emotions and an enhanced sensitiveness to mental and also physical pain, even greater impatience in the presence of obstacles, or greater resentment of mere disturbances. All this contributes much to an enhancement of the whole range of thoughts and conceptions, and so too of repulsive ideas the liveliness of which springs from a powerful imagination. This holds good relatively of all the intermediate stages between the two extremes of the dullest blockhead and the greatest genius. Accordingly, both objectively and subjectively, everyone is the nearer to the one source of suffering in human life, the more remote he is from the other. In keeping with this, his natural tendency will in this respect direct him to adapt as far as possible the objective to the subjective and thus to make greater provision against *that* source of suffering to which he is more susceptible. The clever and intelligent man will first of all look for painlessness, freedom from molestation, quietness, and leisure and consequently for a tranquil and modest life that is as undisturbed as possible. Accordingly, after some acquaintance with human beings so called, he will choose seclusion and, if of greater intellect, even solitude. For the more a man has within himself, the less does he need from without and also the less other people can be to him. Therefore eminence of intellect leads to unsociability. Indeed if the quality of society could be replaced by quantity, it would be worthwhile to live in the world at large; but unfortunately a hundred fools in a crowd still do not produce one intelligent man. On the other hand, as soon as want and privation give a man from the other extreme a breathing space, he will look for pastime and society at any price and will readily put up with anything, wishing to escape from nothing so much as from himself. For in solitude, where everyone is referred back to himself, he then sees what he has *in himself*. For the fool in purple groans under the burden of his wretched individuality that cannot be thrown off, whereas the man of great gifts populates and animates with his ideas the most dreary and desolate environment. What Seneca says is, therefore, very true: *omnis stultitia laborat fastidio sui*[10] (*Epistulae*, 9), as also the statement of Jesus ben Sirach: "The life of the fool is worse than death." Accordingly, we shall find on the whole that everyone is sociable to the extent that he is intellectually poor and generally common.[11] For in this world we have little more than a choice between solitude and vulgarity. The most sociable of all human beings are said to be the Negroes who intellectually are decidedly inferior. According to accounts from North America in the French paper (*Le Commerce*, October 19, 1837), the blacks shut themselves up in large numbers in the smallest space, free men and slaves all together, because they cannot see enough of their black flat-nosed faces.

Accordingly, the brain appears as the parasite or pensioner of the entire organism and a man's hard-won *leisure*, by giving him the free enjoyment of his own consciousness and individuality, is the fruit and produce of his whole existence that is in other respects only toil and effort. But what does the leisure of most men yield? Boredom and dullness, except when there are sensual pleasures or follies for filling up the time. How utterly worthless this leisure is, is seen by the way in which such people spend it; it is precisely Ariosto's *ozio lungo d'uomini ignoranti*.[12] Ordinary men are intent merely on how to *spend* their time; a man with any talent is interested in how to *use* his time. Men of limited intelligence are so exposed to boredom and this is due to their intellect's being absolutely nothing but the *medium of motives* for their will. Now if at

10. Stupidity suffers from its own weariness.—Tr.
11. The very thing that makes people sociable is their inner poverty.
12. The boredom of the ignorant.—Tr.

the moment there are no motives to be taken up, the will rests and the intellect takes a holiday since the one, like the other, does not become active of its own accord. The result is a terrible stagnation of all the powers of the entire man, in a word boredom. To ward off this, men now present the will with trivial motives that are merely temporary and are taken at random in order to rouse it and thus bring into action the intellect that has to interpret them. Accordingly, such motives are related to real and natural ones as paper money to silver, for their value is arbitrarily assumed. Now such small motives are *games,* with cards and so on, which have been invented for this very purpose. And if these are wanting, the man of limited intelligence will resort to rattling and drumming with anything he can get hold of. For him even a cigar is a welcome substitute for ideas. And so in all countries the principal entertainment of all society has become card playing; it is a measure of the worth of society and the declared bankruptcy of all ideas and thoughts. Thus since they are unable to exchange any ideas, they deal out cards and attempt to take one another's half crowns. What a pitiful race! But not to be unjust here, I will not refrain from saying that, in defense of card playing, it could at any rate be said that it is a preliminary training for life in the world of business insofar as in this way we learn to make clever use of the accidentally but unalterably given circumstances (cards in this case) in order to make therefrom what we can. For this purpose we become accustomed to showing a bold front by putting a good face on a bad game. But for this very reason, card playing has a demoralizing effect since the spirit of the game is to win from another what is his and to do so in every possible way and by every trick and stratagem. But the habit, acquired in play, of acting in this way strikes root, encroaches on practical life, and we gradually come to act in the same way with respect to the affairs of mine and thine and to regard as justifiable every advantage we have in our hands whenever we are legally permitted to do so. Proofs of this are furnished by ordinary everyday life. And so, as I have said, *free* leisure is the flower, or rather the fruit, of everyone's existence, since it alone puts him in possession of himself. Therefore those are to be called happy who in themselves then preserve something of value; whereas for the majority leisure yields only a good-for-nothing fellow who is terribly bored and a burden to himself. Accordingly, we rejoice "dear brethren that we are not children of the bondwoman, but of the free" (Galatians 4:31).

Further, just as that country is the best off that requires few or no imports, so too is that man the most fortunate who has enough in his own inner wealth and for his amusement and diversion needs little or nothing from without. For imports are expensive, make us dependent, entail danger, occasion trouble and annoyance, and in the end are only an inferior substitute for the products of our own soil. For on no account should we expect much from others or generally from without. What one man can be to another is very strictly limited; in the end, everyone remains alone and then the question is *who* is now alone. Accordingly, Goethe's general remarks (*Dichtung und Wahrheit*, vol. 3, p. 474) here apply, namely, that in all things everyone is ultimately referred back to himself, or as Oliver Goldsmith says:

> Still to ourselves in ev'ry place consign'd,
> Our own felicity we make or find.
> > *The Traveler*, 2:431f

Therefore everyone must himself be the best and most that he can be and achieve. Now the more this is so and consequently the more he finds within himself the sources of his pleasures, the happier he will be. Therefore Aristotle is absolutely right when he says (*Eudemian Ethics*, 7:2) that happiness belongs to those who are easily contented. For all the external sources of happiness and pleasure are by their nature exceedingly uncertain, precarious, fleeting, and subject to chance; therefore, even under the most favorable circumstances, they could easily come to an end; indeed this is inevitable insofar as they cannot always be close at hand. In old age almost all these sources necessarily dry up, for we are deserted by love, humor, desire to travel, delight in horses, aptitude for social intercourse, and even our friends and relations are taken from us by death. Then more than ever does it depend on what we have in ourselves, for this will last longest; but even at any age it is and remains the genuine and only permanent source of happiness. There is not much to be got anywhere in the world; it is full of privation and pain and for those who have escaped therefrom boredom lurks at every corner. In addition, baseness and wickedness have as a rule the upper hand and folly makes the most noise. Fate is cruel and mankind pitiable. In a world so constituted the man who has much within himself is like a bright, warm, cheerful room at Christmas amid the snow and ice of a December night. Accordingly, the happiest destiny on earth is undoubtedly to have a distinguished and rich individuality and in particular a good endowment of intellect, however differently such a destiny may turn out from the most brilliant. It was, therefore, a wise statement that the nineteen-year-old Queen Christina of Sweden made about Descartes with whom she had become acquainted merely through one essay and from verbal accounts and who at that time had for twenty years lived in Holland in the deepest seclusion. *Mr. Descartes est le plus heureux de tous les hommes, et sa condition me semble digne d'envie.*[13] (*Vie de Descartes*, par Baillet, Liv 7, chap. 10) Of course, as was the case with Descartes, external circumstances must be favorable to the extent of enabling a man to be master of his own life and to be satisfied therewith. Therefore Ecclesiastes 7:11 says: "Wisdom is good with an inheritance; and by it there is profit to them that see the sun." Whoever has been granted this lot through the favor of nature and fate will be anxious and careful to see that the inner source of his happiness remains accessible to him and for this the conditions are independence and leisure. And so he will gladly purchase these at the price of moderation and thrift, the more so as he is not, like others, dependent on the external sources of pleasure. Thus he will not be led astray by the prospects of office, money, favor, and approbation of the world into surrendering himself in order to conform to the sordid designs or bad taste of people.[14] When the occasion occurs, he will do what Horace suggested in his epistle to Maecenas (lib. 1, ep. 7). It is a great folly to lose the *inner* man in order to gain the *outer*, that is, to give up the whole or the greater part of one's quiet,

---

13. M. Descartes is the happiest and most fortunate of men and his condition seems to me to be most enviable.—Tr.

14. They achieve their welfare at the expense of their leisure; but of what use to me is welfare if for it I have to give up that which alone makes it desirable, namely, my leisure?

leisure, and independence for splendor, rank, pomp, titles, and honors. But this is what Goethe did; my genius has definitely drawn me in the other direction.

The truth, here discussed, that the chief source of human happiness springs from within ourselves, is also confirmed by the very correct observation of Aristotle in the *Nicomachean Ethics* (1:7; and 7:13, 14), namely, that every pleasure presupposes some activity and hence the application of some power, and without this it cannot exist. This teaching of Aristotle that a man's happiness consists in the unimpeded exercise of his outstanding ability, is also given again by Stobaeus in his description of the Peripatetic ethics (*Eclogae ethicae*, lib. 2, c. 7, pp. 268-78), for example: *Happiness is a virtuous activity in those affairs that have the desired result.* Generally in even briefer statements he explains that is any supreme skill. Now the original purpose of the forces with which nature endowed man is the struggle against want and privation that beset him on all sides. When once this struggle is over, the unemployed forces then become a burden to him and so now he must *play* with them, that is, use them aimlessly, for otherwise he falls at once into the other source of human suffering, namely, boredom. Thus the wealthy upper classes are primarily martyrs to this evil and Lucretius has given us a description of their pitiable condition. Even now in every great city we daily have instances of the aptness of this description:

> *Exit saepe foras magnis ex aedibus ille,*
> *Esse domi quem pertaesum est, subitoque reventat;*
> *Quippe foris nihilo melius qui sentiat esse.*
> *Currit, agens mannos, ad villam praecipitanter,*
> *Auxilium tectis quasi ferre ardentibus instans:*
> *Oscitat extemplo, tetigit quum limina villae;*
> *Aut abit in somnum gravis, atque oblivia quaerit;*
> *Aut etiam properans urbem petit, atque revisit.*[15]
>
> 3:1060-67

15. Frequently he quits the large palace and hurries into the open, for the house disgusts him, until he suddenly returns because out of doors he feels no better off. Or else he gallops off to his country house, as if it were on fire and he were hurrying to put it out. But as soon as he has crossed the threshold, he yawns with boredom or falls asleep and tries to forget himself, unless he prefers to return to the city.—Tr.

In youth these gentlemen must have muscular strength and procreative power. In later years, we are left with only mental powers; but these they lack or the development thereof and the accumulated material for their activity; and their plight is pitiable. Now since the *will* is the only inexhaustible force, it is roused by a stimulation of passions, for example, by games of chance for high stakes, this truly degrading vice. But generally speaking, every unoccupied individual will choose a game for the exercise of those powers wherein he excels; it may be skittles or chess, hunting or painting, horse racing or music, cards or poetry, heraldry or philosophy, and so on. We can even investigate the matter methodically by going to the root of all the manifestations of human force and thus to the *three physiological fundamental forces*. Accordingly, we have here to consider them in their aimless play wherein they appear as the sources of three kinds of possible pleasures. From these every man will choose the ones that suit him according as he excels in one or other of those forces. First we have the pleasures of the *power of reproduction* that consist in eating, drinking, digesting, resting, and sleeping. There are even whole nations in whom these are regarded as national pleasures. Then we have the pleasures of *irritability* that consist in walking, jumping, wrestling, dancing, fencing, riding, and athletic games of every kind, also in hunting and even conflict and war. Finally, we have the pleasures of *sensibility* that consist in observing, thinking, feeling, writing poetry, improving the mind, playing music, learning, reading, meditating, inventing, philosophizing, and so on. On the value, degree, and duration of each of these kinds of pleasure remarks of many kinds can be made that are left to the reader himself to supply. But it will be clear to everyone that, the nobler the nature of the power that conditions our pleasure, the greater this will be; for it is conditioned by the use of our own powers and our happiness consists in the frequent recurrence of our pleasure. Again no one will deny that, in this respect, sensibility, whose decided preponderance is man's superiority to the other animal species, ranks before the other two fundamental physiological forces that in an equal and even greater degree are inherent in animals. Our cognitive powers are related to sensibility; and so a preponderance thereof qualifies us for the so-called *intellectual* pleasures that consist in *knowledge;* and indeed such pleasures will be the greater, the more decided that preponderance. . . .

What a Man Represents

This, in other words, what we are in the opinion of others, is generally much overrated in consequence of a peculiar weakness of our nature; although the slightest reflection could tell us that, in itself, it is not essential to our happiness. Accordingly, it is difficult to explain why everyone is at heart very pleased whenever he sees in others signs of a favorable opinion and his vanity is in some way flattered. If a cat is stroked it purrs; and just as inevitably if a man is praised sweet rapture and delight are reflected in his face; and indeed in the sphere of his pretensions the praise may be a palpable lie. Signs of other people's approbation often console him for real misfortune or for the scantiness with which the other two sources of our happiness, previously discussed, flow for him. Conversely it is astonishing how infallibly he is annoyed and often deeply hurt by every injury to his ambition in any sense, degree, or circumstance, and by any disdain, disrespect, or slight. Insofar as the feeling of honor rests on this peculiar characteristic, it may have salutary effects on the good conduct of many as a substitute for their morality; but on the man's own *happiness* and above all on the peace of mind and independence essential thereto, its effect is more disturbing and detrimental than beneficial. Therefore, from our point of view, it is advisable to set limits to this characteristic and to moderate as much as possible, through careful consideration and correct assessment of the value of good things, that great susceptibility to the opinions of other people, not only where it is flattered, but also where it is injured, for both hang by the same thread. Otherwise we remain the slave of what other people appear to think:

> *Sic leve, sic parvum est, animum quod laudis avarum*
> *Subruit ac reficit.*[16]

---

16. How trifling and insignificant is that which depresses or elates the man who thirsts for praise! (Horace, *Epistles*, 2:1:179).—Tr.

Accordingly, a correct comparison of the value of what we are *in and by ourselves* with what we are in the eyes *of others* will greatly contribute to our happiness. Belonging to the former is everything that fills up the whole time of our existence, its inner content and consequently every blessing that was considered by us in the two chapters "what a man is" and "what a man has." For the place wherein all this has its sphere of activity is our own consciousness. On the other hand, the place of what we are *for others* is their consciousness; it is the kind of figure in which we appear in that consciousness together with the notions and concepts that are applied to it.[17] Now this is something that certainly does not directly exist for us but only indirectly, namely, insofar as the behavior of others toward us is thereby determined. And this is also taken into consideration only insofar as it influences anything whereby what we are *in and by ourselves* can be modified. Besides, what goes on in the consciousness of others is as such a matter of indifference to us; and to it we shall gradually become indifferent when we acquire an adequate knowledge of the superficial and futile nature of the thoughts in the heads of most people, of the narrowness of their views, of the paltriness of their sentiments, of the perversity of their opinions, and of the number of their errors. We shall also become indifferent to the opinions of others when from our own experience we learn with what disrespect one man occasionally speaks of another as soon as he no longer has to fear him or thinks that what he says will not come to the ears of the other man; but we shall become indifferent especially after we have once heard how half a dozen blockheads speak with disdain about the greatest man. We shall then see that whoever attaches much value to the opinions of others pays them too much honor.

In any case, that man is in a pretty poor way who does not find his happiness in the two classes of blessings already considered, but has to look for it in the third, thus in what he is not in reality but in the minds of others. For in general, the basis of our whole being, and therefore of our happiness, is our animal nature; and so health is the most essential factor for our welfare and after it come the means for maintaining ourselves and thus for having a

17. In their brilliance, their pomp and splendor, their show and magnificence of every kind, the highest in the land can say: "Our happiness lies entirely outside ourselves; its place is in the heads of others."

livelihood that is free from care. Honor, pomp, rank, and reputation, however much value many of us may attach to them, cannot compete with or replace those essential blessings for which, in case of necessity, they would unquestionably be given up. For this reason, it will contribute to our happiness if at times we reach the simple view that everyone lives primarily and actually within his own skin, not in the opinion of others, and that accordingly our real and personal condition, as determined by health, temperament, abilities, income, wife, family, friends, dwelling place, and so on, is a hundred times more important to our happiness than what others are pleased to make of us. The opposite notion will make us unhappy. If it is emphatically exclaimed that honor is dearer than life itself, this really means that existence and well-being are nothing and the real thing is what others think of us. At all events, the statement can be regarded as a hyperbole whose basis is the prosaic truth that honor, that is, other people's opinion of us, is often absolutely necessary for us to live and make our way in the world. I shall later return to this. On the other hand, when we see how almost everything, assiduously sought by people throughout their lives with restless energy and at the cost of a thousand dangers and hardships, has as its ultimate object the enhancement of themselves in the opinion of others; thus when we see how they strive not only for offices, titles, and decorations, but also for wealth, and even science[18] and art, basically and mainly for the same reason, and how the greater respect of others is the ultimate goal to which they work, then this alas merely shows us the magnitude of human folly. To set too high a value on the opinion of others is an erroneous idea that prevails everywhere. Now it may be rooted in our nature itself or may have arisen in consequence of society and civilization. In any case, it exerts on all our actions an influence that is wholly immoderate and inimical to our happiness. We can follow it from the anxious and slavish regard for the *qu'en dira-t-on*[19] to the case where Virginius plunges the dagger into his daughter's heart, or where, for posthumous fame, a man is induced to sacrifice peace, wealth, health, and even life itself. This erroneous idea certainly offers a convenient handle to

18. *Scire tuum nihil est, nisi te scire hoc sciat alter.* (What you know is worthless, unless others also know that you know it.)—TR.
19. What will people say?—TR.

the man who has to control or otherwise direct people; and so, in every scheme for training humanity, instructions for maintaining and strengthening the feeling of honor occupy a prominent place. But it is quite a different matter as regards a man's own happiness that we intend here to consider; on the contrary, one should be dissuaded from placing too high a value on the opinion of others. Daily experience, however, tells us that this is done and that most people attach the highest importance precisely to what others think of them. They are more concerned about this than about what immediately exists for them because it occurs *in their own consciousness.* Accordingly, they reverse the natural order of things and the opinion of others seems to them to be the real part of their existence, their own consciousness being merely the ideal part. They therefore make what is derived and secondary the main issue and the picture of their true nature in the minds of others is nearer to their hearts than is this true nature itself. Consequently, this direct regard for what certainly does not exist directly for us is that folly that has been called *vanity, vanitas,* in order to indicate the empty and insubstantial nature of this striving. It is also easy to see from the above remarks that vanity, like avarice, causes us to forget the end in the means.

In fact, the value we attach to the opinion of others and our constant concern in respect thereof exceed almost every reasonable expectation, so that it can be regarded as a kind of mania that is widespread or rather inborn. In everything we do or omit to do, almost the first thing we consider is the opinion of other people and, if we examine the matter more closely, we shall see that almost half the worries and anxieties we have ever experienced have arisen from our concern about it. For it is at the root of all our self-esteem that is so often mortified because it is so morbidly sensitive, of all our vanities and pretensions, and also of our boasting and ostentation. Without this concern and craze, there would be hardly a tithe of the luxury that exists. Pride in every form, *point d'honneur,* and *puntiglio,* however varied their sphere and nature, are due to this opinion of others, and what sacrifices it often demands! It shows itself even in the child and then at every age, yet most strongly in old age because when the capacity for sensual pleasures fails, vanity and pride have only to share their dominion with avarice. It can be most clearly observed in the French in whom it is quite endemic and often becomes the absurdest ambition, the most ludicrous national vanity, and the most shameless boasting. But then in this way they defeat their own efforts, for they have been made fun of by other nations and nicknamed *la grande nation.* Now to furnish a special illustration of the perverse nature of that excessive concern about the opinion of others, a really superlative example may here be given of that folly that is rooted in human nature. Through the striking effect of the coincidence of the circumstances with the appropriate character, it is suitable to a rare degree, for in it we are able wholly to estimate the strength of this very strange motive. It is the following passage that comes from a detailed report of the execution of Thomas Wix, which had just taken place, and it appeared in the *Times* of March 31, 1846. Wix, a journeyman, had out of revenge murdered his master. "On the morning fixed for the execution, the rev. ordinary was early in attendance upon him, but Wix, beyond a quiet demeanor, betrayed no interest in his ministrations, appearing to feel anxious only to acquit himself bravely before the spectators of his ignominious end.—This he succeeded in doing. In the procession Wix fell into his proper place with alacrity, and, as he entered the chapel-yard, remarked, sufficiently loud to be heard by several persons near him, 'Now, then, as Dr. Dodd said, I shall soon know the grand secret.' On reaching the scaffold, the miserable wretch mounted the drop without the slightest assistance, and when he got to the center, he bowed to the spectators twice, a proceeding that called forth a tremendous cheer from the degraded crowd beneath." This is an excellent example of a man with death in its most terrible form before his eyes and eternity behind it, not caring about anything except the impression he would make on a crowd of gapers and the opinion that would remain in their minds! And indeed, in the same year, Lecomte in France was executed for an attempt on the king's life. At the trial he was annoyed mainly because he could not appear in decent attire before the chamber of peers; and even at his execution his main worry was that he had not been allowed to shave beforehand. Even in former times, it was just the same, as is seen from what Mateo Alemán says in the introduction (*declaracion*) to his famous novel, *Guzman de Alfarache,* that many infatuated criminals used their last hours that should have been devoted exclusively to the salvation of their souls, for the preparation and committing to memory of a short sermon that they intended to deliver on the steps of the gallows. Yet in such characteristics we can see a reflection of ourselves, for extreme cases always give us the clearest illustration. The anxieties of all of us, our worries, vexations, bothers, troubles, fears, exertions, and so on, are really concerned with someone else's opinion, perhaps in the majority of cases, and are just as absurd as is the behavior of those miserable sinners. For the most part, our envy and hatred also spring from the same root.

Now it is obvious that our happiness, resting as it does mainly on peace of mind and contentment, could scarcely be better promoted than by limiting and moderating these motives to reasonable proportions that would possibly be a fiftieth of what they are at present, and thus by extracting from our flesh this thorn that is always causing us pain. Yet this is very difficult, for we are concerned with a natural and innate perversity. Tacitus says: *Etiam sapientibus cupido gloriae novissima exuitur*[20] (*Historiae*, 4:6). The only way to be rid of this universal folly is clearly to recognize it as such and for this purpose to realize how utterly false, perverse, erroneous, and absurd most of the opinions usually are in men's minds, which are, therefore, in themselves not worth considering. Moreover, other people's opinions can in most cases and things have little real influence on us. Again, such opinions generally are so unfavorable that almost everyone would worry himself to death if he heard all that was said about him or the tone in which people spoke of him. Finally, even honor itself is only of indirect not direct value. If we succeeded in such a conversion from this universal folly, the result would be an incredibly great increase in our peace of mind and cheerfulness, likewise a firmer and more positive demeanor, and generally a more natural and unaffected attitude. The exceedingly beneficial influence a retired mode of life has on our peace of mind is due mainly to the fact that we thereby escape having to live constantly in the sight of others and consequently having always to take into consideration the opinions they happen to have; it restores to a man his true self. Similarly, we should avoid a great deal of real misfortune into which we are drawn simply by that purely ideal endeavor, or more correctly that incur-

---

20. The thirst for fame is the last thing of all to be laid aside by wise men.—TR.

able folly. We should also be able to devote much more attention to solid blessings and then enjoy them with less interruption. But as they say: *What is noble is difficult.*

The folly of our nature, here described, puts forth three main offshoots, ambition, vanity, and pride. The difference between the last two is that *pride* is the already firm conviction of our own paramount worth in some respect; *vanity,* on the other hand, is the desire to awaken in others such a conviction, often accompanied by the secret hope of being able thereby to make it our own. Accordingly, pride is self-esteem that comes from *within* and so is direct; vanity, on the other hand, is the attempt to arrive at such esteem from *without* and thus indirectly. Accordingly, vanity makes us talkative, whereas pride makes us reserved and reticent. The vain man, however, should know that the high opinion of others that is coveted by him can be gained much more easily and certainly by persistent silence than by speech, even if he has the finest things to say. Anyone wishing to affect pride is not necessarily proud, but at most can be; yet he will soon drop this, as he will every assumed role. For only the firm, inner, unshakable conviction of preeminent qualities and special worth makes us really proud. Now this conviction may be mistaken or rest on merely external and conventional advantages; that makes no difference to pride if only the conviction is present in real earnest. Therefore since pride is rooted in *conviction,* it is, like all knowledge, not within our *arbitrary power.* Its worst foe, I mean its greatest obstacle, is vanity that solicits the approval of others in order to base thereon our own high opinion of ourselves, wherein the assumption of pride is already quite firmly established.

Now however much pride is generally censured and decried, I suspect that this has come mainly from those who have nothing whereof they could be proud. In view of the effrontery and impudence of most men, anyone who has virtues and merits will do well to keep them in mind in order not to let them fall into oblivion. For whoever mildly ignores such merits and associates with most men, as if he were entirely on their level, will at once be frankly and openly regarded by them as such. But I would like to recommend this especially to those whose merits are of the highest order, that is to say, are real and therefore purely personal, for, unlike orders and titles, such merits are not brought to men's minds at every moment by an impression on their senses; otherwise they will see often enough exemplified the *sus Minervam*.[21] "Joke with a slave, and he will soon show you his backside" is an admirable proverb of the Arabs, and the words of Horace should not be rejected: *sume superbiam, quaesitam meritis*.[22] But the virtue of modesty is, I suppose, a fine invention for fools and knaves; for according to it everyone has to speak of himself as if he were a fool; and this is a fine leveling down since it then looks as if there were in the world none but fools and knaves.

On the other hand, the cheapest form of pride is national pride; for the man affected therewith betrays a want of *individual* qualities of which he might be proud, since he would not otherwise resort to that which he shares with so many millions. The man who possesses outstanding personal qualities will rather see most clearly the faults of his own nation, for he has them constantly before his eyes. But every miserable fool, who has nothing in the world whereof he could be proud, resorts finally to being proud of the very nation to which he belongs. In this he finds compensation and is now ready and thankful to defend, tooth and nail, all the faults and follies peculiar to it. For example, of fifty Englishmen hardly more than one will be found to agree with us when we speak of the stupid and degrading bigotry of his nation with the contempt it deserves; but this one exception will usually be a man of intelligence. The Germans are free from national pride and thus furnish a proof of the honesty that has been said to their credit; but those of them are not honest who feign and ludicrously affect such pride. This is often done by the "German Brothers" and democrats who flatter the people in order to lead them astray. It is said that the Germans invented gunpowder, but I cannot subscribe to this view. Lichtenberg asks: "Why is it that a man who is not a German does not readily pass himself off as one, but usually pretends to be a Frenchman or an Englishman when he wants to give himself out as something?" For the rest, individuality far outweighs nationality and in a given man merits a thousand times more consideration than this. Since national character speaks of the crowd, not much good will ever be honestly said in its favor.

21. The swine (instructs) Minerva. (Cicero).—Tr.
22. Arrogate to yourself the pride you earned through merit. (*Od.* 3:30:14)—Tr.

On the contrary, we see in a different form in each country only human meanness, perversity, and depravity, and this is called national character. Having become disgusted with one of them, we praise another until we become just as disgusted with it. Every nation ridicules the rest and all are right.

The subject of this chapter, namely, what we *represent* in the world, that is, what we are in the eyes of others, may now be divided, as already observed, into *honor, rank, and fame.*

For our purpose, *rank* may be dismissed in a few words, however important it may be in the eyes of the masses and of Philistines, and however great its use in the running of the State machine. Its value is conventional, that is to say, it is really a sham; its effect is a simulated esteem and the whole thing is a mere farce for the masses. Orders are bills of exchange drawn on public opinion; their value rests on the credit of the drawer. However, quite apart from the great deal of money they save the state as a substitute for financial rewards, they are a thoroughly suitable institution provided that they are distributed with discrimination and justice. Thus the masses have eyes and ears, but not much else, precious little judgment and even a short memory. Many merits lie entirely outside the sphere of their comprehension; others are understood and acclaimed when they make their appearance, but are afterwards soon forgotten. I find it quite proper through cross or star[22] always and everywhere to exclaim to the crowd: "This man is not like you; he has merits!" But orders lose such value when they are distributed without justice or judgment or in excessive numbers. And so a prince should be as cautious in conferring them as a businessman is in signing bills. The inscription *pour le mérite* on a cross is a pleonasm; every order should be *pour le mérite, ça va sans dire.*[23]

The discussion of *honor* is much more difficult and involved than that of rank. First we should have to define it. Now if for this purpose I said that honor is external conscience and conscience internal honor, this might perhaps satisfy a number of people; yet it would be an explanation that is more showy than clear and thorough. And so I say that objectively honor is other people's

22. I.e., decorations.—Tr.
23. That goes without saying.—Tr.

opinion of our worth and subjectively our fear of that opinion. In the latter capacity, it often has in the man of honor a very wholesome, though by no means a purely moral, effect.

The feeling of honor and shame, inherent in everyone who is not utterly depraved, and the great value attributed to the former, have their root and origin in the following. By himself alone man is capable of very little and is like Robinson Crusoe on a desert island; only in the society of others is he a person of consequence and capable of doing much. He becomes aware of this state of affairs as soon as his consciousness begins to develop in some way and there at once arises in him the desire to be looked upon as a useful member of society, as one capable of playing his part as a man, *pro parte virili,* and thus as one entitled to share in the advantages of human society. Now he is a useful member of society firstly by doing what all are everywhere expected to do and secondly by doing what is demanded and expected of him in the particular position he occupies. But he recognizes just as quickly that here it is not a question whether he is useful in his own opinion, but whether he is so in that of others. Accordingly, there spring from this his keen desire for the favorable *opinion* of others and the great value he attaches to this. Both appear with the original nature of an innate feeling, called a feeling of honor, and, according to circumstances, a feeling of shame [*verecundia*]. It is this that makes a man blush at the thought of having suddenly to fall in the opinion of others even when he knows he is innocent, or where the fault that comes to light concerns only a relative obligation and thus one arbitrarily undertaken. On the other hand, nothing stirs his courage and spirits more than does the attained or renewed certainty of other people's favorable opinion because it promises him the protection and help of the united forces of all that are against the evils of life an infinitely greater bulwark than his own forces.

From the different relations in which a man may stand to others, and in respect of which they must show him confidence and therefore have a certain good opinion of him, there arise several *kinds of honor.* These relations are mainly mine and thine, then the fulfillment of pledges, and finally the sexual relation. Corresponding to them we have civic honor, official honor, and sexual honor, each of which again has subspecies.

Civic honor has the widest sphere; it consists in the assumption that we respect absolutely the rights of everyone and therefore shall never use for our own advantage unjust or unlawful means. It is the condition for our taking part in all amicable intercourse. It is lost through a single action that openly and violently runs counter thereto and so through every criminal punishment, yet only on the assumption that this was just. In the last resort, however, honor always rests on the conviction that moral character is unalterable by virtue whereof a single bad action is a sure indication of the same moral nature of all subsequent actions as soon as similar circumstances occur. This is also testified by the English expression *character* for fame, reputation, honor. For this reason, honor once lost cannot be recovered unless the loss had rested on a mistake, such as slander or a false view of things. Accordingly, there are laws against slander, libel, and also insults; for an insult, mere abuse, is a summary slander without any statement of the reasons. The man who is abusive shows, of course, that he has no real and true complaint against the other man since he would otherwise give this as the premises and confidently leave the conclusion to the hearers; instead of which he gives the conclusion and leaves the premises unsaid. But he relies on the presumption that this is done merely for the sake of brevity. It is true that civic honor has its name from the middle classes, but it applies without distinction to all classes, even to the highest. No one can dispense with it and it is a very serious matter that everyone should guard against taking lightly. Whoever breaks trust and faith has forever lost trust and faith, whatever he may do and whoever he may be, and the bitter fruits, entailed in this loss, will not fail to come.

In a certain sense, *honor* has a *negative* character in contrast to *fame* that has a *positive*. For honor is not the opinion of particular qualities that belong to this subject alone, but only of those that, as a rule, are to be assumed as qualities in which he should not be wanting. Therefore honor asserts merely that this subject is not an exception, whereas fame asserts that he is. Thus fame must first be acquired; honor, on the other hand, has simply not to be lost. According to this, want of fame is obscurity and something negative; want of honor is shame and something positive. This negativity, however, must not be confused with passivity; on the contrary, honor has quite an active character. Thus it proceeds solely from its *subject;* it rests on *his* actions, not on what others do and on what befalls him; it is therefore *part of what depends on us*.[24] This is, as we shall see in a moment, the mark of distinction between true honor and chivalry or sham honor. Only through slander is an attack on honor possible from without, and the only way to refute it is to give it proper publicity and unmask the slanderer.

The respect shown to old age appears to be due to the fact that the honor of young people is, of course, assumed but has not yet been put to the test; it therefore really exists on credit. But with older people it had to be shown in the course of their lives whether through their conduct they could maintain their honor. For neither years in themselves, which are also attained by animals and even greatly exceeded by some, nor even experience, as being merely a more detailed knowledge of the ways of the world, are a sufficient ground for the respect that the young are required everywhere to show to their elders. Mere feebleness of old age would entitle a man to indulgence and consideration rather than respect. But it is remarkable that a certain respect for white hair is inborn and therefore really instinctive in man. Wrinkles, an incomparably surer sign of old age, do not inspire this respect at all. One never speaks of venerable wrinkles, but always of venerable white hair.

The value of honor is only indirect; for, as already explained at the beginning of this chapter, other people's opinion of us can be of value only insofar as it determines or can at times determine their behavior to us. Yet this is the case so long as we live with or among them. For, as in the civilized state we owe our safety and possessions simply to society and moreover we need others in all our undertakings and they must have confidence in us in order to have any dealings with us, their opinion of us is of great value, although this is always only indirect, and I cannot see how it can be direct. In agreement with this Cicero also says: *De bona autem fama Chrysippus quidem et Diogenes, detracta utilitate, ne digitum quidem, ejus causa, porrigendum esse dicebant. Quibus ego vehementer assentior.*[25] (*De finibus*, 3:17.) In the same way, Helvétius gives us a lengthy explanation of this truth in his masterpiece *De l'esprit* (Disc., pt. 3, chap. 13) the result of which is: *Nous n'aimons*

24. Term used by the Stoics.—Tʀ.
25. But Chrysippus and Diogenes said of a good reputation that, apart from its being useful, one should not even raise a finger for its sake. I entirely agree with them.—Tʀ.

pas l'estime pour l'estime, mais uniquement pour les avantages qu'elle procure.[26] Now as the means cannot be worth more than the end, the statement "honor is dearer than life itself," of which so much is made, is, as I have said, an exaggeration.

So much for civic honor. *Official honor* is the general opinion of others that a man who holds an office actually has the requisite qualities and also in all cases strictly fulfills his official duties. The greater and more important a man's sphere of influence in the State and so the higher and more influential the post occupied by him, the greater must be the opinion of the intellectual abilities and moral qualities that render him fit for the post. Consequently, he has a correspondingly higher degree of honor, as expressed by his titles, orders, and so on, and also by the deferential behavior of others to him. Now by the same standard, rank or status determines the particular degree of honor, although this is modified by the ability of the masses to judge of the importance of the rank. But greater honor is always paid to the man who has and fulfills special obligations than to the ordinary citizen whose honor rests mainly on negative qualities.

Official honor further demands that whoever holds an office will for the sake of his colleagues and successors maintain respect for it. This is done by the strict observance of his duties and also by the fact that he never allows to go unchallenged any attacks on himself or the office while he is holding it, in other words, that he does not allow statements to the effect that he is not strictly carrying out his duties or that the office itself does not contribute to the public welfare. On the contrary, he must prove by legal penalties that such attacks were unjust.

Under official honor we have also that of the man serving the state, the doctor, the lawyer, every public teacher or even graduate, in short, everyone who has been declared publicly qualified for a certain kind of mental proficiency and has, therefore, promised to carry it out; in a word, the honor of all who, as such, have publicly undertaken to do something. Here, then we have true *military honor;* it consists in the fact that whoever has undertaken to defend his country actually possesses the requisite qualities, above all,

---

26. We do not like esteem for its own sake, but simply for the advantage that it brings us.—TR.

courage, bravery, and strength, and that he is in fact ready to defend his country to the death, and will not for anything in the world desert the flag to which he has once sworn allegiance. Here I have taken *official honor* in a wider sense than the usual one, namely, where it indicates the citizens' respect that is due to the office itself.

It seems to me that *sexual honor* calls for a more detailed consideration and a reference of its principles to their root. At the same time, this will confirm that all honor ultimately rests on considerations of expediency.

By its nature *sexual honor* is divided into that of women and that of men, and from both angles it is a well understood *esprit de corps*. The former is by far the more important of the two because in a woman's life the sexual relation is the essential thing. Hence female honor is the general opinion in regard to a girl that she has never given herself to a man and in regard to a wife that she has devoted herself solely to her husband. The importance of this opinion depends on the following. The female sex demands and expects from the male everything, thus all that it desires and needs; the male demands from the female primarily and directly one thing only. Therefore the arrangement had to be made whereby the male sex could obtain from the female that one thing only by taking charge of everything and also of the children springing from the union. The welfare of the whole female sex rests on this arrangement. To carry it out, this sex must necessarily stick together and show *esprit de corps*. But in its entirety and in closed ranks it then faces the whole male sex as the common foe who is in possession of all the good things of the earth through a natural superiority in physical and mental powers. The male sex must be subdued and taken captive so that the female sex, by holding it, may come to possess those good things. Now to this end the maxim of honor of the whole female sex is that all illicit intercourse is absolutely denied to the male so that every man is forced into marriage as into a kind of capitulation, and the whole female sex is provided for. This end can be completely attained, however, only by the strict observance of the above maxim; and therefore the whole female sex sees with true *esprit de corps* that that maxim is upheld by all its members. Accordingly, every girl who through illicit intercourse has betrayed the whole female sex, since its welfare would be undermined if this kind of conduct were to become general, is expelled by her sex and is branded with shame; she has lost her honor. No woman may have anything more to do with her; she is avoided like the plague. The same fate befalls the woman who commits adultery since for the husband she has not maintained the capitulation into which he entered; but through such an example men are discouraged from entering it; yet on such a capitulation depends the salvation of the whole female sex. Moreover, because of her gross breach of faith and of the deception of her deed, the adulteress loses not only her sexual honor but also her civic. Thus we may well excuse a girl by saying that she has "fallen," but we never speak of a "fallen wife." In the former case the seducer can restore the girl's honor by marrying her, but this the adulterer cannot do after the wife has been divorced. Now if in consequence of this clear view, we recognize as the foundation of the principle of female honor an *esprit de corps* that is wholesome and indeed necessary but is also well calculated and based on interests, it will be possible for us to attribute to such honor the greatest importance for woman's existence and hence a value that is great and relative yet not absolute, not one that lies beyond life and its aims and is accordingly to be purchased at the price of this. And so there will be nothing to applaud in the extravagant deeds of Lucretia and Virginius, which degenerate into tragic farces. Thus there is something so shocking at the end of *Emilia Galotti* that we leave the theater in a wholly dejected mood. On the other hand, in spite of sexual honor, we cannot help sympathizing with Clara in *Egmont*. To push the principle of female honor too far is, like so many things, equivalent to forgetting the end for the means. For such exaggeration attributes to sexual honor an absolute value, whereas even more than any other it has a merely relative value. In fact it might be said that it has only a conventional value, when we see from Thomasius's *De concubinatu* how in almost all countries and at all times down to the Lutheran Reformation concubinage was a relation permitted and recognized by law in which the concubine retained her honor; not to mention the temple of Mylitta at Babylon (Herodotus, lib. 1, c. 199) and other instances. Of course, there are also civil circumstances that render impossible the external form of marriage, especially in Catholic countries where no divorce occurs. In my opinion ruling sovereigns always act more morally when they have a mistress than when they contract a morganatic marriage whose descendants might one day raise claims if the legitimate descendants happen to die out. Thus however remote it may be, the possibility of civil war is brought about by such a marriage. Moreover, a morganatic marriage, that is, one contracted actually in defiance of all external circumstances, is at bottom a concession made to women and priests, two classes to whom we should be careful to concede as little as possible. Further, it should be borne in mind that everyone in the land may marry the woman of his choice except one to whom this natural right is denied; this poor man is the prince. His hand belongs to his country and is given in marriage for reasons of state, that is, for the good of the country. But yet he is human and wants one day to follow the inclinations of his heart. It is, therefore, as unjust and ungrateful as it is narrowminded to prevent him from having a mistress, or to want to reproach him with this; it must always be understood, of course, that she is not permitted to have any influence on the government. As regards sexual honor, such a mistress is from her point of view to a certain extent an exception, as being exempt from the universal rule. For she has given herself merely to a man who loves her and whom she loves but could never marry. In general, however, the many bloody sacrifices that are made to the principle of female honor, such as the murder of children and the suicide of mothers, are evidence that this principle has not a purely natural origin. Of course a girl who surrenders illicitly thereby commits against her whole sex a breach of faith that is nevertheless only tacitly assumed and not affirmed on oath. And since in the usual case her own advantage suffers directly from this, her folly is here infinitely greater than her depravity.

The sexual honor of men is brought about by that of women as the opposite esprit de corps. This demands that everyone who has entered marriage, that capitulation so favorable to the opposite party, must now see that it is upheld so that not even this pact may lose its strength through any laxity in its observance and that men, by giving up everything, may be assured of the one thing for which they bargain, namely, the sole possession of the woman. Accordingly, man's honor demands that he shall resent his wife's breach of the marriage tie and shall punish it at any rate by separating from her. If he tolerates it with his eyes open, he is discredited and disgraced by the entire community of men. Nevertheless, this shame is not nearly so grave as that of the woman who has lost her sexual honor; on the contrary, it is only a *levioris notae macula*[27] since with man the sexual relation is subordinate and he has many others that are more important. The two great dramatic poets of modern times have each twice taken as their theme man's honor in this sense; Shakespeare in *Othello* and *The Winter's Tale*, and Calderón in *El medico de su honra* (the Physician of his Honor) and *A secreto agravio secreta venganza* (for Secret Insult Secret Vengeance). For the rest, this honor demands only the woman's punishment not her lover's that is merely an *opus supererogationis*.[28] In this way is confirmed the statement that such honor originates from men's esprit de corps.

Translated by E. F. J. Payne

27. A belmish of less importance.—Tr.
28. A piece of work going beyond what was required.—Tr.

15

On Death and Its Relation to the Indestructibility of Our Inner Nature

We know, of course, of no higher gamble than that for life and death. We watch with the utmost attention, interest, and fear every decision concerning them; for in our view all in all is at stake. On the other hand, *nature,* which never lies, but is always frank and sincere, speaks quite differently on this theme, as Krishna does in the *Bhagavadgita.* Her statement is that the life or death of the individual is of absolutely no consequence. She expresses this by abandoning the life of every animal, and even of man, to the most insignificant accidents without coming to the rescue. Consider the insect on your path; a slight unconscious turning of your foot is decisive as to its life or death. Look at the wood-snail that has no means of flight, of defence, of practicing deception, of concealment, a ready prey to all. Look at the fish carelessly playing in the still-open net; at the frog prevented by its laziness from the flight that could save it; at the bird unaware of the falcon soaring above it; at the sheep eyed and examined from the thicket by the wolf. Endowed with little caution, all these go about guilelessly among the dangers that at every moment threaten their existence. Now, since nature abandons without reserve her organisms constructed with such inexpressible skill, not only to the predatory instinct of the stronger, but also to the blindest chance, the whim of every fool, and the mischievousness of every child, she expresses that the annihilation of these individuals is a matter of indifference to her, does her no harm, is of no significance at all, and that in these cases the effect is of no more consequence than is the cause. Nature states this very clearly, and she never lies; only she does not comment on her utterances, but rather expresses them in the laconic style of the oracle. Now if the universal mother carelessly sends forth her children without protection to a thousand threatening dangers, this can be only because she knows that, when they fall, they fall back into her womb, where they are safe and secure; therefore their fall is only a jest. With man she does not act otherwise than she does with the animals; hence her declaration extends also to him; the life or death of the individual is a matter of indifference to her. Consequently, they should be, in a certain sense, a matter of indifference to us; for in fact, we ourselves are nature. If only we saw deeply enough, we should certainly agree with nature, and regard life or death as indifferently as does she. Meanwhile, by means of reflection, we must attribute nature's careless and indifferent attitude concerning the life of individuals to the fact that the destruction of such a phenomenon does not in the least disturb its true and real inner being.

As we have just been considering, not only are life and death dependent on the most trifling accidents, but the existence of organic beings generally is also ephemeral; animal and plant arise today and tomorrow pass away; birth and death follow in quick succession, whereas to inorganic things, standing so very much lower, an incomparably longer duration is assured, but an infinitely long one only to absolutely formless matter, to which we attribute this even a priori. Now if we ponder over all this, I think the merely empirical, but objective and unprejudiced, comprehension of such an order of things must be followed as a matter of course by the thought that this order is only a superficial phenomenon, that such a constant arising and passing away cannot in any way touch the root of things, but can be only relative, indeed only apparent. The true inner being of everything, which, moreover, evades our glance everywhere and is thoroughly mysterious, is not affected by that arising and passing away, but rather continues to exist undisturbed thereby. Of course, we can neither perceive nor comprehend the way in which this happens, and must therefore think of it only generally as a kind of *tour de passe-passe*[1] that took place here. For whereas the most imperfect thing, the lowest, the inorganic, continues to exist unassailed, it is precisely the most perfect beings, namely, living things with their infinitely complicated and inconceivably ingenious organizations, which were supposed always to arise afresh from the very bottom, and after a short span of time to become absolutely nothing, in order to make room once more for new ones like them coming into existence out of nothing. This is something so obviously absurd that it can never be the true order of things, but rather a mere veil concealing such an order, or more correctly a phenomenon conditioned by the constitution of our intellect. In fact, the entire existence and nonexistence of these individual beings, in reference to which life and death are opposites, can be only relative. Hence the language of nature, in which it is given to us as something absolute, cannot be the true and ultimate expression of the quality and constitution of things and of the order of the world, but really only a *patois du pays*,[2] in other words, something merely relatively true, something self-styled, to be understood *cum grano salis*, or properly speaking, something conditioned by our intellect. I say that an immediate, intuitive conviction of the kind I have here tried to describe in words will force itself on everyone, of course only on everyone whose mind is not of the utterly common species. Such common minds are capable of knowing absolutely only the particular thing, simply and solely as such, and are strictly limited to knowledge of individuals, after the manner of the animal intellect. On the other hand, whoever, through an ability of an only somewhat higher power, even just begins to see in individual beings their universal, their ideas, will also to a certain extent participate in that conviction, a conviction indeed that is immediate and therefore certain. Indeed, it is also only small, narrow minds that quite seriously fear death as their annihilation; those who are specially favored with decided capacity are entirely remote from such terrors. Plato rightly founded the whole of philosophy on knowledge of the doctrine of ideas, in other words, on the perception of the universal in the particular. But the conviction here described and arising directly out of the

1. Conjuring trick.—Tr.
2. Provincial dialect.—Tr.

apprehension of nature must have been extremely lively in those sublime authors of the *Upanishads* of the *Vedas,* who can scarcely be conceived as mere human beings. For this conviction speaks to us so forcibly from an immense number of their utterances that we must ascribe this immediate illumination of their mind to the fact that, standing nearer to the origin of our race as regards time, these sages apprehended the inner essence of things more clearly and profoundly than the already enfeebled race, *as mortals now are,* is capable of doing. But, of course, their comprehension was also assisted by the natural world of India, which is endowed with life in quite a different degree from that in which our northern world is. Thorough reflection, however, as carried through by Kant's great mind, also leads to just the same result by a different path; for it teaches us that our intellect, in which that rapidly changing phenomenal world exhibits itself, does not comprehend the true, ultimate essence of things, but merely its appearance or phenomenon; and indeed, as I add, because originally such an intellect is destined only to present motives to our will, in other words, to be serviceable to it in the pursuit of its paltry aims.

But let us continue still farther our objective and unprejudiced consideration of nature. If I kill an animal, be it a dog, a bird, a frog, or even only an insect, it is really inconceivable that this being, or rather the primary and original force by virtue of which such a marvelous phenomenon displayed itself only a moment before in its full energy and love of life, could through my wicked or thoughtless act have become nothing. Again, on the other hand, the millions of animals of every kind that come into existence at every moment in endless variety, full of force and drive, can never have been absolutely nothing before the act of their generation, and can never have arrived from nothing to an absolute beginning. If in this way I see one of these creatures withdraw from my sight without my ever knowing where it goes to, and another appear without my ever knowing where it comes from; moreover, if both still have the same form, the same inner nature, the same character, but not the same matter, which they nevertheless continue to throw off and renew during their existence; then of course the assumption that what vanishes and what appears in its place are one and the same thing, which has experienced only a slight change, a renewal of the form of its existence, and consequently that death is for the species what sleep is for the individual—this assumption, I say, is so close at hand, that it is impossible for it not to occur to us, unless our minds, perverted in early youth by the impression of false fundamental views, hurry it out of the way, even from afar, with superstitious fear. But the opposite assumption that an animal's birth is an arising out of nothing, and accordingly that its death is an absolute annihilation, and this with the further addition that man has also come into existence out of nothing, yet has an individual and endless future existence, and that indeed with consciousness, whereas the dog, the ape, and the elephant are annihilated by death—is really something against which the sound mind must revolt, and must declare to be absurd. If, as is often enough repeated, the comparison of a system's result with the utterances of common sense its supposed to be a touchstone of its truth, I wish that the adherents of that fundamental view, handed down by Descartes to the preKantian eclectics, and indeed still prevalent even now among the great majority of cultured people in Europe, would once apply this touchstone here.

The genuine symbol of nature is universally and everywhere the circle, because it is the schema or form of recurrence; in fact, this is the most general form in nature. She carries it through in everything from the course of the constellations down to the death and birth of organic beings. In this way alone, in the restless stream of time and its content, a continued existence, i.e., a nature, becomes possible.

In autumn we observe the tiny world of insects, and see how one prepares its bed, in order to sleep the long, benumbing wintersleep; another spins a cocoon, in order to hibernate as a chrysalis, and to awake in spring rejuvenated and perfected; finally, how most of them, intending to rest in the arms of death, carefully arrange a suitable place for depositing their eggs, in order one day to come forth from these renewed. This is nature's great doctrine of immortality, which tries to make it clear to us that there is no radical difference between sleep and death, but that the one endangers existence just as little as the other. The care with which the insect prepares a cell, or hole, or nest, deposits therein its egg, together with food for the larva that will emerge from it in the following spring, and then calmly dies, is just like the care with which a person in the evening lays out his clothes and his breakfast ready for the following morning, and then calmly goes to bed; and at bottom it could not take place at all, unless the insect that dies in autumn were in itself and according to its true essence just as identical with the insect hatched in spring as the person who lies down to sleep is with the one who gets up.

After these considerations, we now return to ourselves and our species; we then cast our glance forward far into the future, and try to picture to ourselves future generations with the millions of their individuals in the strange form of their customs and aspirations. But then we interpose with the question: Whence will all these come? Where are they now? Where is the abundant womb of that nothing that is pregnant with worlds, and that still conceals them, the coming generations? Would not the smiling and true answer to this be: Where else could they be but there where alone the real always was and will be, namely, in the present and its content?—hence with you, the deluded questioner, who in this mistaking of his own true nature is like the leaf on the tree. Fading in the autumn and about to fall, this leaf grieves over its own extinction, and will not be consoled by looking forward to the fresh green that will clothe the tree in spring, but says as a lament: "I am not these! These are quite different leaves!" Oh, foolish leaf! Whither do you want to go? And whence are the others supposed to come? Where is the nothing, the abyss of which you fear? Know your own inner being, precisely that which is so filled with the thirst for existence; recognize it once more in the inner, mysterious, sprouting force of the tree. This force is always *one* and the same in all the generations of leaves, and it remains untouched by arising and passing away. And now

As the leaves on the tree, so are the generations of human beings.[3]
(*Qualis foliorum generatio, talis et hominum.*)

Whether the fly now buzzing round me goes to sleep in the evening and buzzes again the following morning, or whether it dies in the evening and in spring another fly buzzes that has emerged from its egg, this in itself is the same thing. But then the knowledge that presents these as two fundamentally different things is not unconditioned, but relative, a knowledge of the phenomenon, not of the

3. (*Iliad*, 6: 146.)—Tr.

thing-in-itself. In the morning the fly exists again; it also exists again in the spring. For the fly what distinguishes the winter from the night? In Burdach's *Physiologie*, vol. 1, section 275, we read: "Up till ten o'clock in the morning no *Cercaria ephemera* (one of the infusoria) is yet to be seen (in the infusion), and at twelve the whole water swarms with them. In the evening they die, and the next morning new ones come into existence again. It was thus observed for six days in succession by Nitzsch."

Thus everything lingers only for a moment, and hurries on to death. The plant and the insect die at the end of the summer, the animal and man after a few years; death reaps unweariedly. But despite all this, in fact as if this were not the case at all, everything is always there and in its place, just as if everything were imperishable. The plant always flourishes and blooms, the insect hums, animal and man are there in evergreen youth, and every summer we again have before us the cherries that have already been a thousand times enjoyed. Nations also exist as immortal individuals, though sometimes they change their names. Even their actions, what they do and suffer, are always the same, though history always pretends to relate something different; for it is like the kaleidoscope, that shows us a new configuration at every turn, whereas really we always have the same thing before our eyes. Therefore, what forces itself on us more irresistibly than the thought that that arising and passing away do not concern the real essence of things, but that this remains untouched by them, hence is imperishable, consequently that each and every thing that *wills* to exist actually does exist continuously and without end? Accordingly, at every given point of time all species of animals, from the gnat to the elephant, exist together complete. They have already renewed themselves many thousands of times, and withal have remained the same. They know nothing of others like them who have lived before them, or who will live after them; it is the species that always lives, and the individuals cheerfully exist in the consciousness of the imperishability of the species and their identity with it. The will-to-live manifests itself in an endless present, because this is the form of the life of the species, which therefore does not grow old, but remains always young. Death is for the species what sleep is for the individual, or winking for the eye; when the Indian gods appear in human form, they are recognized by their not winking.

Just as at nightfall the world vanishes, yet does not for a moment cease to exist, so man and animal apparently pass away through death, yet their true inner being continues to exist just as undisturbed. Let us now picture to ourselves that alternation of birth and death in infinitely rapid vibrations, and we have before us the persistent and enduring objectification of the will, the permanent ideas of beings, standing firm like the rainbow on the waterfall. This is temporal immortality. In consequence of this, in spite of thousands of years of death and decay, there is still nothing lost, no atom of matter, still less anything of the inner being exhibiting itself as nature. Accordingly we can at any moment cheerfully exclaim: "In spite of time, death, and decay, we are still all together!"

Perhaps an exception would have to be made of the man who should once have said from the bottom of his heart with regard to this game: "I no longer like it." But this is not yet the place to speak of that.

Attention, however, must indeed be drawn to the fact that the pangs of birth and the bitterness of death are the two constant conditions under which the will-to-live maintains itself in its objectification, in other words, our being-in-itself, untouched by the course of time and by the disappearance of generations, exists in an everlasting present, and enjoys the fruit of the affirmation of the will-to-live. This is analogous to our being able to remain awake during the day only on condition that we sleep every night; indeed, this is the commentary furnished by nature for an understanding of that difficult passage. For the suspension of the animal functions is sleep; that of the organic functions is death.

Translated by E. F. J. Payne

16
Manuscript Remains

[75a] By the very fact that he lives and creates, the man gifted with *genius* sacrifices himself entirely for the whole of mankind. He is therefore free from the obligation of making particular sacrifices for individuals. For this reason he can refuse many a demand that others must reasonably fulfil. Yet he suffers and achieves more than all the others.

Men are puppets that are not drawn by external threads, but driven by an *inner* clockwork, and therefore to the outside spectator their movements are inexplicable. What I mean is that, if we compare the restless, assiduous and serious efforts of men with what they get from these, indeed with what they can ever get, then the former is out of all proportion to the latter. This goal to be attained, taken as the motive force to explain that movement (the constant activities of all men), is entirely inadequate and far too weak. [183] For what are a brief postponement of death, a small alleviation of need and want, a deferment of pain, a momentary satisfaction of desires, with such a frequent victory of all those evils and the certain triumph of death? What are all these, considered as causes of movement of a world of men who are innumerable and endlessly renew themselves? At every moment this world is astir, pushes, presses, struggles, indeed performs the entire tragicomedy of world history; and, what says more than anything else, it *perseveres* as long as possible in such a mock existence!—Obviously this movement and perseverance cannot possibly be explained, if we look for the moving cause outside the figures and conceive the human race as striving, in consequence of rational deliberation or something (as pulling threads), after the good things that are presented to it and whose attainment would be an adequate reward for its efforts and troubles. If matters were thus, then everyone would say "le jeu ne vaut pas la chandelle," and would quit life. However, as I have just stated, these puppets are not drawn and moved from outside, [184] but each of them carries within itself a clockwork whereby the movements follow quite independently of the external objects to which they are directed. This clockwork is the *will-to-live,* an untiring and irrational impulse, in other words something about which the external world gets no explanation and account or any other sufficient reason or ground. This will is the *deus in machina* that drives them, whereas only apparently are they drawn by objects that in themselves certainly do not have the power to do this. It holds them firmly on a scene from which they would otherwise immediately fly away. The external objects, as *motives,* determine merely the *direction* of the movement of these puppets; they certainly do not contain the sufficient reason or ground of the *movement* itself, otherwise the cause would not be at all appropriate to the effect.

The result of all this is that life is obviously not worth the effort and therefore cannot itself be the goal.

[277] If we rise to a very universal point of view, we shall find that the principal characteristic of the *Kantian philosophy* is negative and is directed against the fundamental false doctrines of European nations that had to be removed so that for truth space would exist only for the time being. Thus, for example, in the *Critique of Judgment* he does not show, as he could have shown, that the fitness of things, in other words, the suitability of the parts to the whole and of each thing to the others, admits of many other and better explanations than the one that a *Deus creator* produced them in accordance with previous concepts. On the contrary, he is content to demonstrate that that fitness is not entitled to conclude that things must be produced in that way. [278] In general, therefore, the true title of the Critiques of Pure Reason and Judgment together would be "Critique of Occidental Theism."—Even Kant regarded the doctrines of this as errors into which the faculty of reason necessarily falls, whereas they are merely fixed prejudices implanted in the mind of every Euopean before the age of thinking.

In India it would never have occurred to Kant to write such a critique of reason.—He would have produced its positive doctrines in quite a different form. In their present form the Critiques of Reason and of Judgment have therefore a local reference and a qualified and conditional purpose.

Intuitive knowledge can guide our actions and conduct directly and by itself; on the other hand, *abstract knowledge* can do so only by means of the *memory*. From this springs the superiority of intuitive knowledge for all those actions [320] where their execution at once follows our resolve; especially in our association with others intuitive knowledge is infinitely more helpful than abstract, and hence women excel here. Only the person who has intuitively grasped the real nature of men as they generally are and then the modifications of the individual in front of him, will know how to treat him with certainty and according to his deserts. Another man may be able to repeat by heart all the three hundred rules of Gracián, but this will be of little use to him if he lacks this intuitive knowledge. For in the first place all abstract knowledge gives merely universal rules that the memory should first bring to mind at the right time. This is seldom done promptly; and then from the present case [321] the *propositio minor* should be formed and finally the conclusion drawn. Before all this is done, the opportunity for its application has already vanished. On the other hand, intuitive knowledge gives at once and at a single stroke all that is necessary and gives it in direct reference to the present case without any extraneous admixture. It gives rule, case and application in a nutshell and therefore action rapidly goes ahead. This explains why in real life the scholar, whose merit consists in an abundance of abstract knowledge, is so inferior to the man of the world whose merit consists in a more perfect intuitive knowledge, which an original disposition has bestowed on him and a wealth of experience has developed.

[322] Always and everywhere intuitive knowledge is related to abstract as hard cash is to paper money. Therefore since only intuitive knowledge has direct reference to the present, it is also only such knowledge that finds its expression on the face and gives that look of intelligence. But just as for many cases and affairs paper money is preferable to hard cash, so also for certain things abstract knowledge is much more useful than intuitive; they are the things spoken about on page 83 of the work.

[338] What makes the first quarter of life so happy is that we behave more as knowing than as willing beings. *All things are delightful to see and frightful to be.* In childhood we see much indeed everything, but we are little, have few connections, few needs, and little will. On the other hand, the intellect is developed early although it is not mature, and it looks incessantly for nourishment in a whole world of fresh existence where literally everything is varnished over with the lure and appeal of novelty. And not yet satisfied even with this, the intellect thoroughly examines the works of art and of knowledge that lie in the realm of its powers. Therefore at an early age we become ever so much more acquainted with things from the side of seeing, of the representation and of objectivity than from the side of being that is that of the will. And since all things, as I have said, are delightful to *behold* and are frightful only to be, the young intellect regards as just so many *blissful entities* all those forms that reality and art place before it. [339] It imagines that, as they are so beautiful to behold, they must indeed be even more beautiful to be. The world lies before it like a garden of Eden, and this is the Arcadia in which we are all born. From this there then arises the thirst for real life, the eagerness for deeds and sufferings, which drives us into the hurly-burly of the world. But here we first become acquainted with the other side, the side of being, i.e., of the will, which is thwarted and frustrated a thousandfold. The great *desengaño* gradually appears, according to which it says that l'áge des illusions est passé.

Essentially it is all the same whether we fear harm or look for enjoyment; in both cases care for the satisfaction of the will fills our consciousness. For a time will-less knowledge alone is liberation from the suffering of life and it alone is the painless state of Epicurus. Hunting (for pleasure) and fleeing (from pain) are equally far from it.

What I call *eternal justice* and have described, differs from *human justice* by the fact that the latter requires *time* in order to come to light, for it is the evil *consequence* of the evil deed. Eternal justice, however, requires no time; the deed is already the punishment, for the tormentor and tormented are one and their difference is only phenomenon, Maya. The concept of *retaliation* includes that of time, and therefore *eternal* justice cannot be *retaliative,* as temporal or human justice is.

We experience a feeling of inexpressible well-being when we are delivered for only a few moments from the fierce pressure and burden of the will; for the aesthetic contemplation of the beauty of nature or of some work of art puts us into the state of will-free knowledge in which for the most part the effect of the beautiful consists. Such moments, in which we emerge, so to speak, from the heavy atmosphere of the earth only temporarily, are the most blissful that we know. From all this we can infer how [274] blessed must be the life of a man whose will is silenced, not for a few moments, but forever and is completely extinguished except for the last glimmering spark in the ashes, which is first extinguished with the death of the body. After such a man has completely overcome his will, he is now left only as a purely knowing being, the pure mirror of the world. He is liberated from all the misery of desiring and fearing, and with a smile he looks back on the phantasmagoria of this world, which once could agitate and agonize even his mind, as he does at the overturned chessmen after the end of a game. These figures still stand before him like a light morning dream through which reality already is faintly discerned and which no longer deceives. [274a] If we picture to ourselves the heavenly peace and calm of such a life, we then look longingly up to it from the deep distress and corruption in which we are still enmeshed. Here willing in the form of desire, fear, envy, and anger holds us captive with a thousand strings and tugs us most painfully in all directions, so that our understanding, bewildered and perplexed in this way, gets involved in many kinds of errors that we shall one day have to atone for.

The turning of the will-to-live is for us certainly a transition *into nothing,* for everything we describe as *existing,* namely, this world, is just the phenomenon of the will-to-live. The basis of this phenomenon, or its universal form, is always something known and a knower, and its content where it stands out most clearly and completely is man, who is the most perfect objectity of the will-to-live [194] and who declares himself to be a concrete willing, i.e., concrete neediness, to be a concretion of a thousand wants. His existence is a constant wanting whose satisfaction cultivates and constitutes his life. Accordingly, this is a constant transition from need to satisfaction and from this to a fresh need.

The same thing still appears in all animals, but the more simply and with less exuberance and abundance, the more remote they are by degree from man. We again perceive essentially the same thing in plants, yet only as a dull and obscure impulse devoid of knowledge, as vegetation. The same thing is expressed even less distinctly by all so-called dead natural forces and bodies ultimately only as gravity, rigidity, and persistence in a state once assumed. Here the will appears only as a quite obscure urge, far removed from any possibility of being directly known.

Now with the abolition of the will all these phenomena are abolished, and hence also the fundamental condition of them as phenomena, the form of appearance, and thus subject and object. That constant pressure and effort without end and aim, which appears in this whole world in all its parts and in which the *will,* the *essence-in-itself of the world,* objectifies itself—all this too is now abolished. The turning and abolition of the will are therefore identical with the abolition of the world. What is left is called by us *nothing* and our whole nature struggles against this transition into nothing. But the reason for this is simply that we are the will-to-live itself and what is knowable in us is its phenomenon. We abhor nothingness and this is identical with the fact that we will life and are nothing but this will. But now let us turn our glance from our own needy and perplexed nature to those who have overcome the world and have wholly abolished the will-to-live, in other words, to the saints who, after the will hardly exists anymore, only await the dissolution of its phenomenon, the body, and with this the complete decline and death of the will [195]. We then see in them, instead of the restless pressure, the rapturous joy and violent suffering that make up the actions of the man who loves life, an unshakable calm and inner serenity, a state we cannot look at without yearning and that we are bound to acknowledge as infinitely superior and as the only right thing in face of which the emptiness of everything else becomes apparent. This consideration is the only one that can console us when, on the other hand, we contemplate the endless misery making up the phenomenon of the will, i.e., the world, and, on the other, think of the abolition of the will along with its phenomenon and have before us empty nothingness. Thus in this way by considering saints who, of course, are brought to our notice rarely in real life, but through history and through art with a truth that is better vouched for and manifestly evident, we will banish the somber impression of that nothingness that stands out as the goal of all virtue and holiness and that we feared as children fear the dark.

Translated by E. F. J. Payne